The Scottish Settlers of America
The 17th and 18th Centuries

BY

Stephen M. Millett, Ph.D., FSA Scot

CLEARFIELD

Chapters of this book were originally published in *U.S. Scots Magazine*:

The Scottish Settlers of America. The 17th and 18th Centuries.
by Stephen M. Millett, Ph.D., FSA Scot
Copyright © 1996 U.S. Scots
All rights reserved

Originally published
U.S. Scots
Columbus, Ohio, 1996

Reprinted with permission of
Stephen M. Millett
U.S. Scots
Columbus, Ohio

Reprinted for
Clearfield Company, Inc. by
Genealogical Publishing Co., Inc.
Baltimore, Maryland
1998, 1999, 2004

International Standard Book Number: 0-8063-4761-9

Made in the United States of America

Contents

About the Author:

STEPHEN M. MILLETT is the editor and publisher of *U.S. Scots. The Magazine of the Scottish-American Community*, which serialized *The Scottish Settlers of America* from the Winter 1992 to Winter 1995. He was graduated from Miami University (Oxford, Ohio) in 1969 and received his M.A. and Ph.D. in history from The Ohio State University in 1970 and 1972, respectively. After serving more than six years on active duty as a regular officer of the U.S. Air Force, in 1979 Dr. Millett joined the professional staff of the Battelle Memorial Institute, a technology research and development house in Columbus, Ohio. He is currently the Managing Principal of the Technology Management Group at Battelle. He consults with industrial clients around the world on technology and market futuring, and he is an internationally respected authority on scenario analysis for long-term R&D investments.

Dr. Millett is a past convener of the Mid-Ohio Scottish Heritage Association and a past regional commissioner of the Clan MacDougall Society. He is an elected Fellow of the Society of Antiquaries of Scotland (FSA Scot), located in Edinburgh. Dr. Millett has lectured widely on the topic of Scottish-Americans and has published numbers papers on the subject. He spent five years in the research and writing of *The Scottish Settlers of America*. In addition to *U.S. Scots*, which began publication in 1992, Dr. Millett founded the Scottish-American Studies Center to promote continuous eduation for adults in Scottish and American history, geography, and culture.

U.S. Scots Magazine is a quarterly publication available at the annual subscription price of $9.95. Its mailing address is P. O. Box 20217, Columbus, OH 43220.

CHAPTER ONE:

THE SCOTTISH HOMELAND

For a great many Scots, leaving their ancestral homeland and hazarding the voyage to a strange land was a great act of courage. They left Scotland for many reasons, and they came to America for many reasons. We generally call the reasons to leave the "push" of emigration and the reasons for going to America the "pull" of immigration. And yet for all of the unique, individual reasons, there existed several common themes to Scottish emigration to the New World. Among these common themes was the fact that the Scots were historically migrant peoples. They were not the first and only inhabitants of Scotland. They were from wanderers in whose hearts the urge to move on still beat.

An understanding of the Scottish people begins with an appreciation for their homeland, the part of the world that they have inhabited for about 3,000 years. The physical location and environment of Scotland may be characterized as being a far northern, although surprisingly temperate, corner of the globe on the fringe of European civilization, whose mountains and glens have protected, isolated, and frequently impoverished its people. Having lived in this environment for some 30 centuries, the Scots developed a national spirit of determination to survive the elements and preserve their unique identity in the face of both natural and human oppression. This Scottish spirit shaped by the Scottish environment became inborn to its people and remained with them even as they relocated to various other environments around the world.

Three features of the Scottish environment particularly influenced the character of the Scottish people: 1) the geographical location of the British Isles at the end of the Gulf Stream, which makes the climate unexpectedly mild and wet given their far northern position on the globe, 2) the geographical location at the farthest northwest corner of the Eurasian land mass and hence its status as a fringe of European civilization, and 3) Scotland's landscape of mountains, rolling hills, sea coast, lochs (lakes), and valleys that provides spectacular scenery but yields sustenance sparingly.

The Temperate Climate

If the British Isles could be shifted westward and transposed upon North America, they would just about fit within Hudson Bay. They are much farther north on the globe than the U.S. London sits close to the 51st parallel of latitude. Edinburgh is 380 miles farther north and rests above the 55th parallel. In contrast, New York City and Columbus, Ohio, are located at about the 40th parallel (which is as far south on the globe as Madrid, Spain).

Yet, for as far north as the British Isles are, they are surprisingly mild, without the extreme winter cold or summer heat of North America. The average daily low temperature in January in both London and Edinburgh is 35 degrees Fahrenheit. The average daily high in July is 73 degrees in London and 65 degrees in Edinburgh. The Scottish capital experiences a temperature range from an extreme low of 15 degrees in winter to an extreme high of 83 degrees in summer. In contrast, the January average daily low is 27 degrees in New York City, and the July average daily high is 85 degrees. New York experiences the temperature range from an extreme low of -15 in winter to an extreme high of 99 degrees in summer. While cold winds and snow are well known in the Scottish Highlands, the entire British Isles are temperate indeed compared with the bitter sub-freezing winters traditional to the northern U.S. Likewise, Scotland enjoys warm summers, but escapes the blistering heat of American summers.

To the Scots who relocated on the western side of the Atlantic, the North American summers felt tropical and the winters arctic. Highlanders who may have brought their kilts with them quickly put them away in favor of warm trousers when autumn turned to winter, as indeed the native Indians covered their legs, too. In many cases, the Scots had more difficulty adjusting to the cold than to the heat, which may explain, at least in part, why more Scots settled in the warmer colonies of Virginia, the Carolinas, Georgia, and the Caribbean islands than in the colder colonies of New England and New York.

The reason for the temperate climate of the British Isles is their location at the western end of the Gulf Stream, with its warm Caribbean currents flowing to the northeast across the Atlantic Ocean. The Gulf Stream bathes Ireland and flows up the Irish Sea to the Scottish west coast. It makes the area far warmer and wetter than one would expect of a land so far north. The temperature rarely falls below freezing during the winter, although the short winter days may be damp and chilling to the bone. At the small fishing village of Plocton, in a sheltered harbor near the Isle of Skye, there stands a row of palm trees. In the mountains, of course, the air is colder than in the plains and snow often falls during the winter. In addition, the east side of Scotland is typically cooler and drier than the west side. Generally, the dampness of the air and the biting chill of the wind combined with long hours of darkness and dusk give Scotland its bad reputation for about five months during the year, when in reality the Scottish cold season is milder than the New York cold season.

The average annual precipitation in London is only 23 inches, which is considerably less than the average annual rainfall of over 42 inches in New York City. London's reputation as a wet city is based more upon frequent light mists than driving rain storms. Similarly, Edinburgh has a typical annual precipitation of about 27 inches and Aberdeen, also on the east side, has about 33 inches. The west side, however, which is exposed to the Gulf Stream, has much more rain. Glasgow, just about 45 miles to the west of Edinburgh, has an average annual rainfall of over 40 inches, and Fort William, at the western base of the Great Glen, has nearly 80 inches. Over two-thirds of Scotland receives more than 40 inches of rainfall per year, and some mountainous areas of the north receive over 100 inches a year. Hard rainfall can last days, resulting in permanently soggy ground. Throughout Scotland, rain can be a daily event. Sunshine averages only 3.5 hours per day over the entire year. The skies can change continuously from rain to shine back to rain. Sometimes the sun shines and rain falls at the same time (called "brightly showering" by contemporary weather reporters) as the clouds quickly pass overhead. The winds off of the Atlantic contribute much to the chill in the air.

The variable weather of Scotland has been blamed for the variable moods of the Scots. Sometimes the Scots are very warm and hospitable; at moments, they can be almost manic, such as the exuberance of Robert Burns' poetry. At other times, the Scots can be very dour and downright depressing, such as the occasional excesses in the hell-and-damnation theology of John Knox. Scottish history is full of stories from both sides of this dual emotionalism, from highly romanticized tales of Bonnie Prince Charlie to the cold treachery of the Glencoe Massacre. Although it seems hard to imagine the "brightly showering" of human emotions, the Scots certainly can be temperamentally volatile.

As H.V. Morton, the celebrated travel writer of the 1930s, observed over 50 years ago, "Scotland is two absolutely different countries: Scotland in sunlight and Scotland in rain. One is the most beautiful country in the world and the other is the most awesome....It is to these grey fearful days that one can trace the moody, poetic, sensitive temperament of the Gael." One should only add that it is to the sunshine that one can trace the parallel energetic, optimistic, and joyful spirit of the Scot.

The Remote Corner

While the British Isles enjoy the climatic benefits of their location at the terminus of the Gulf Stream on the Atlantic Ocean, they have historically suffered from being at the far northwest corner of mainstream European culture. Located at the far northern and mountainous edge of the principal British island, the remoteness and isolation of Scotland has been particularly significant. It was the farthest northwest reach of the great Indo-European migrations, which arrived from the great Steppes of the Eurasian heartland to the British Isles during the first millennium B.C. Scotland was the farthest extent of the Celtic culture, which was the dominating Indo-European presence north of the Alps from Iberia (Spain) to Germania (Germany). Later, it was beyond the farthest outpost of the Roman Empire. What the Romans called Caledonia extended north of Hadrian's Wall, a demarcation line of Latin civilization. Roman armies once occupied the land as far north as the present Glasgow-Edinburgh line, and they may have penetrated as far north as the present Inverness-Aberdeen line, but they never subdued the wild Celtic tribes of the far north. The language of Rome was not introduced by centurions at the point of a sword, but by Church fathers carrying the Word. It was Christianity that eventually tied the Celtic fringe to the mainstream of European culture less than 2,000 years ago.

After the Romans left Britain in the fifth century A.D., the invading Anglo-Saxons from the continent failed to overrun Scotland as they did England. They penetrated the eastern Lowlands, but not beyond the Forth. Once again, Scotland lay beyond the dominant culture of the British Isles. In historical times, Scotland was often invaded and pillaged, but never successfully occupied by foreign nations — not by Romans, Anglo-Saxons, Vikings, Normans, or English. Scotland remained fiercely independent, alone and apart from other nations.

Because it was positioned at the far northwest corner of the continent, Scotland long enjoyed its independence from the conquerors who swept across western Europe after the fall of Rome. The Scottish spirit of fierce independence was due to both its position on the fringe of Western civilization and its terrain of mountains and lakes. Scotland was both remote and hard to get to. It was also indifferent to the outside world for too long and very slow to modernize. The cost of proud independence was too often poverty for the common people. As the venerable Dr. Samuel Johnson, an English chauvinist of the first order, correctly observed after his tour of the Highlands and islands in 1773, "Mountainous countries commonly contain the original, at least the oldest race of inhabitants, for they are not easily conquered....As mountains are long before they are conquered, they are likewise long before they are civilized."

Yet, Scotland could never be totally isolated from other peoples. It was vulnerable from the sea, which is no farther than about 60 miles from any interior point in Scotland. Even the Highlands were the object of invading Irish, Anglo-Saxons, English, and Vikings. The Scottish people were frequently exposed to these foreigners, often unpleasantly, but usually to some long-term advantage. Scotland was also vulnerable to land attack from the south due to its physical link with England, which posed the longest and most serious threat to Scottish security. The Scots fought bravely for centuries to keep their independence from the English, but they could not escape the growing power of their Anglo-Norman neighbor. Ultimately, Scotland could not resist the roads of commerce that connected the poor mountains to the rich markets of the south. As Johnson once again astutely commented, "...the noblest prospect that a Scotsman ever sees is the high road that leads him to London." For many Scots, Johnson's words were indeed true; but even truer might be that the Scots found their best prospects of all in the routes to America.

Scotland barely averted annexation by the English in the late 13th and early 14th centuries. If it had been subdued, its history may have been more like that of Wales and Ireland. William Wallace uncovered Scottish nationalism in his revolt against the English from 1297 to 1305. Robert the Bruce began another revolt in 1306 by claiming the vacant Scottish throne for himself. The King of Scots in 1314 won a startling victory over the English army at the Battle of Bannockburn (which continues to live in Scottish memories like the Battle of Yorktown lives in American memories). By 1328 the English king finally recognized Scottish independence in the Treaty of Edinburgh.

The spirit of Scottish nationalism, a bellicose sense of separate identity and pride, was captured in the Declaration of Arbroath in 1320 during the war with England. In their recounting of their grievances against the English, the Scottish nobles asserted that "But from these countless evils we have been set free...by our most tireless prince, king and lord, the lord Robert....for, as long as but a hundred of us remain alive, never will we on any conditions be brought under English rule. It is in truth not for glory, nor riches, nor honours that we are fighting, but for freedom — for that alone, which no honest man gives up but with life itself."

When Scotland did become a part of Great Britain with neighboring England, it did so as an independent sovereign country. In 1603, upon the death of Elizabeth the Great, the English throne passed to James VI of Scotland, the son of Mary, Queen of Scots, and a descendant of the Anglo-Welsh Tudor king, Henry VII. For over a century, the Scots continued to hold on to their own parliament, legal system, and church, although their monarch lived in London. Scots came to enjoy all the rights of Englishmen within the British realm. By the Act of Union of 1707, Scotland lost its separate parliament and came under the authority of the parliament of Westminster. In some ways, Scotland gradually became politically, economically, and culturally integrated with England and Wales. In other ways, it has remained aloof with its own peculiar ways, which have become the source of English jokes and Scottish pride.

In simple terms, England, which had long been considered as the backwash of Europe, became a great world power because of its naval power and its commercial empire. It forced itself into the mainstream of world affairs beginning in the 16th century. Scotland, in the meantime, remained in the English shadow without any extraordinary naval power or commerce. It never enjoyed the population size or wealth of its southern neighbor. But it remained independent and proud, even when others viewed Scotland as backward and barbaric. One estimate is that by 1707 Scotland had only 20% as many people and 2.5% as much taxable wealth as England. In time, with its integration into the British Empire, Scottish self-respect, enterprise, and hard work gained Scots much material success. The Act of Union of 1707 was neither English political subversion or the military conquest of Scotland; rather, it was the recognition of a defense imperative for the English to have a secured northern flank and an economic imperative for the Scots to enjoy the opportunities of a single, integrated British market.

Scotland may have been on the northwest fringe of European civilization and it may not have wielded the power of England, with whom it was tied by land and could not escape, but it had a strong sense of independent identity. This feeling of being different but "good different" was carried in the hearts of adventurous Scots around the world.

The Rough Land

Finally, the last physical characteristic of great importance to Scotland was its terrain dominated by mountains and water. Scotland was not a large country: about 30,414 square miles (or 78,784 square kilometers), just about half the size of England and Wales combined and less than the size of the State of South Carolina. With not much space to work within, most of Scotland is not suited for agriculture, despite the relatively mild temperatures and abundant rainfall. Too much Scottish land, especially in the Highlands, is taken by rough mountains and lochs.

Scotland contains the roughest terrain of the British Isles, including its highest point, Ben Nevis (4406 feet). Geologically, the Scottish mountains are extremely old and were once mightier than the Alps. Most were once active volcanoes that left many violent scars upon the land. Remnants of these great mountains and the very early crust of the earth have been found in the Highlands and the Hebrides. For example, rocks have been found that have been dated back 2.5 billion years.

The once great volcanoes and mountains have been worn down and broken up by glaciers, the last of which receded as recently as 10,000 to 12,000 years ago. The last glacier also carved out numerous lochs, many of which are not strictly lakes but actually fjords. As a result of once being under about 8,000 feet of ice, Scotland has some 31,000 lochs and over 5,000 rivers and streams (burns). Some of these lochs are extremely deep: Loch Morar, on the west coast, is at least 1,000 feet deep; Loch Ness, famous for its monster (and Morar has its own monster, too) may be as deep as 975 feet with a mean depth of about 700 feet. Loch Ness also has the largest volume of water, with 26 billion cubic feet. Loch Lomond, not far north of Glasgow, has the largest area of water with 27 square miles.

Not only is Scotland full of rough mountains and lochs carved out from the last glacier, but it is also almost surrounded by sea. Scotland has 6,000 miles of coastline. While the Scots have always been fishermen, they have never been able to live off of the sea alone. Much of the coast is very rough with few good ports. In addition, there are as many as 500 islands, most of them too small, too isolated, and too barren to support whole communities.

Because of the mountains, lochs, sea, and islands, no more than 20% of Scottish land is arable even today, and considerably less would have been productive before the agricultural improvements of the mid-eighteenth century. The rich farm land that does exist is confined to the narrow eastern coast, the Lowlands below the Clyde River-Forth River (Glasgow-Edinburgh) line, and a few river valleys in the Highlands, especially the Spey. The climate was not particularly harsh, but the land was. Subsistence was indeed the right modifier for Scottish agriculture for most Scots at most times.

From an economic perspective, Scotland's greatest natural resource has been its scenery. Its mountains today may not be as high or as peaked as the Alps, nor as massive as the Rockies, but they command respect. They stand majestically with weathered, rugged beauty. They are not so much the mountains of recreation as they are the mountains of hard work. They are not impassible, but they are demanding. These mountains are frequently punctuated with beautiful lochs and rivers with valleys called glens or dales. The west coast and islands in particular are extremely dramatic. Unfortunately, these Scottish visual assets provided no economic advantage until very recent history when tourism, the commercial exploitation of natural scenery, became a principal Scottish industry.

One of Scotland's greatest natural resources was almost entirely eliminated by people, even before the Industrial Revolution. That was the extensive forests. When the Celts first came to Scotland in c.1000 B.C., the land was covered with oaks, pines, birch, ash, elm, and alders. Indeed, the Romans allegedly called Scotland "Caledonia," which meant "wooded heights." Over the centuries the forests were cut down for firewood, building timber, and charcoal. Today, less than one percent of the primeval forest remains. Among this one percent is a yew tree near Edinburgh that is reputedly a thousand years old; in the northern Highland forests, there are still pines at least 400 years old. Modern reforestation has barely recovered the landscape. Even today, Scotland remains 80%-90% defoliated.

In the once extensive Scottish woods lived numerous wild animals long since gone. Brown bears roamed Scotland until they were killed off by the 10th century. Beaver were prevalent and very desirable, but they were exterminated by the 12th century. (Local beaver fur had once been very popular in the British Isles and it became again the object of Scottish pursuit in its first American colony of Nova Scotia in the 1620s.) The wild boar was so common that it became a symbol for both the Picts and the Irish Scots. Wolves existed until the end of the Middle Ages. Today, Scotland still has a large deer population, which has learned to live off of the moors and glens rather than the woods.

In addition to trees, Scotland also has contained large amounts of other biomass fuels, but none has brought any particular wealth to Scots. Peat has provided a fuel for centuries, but it has had little or no commercial value (except, perhaps, for the making of whisky). Scotland had some coal, but never the amounts found in Wales. The Scottish coal supply, like its wood resources, is now virtually gone after only about two centuries of exploitation. The coal mines from Glasgow to Edinburgh and into Fife are now mostly exhausted after the exploitations of the Industrial Revolution. The other important fuel is the oil from the North Sea wells. Oil exploration did not become important until after the energy crisis of 1973. Today it is a major source of income for Scotland, especially Aberdeen, but there is much Scottish resentment that most of the oil profits seem to end up in London.

Beyond the sparse arable land and the extensive pastures, the Scottish land yields little to its people. Even the sea produced relatively little, except for commercial fishing in the North Sea and lobsters on the west coast. During the Napoleonic wars, kelp, a mineral rich seaweed, supported some people. But mostly, beyond subsistence agriculture, the Scots have lived on the land but not off of it. Where the Scots progressed materially was in the value-added activities of the mind and hands, rather than exploitation of the land and sea. The Scots were rich in human resources rather than natural resources. They produced world-class universities for higher education, scholarship, and research and development. They produced skilled craftsmen, who in turn encouraged generations of industrialists. During the Industrial Revolution, Scotland, especially Glasgow and the towns of the Clyde valley, became a major British manufacturing and shipbuilding center. One important industry was textiles, whereby sheep's wool was made into cloth and clothes. Today, Scotland has become a principal area for the British computer and electronics industry, with the Glasgow-Edinburgh corridor called "silicon glen."

Three other traditional Scottish activities have been important moneymakers. One is fighting. What was once sport became business when thousands of Scots hired themselves out to serve in various European armies, including those of Sweden, Russia, and France as well as the armed forces of Great Britain. Another sport which became big business within the last 125 years is golf, which the Scots claim to have originated. And the third major industry is distilling, as true Scotch whiskey can only be made in Scotland.

The wealth of Scotland has not rested on its relatively mild climate, or its geographical position, or its land, but in its people. Their power came from within themselves. The land made a hearty people, and the spirit of freedom and enterprise remained always in their personality. And when many of them left Scotland, for any number of reasons, they took their people-powers with them. The Scottish wealth in many cases became reinvested in American wealth.

The land, its location and its nature, had a profound influence on the Scottish people, even on those who left Scotland to resettle in America. The next chapter will continue the discussion of the Scottish people as background to the story of emigration to the New World.

References

G. W. S. Barrow, *Robert Bruce & The Community of the Realm in Scotland.* Edinburgh: Edinburgh University Press, 1988 (1965) (quoting the Declaration of Arbroath, p. 307).

Central Office of Information, *Britain, 1987.* London: Her Majesty's Stationary Office, 1987.

G. H. Dury, *The British Isles. A Systematic and Regional Geography.* 2nd ed. London: Heinemann, 1963.

Gazetteer of the British Isles. Edinburgh: John Bartholomew & Son, Ltd., 1972.

J. D. Mackie, *A History of Scotland.* Revised and edited by Bruce Lenman and Geoffrey Parker. London: Penguin Books, 1991 (1964). (This is generally considered to be the best one volume, broad-brush history of Scotland.)

Magnus Magnusson and Graham White, eds, *The Nature of Scotland. Landscape, Wildlife and People.* Edinburgh: Canongate Press, 1991.

H.V. Morton, *In Scotland Again.* New York: Dodd, Mead & Company, 1939 (quote on pp. 211-212).

L. Russell Muirhead, ed., *The Blue Guides. Scotland.* London: Ernest Benn Ltd, 1949. [Numerous guides books explain the terrain and monuments of Scotland. *The Blue Guides* have been particularly rich in details. Other worthy periodic guides include *Fodor's, Frommer's,* and *Michelin.*]

Allan Wendt, ed., Samuel Johnson, *A Journey to the Western Islands of Scotland* [1775]
and James Boswell, *The Journal of a Tour to the Hebrides* [1785]. Boston: Houghton Mifflin Co., 1965 (quotes on p. 32 and p. 369.)

12

CHAPTER TWO:

THE SCOTTISH PEOPLES

The Scots historically have never been a single, homogeneous nation. They have always been a mixture of several peoples who crossed paths on the remote northwest corner of the Eurasian land mass. While humans may have inhabited what we know today as Scotland since the dawn of civilization, the peoples whom we now call Scots actually have occupied Scotland for only the last 1,500 years. The wanderlust of Scottish emigrants since the 17th century can, at least in part, be explained by the fact that people have been migrating into and out of the British Isles in general and Scotland in particular for a very long time.

This chapter will briefly overview the ethnic origins of the modern Scots and identify their four principal sub-groups: Highlanders, Lowlanders, Ulster Scots, and Anglo-Scots. This background will help explain the characteristics of the Scots who eventually settled in America and passed on their ways, some of which were very ancient, to American culture.

Ethnic Origins

The Roman historian Tacitus correctly observed in A.D. 98 that "Who were the original inhabitants of Britain, whether they were indigenous or foreign, is, as usual among barbarians, little known." He characterized all

Britons as a mixture of Iberians, Germans, and Gauls. Tacitus further commented that "They were once ruled by kings, but are now divided under chieftains into factions and parties....Seldom is it that two or three states meet together to ward off a common danger. Thus, while they fight singly, all are conquered."

The English churchman and historian Bede wrote in 741 that the Britons were descendants of a Brutus, who was the grandson of Aeneas, a survivor of the fall of Troy who escaped to Italy. Brutus led his "Trojans" by sea around the Iberian peninsula and founded a new culture on the island that was then called "Albion," which he renamed "Britannia" after himself. The Britons once occupied the entire island, but eventually yielded the northern part to another migrating people, the Picts. The Picts were different from their southern Briton neighbors and were barbarians whom the Romans called "Caledonians."

Bede's account was further embellished in Geoffrey of Monmouth's *The History of the Kings of Britain* in 1136. The basic story was that the British Isles had been inhabited long before the Romans by various peoples, the principal group having had a Mediterranean origin.

The early English church historians, including Bede and Geoffrey of Monmouth, emphasized the same basic points: the peoples of the British Isles were very ancient, they had a Mediterranean origin, and they were not homogeneous, with a marked difference especially between the southern Britons and the northern Picts.

The Scots had their own legends of their ethnic origins. In the 1320 Declaration of Arbroath, which was mentioned in Chapter I, the Scottish nobles claimed a fundamental ethnic difference from the English. They claimed that their ancestors had originated in "Scythia the greater," apparently meaning the Black and Caspian Sea area (approximately today's Ukraine). These people migrated by way of the Mediterranean Sea to Spain, from which they circled Europe by water and landed in Scotland within a century of the birth of Christ. They rooted out earlier inhabitants and drove off the Britons, thereby claiming Scotland for themselves.

The Scottish churchman John of Fordun provided more details on this legend in his fourteenth century chronicle of Scottish history. He began the story with a Greek prince named Gaythelos, who was expelled from his home and resettled in Egypt approximate to the time of Moses. He married Scota (from which came the name Scotti, "Scots," and "Scotland"), the daughter of the Pharaoh. Gaythelos himself became the Pharaoh, but he and his followers were driven out of Egypt by hostile mobs. The exiles took with them the highly valued "Stone of Destiny," which was the rock allegedly used as a pillow by Jacob when he experienced his dream of Jacob's Ladder. This stone long remained the holiest object and ultimate symbol of national identity to the Scots.

Gaythelos' followers, having fled Egypt, sailed westward and landed in what is today Spain, where his people lived for many generations. From the son of Gaythelos and Scota, Hyber, derived the names of both Iberia (the peninsula of Spain and Portugal) and Hibernia (the island of Ireland).

According to John of Fordun, the Scots sent small outposts to Ireland while most of the descendants of Gaythelos and Scota's band remained in Spain, primarily in the mountains, where they could defend themselves from hostile natives. The Scots as a nation eventually moved to Ireland, where they reestablished themselves around Tara. The Stone of Destiny was used as a coronation throne to remind the people of their ancient origins in the Mediterranean. While settled in Ireland, the Scots were approached by another displaced people, the Picts, who had migrated westward from Scythia led by a King Humber (who was killed by the son of Brutus, the legendary founder of Britannia). The Scots encouraged the Picts to settle across the sea from them in what is today Scotland. They provided wives for families and required that future Pictish kings be selected according to their maternal rather than paternal lineage. Years later, the Scots themselves crossed over the Irish Sea, established themselves in the Highlands, and eventually merged with the Picts to form Scotland.

As fantastic as these legends seem, some historical facts do lie behind them. In terms of geological history, the entire British Isles remained uninhabited by human beings until just recently. Even relative to the ancient history of the Fertile Crescent, the cultures of Great Britain are new. The historical Irish, Picts, and Britons were all Celts. Although they were not the first inhabitants of the British Isles, the Celts dominated them by the time of recorded history. They were indeed a migratory people who had come from the east. Like many legends, the Scottish genesis was highly condensed in its time frame and personified in its heroes, but it did represent a basic truth that the Celts were a very old and proud people who had traveled a great distance to locate their new "homeland," from which they would be extremely difficult to dislocate again.

The Celtic peoples are believed to have arrived in the British Isles in about 1000 B.C., plus or minus 500 years. For a point of reference, the exodus of the Israelites led by Moses from Egypt is dated to the reign of the Pharaoh Ramesses II, 1304-1237 B.C. The Celts were the far western extent of the migrating Indo-European people, who are believed to have originated in the Black and Caspian Sea region (which was generally known to the Greeks as "Scythia"). These people, who have been called the Kurgans, had lived on the steppes, where they had been herders of flocks (primarily cattle, sheep, and goats) and cultivators of grains (derived from wild grasses) by the use of heavy ploughs with which to break thick turf. They were excellent horsemen and fierce warriors. They were also great craftsmen and loved ornamentations. They lived in small groups with much mobility. They had an elaborate set of religious beliefs centered on spirits who acted through various natural objects. They also had an elaborate social structure divided into three general classes: warriors-leaders, priests-sages, and herders-cultivators.

The Indo-Europeans began their migrations, both to the west and to the east, in the approximate period of 5,000-4,000 B.C. The reasons for their moving in such large numbers from their homeland as far west as Ireland and as far east as India has not yet been reconstructed. Traditionally, when they are called "Kurgans" they are viewed as wild conquerors seeking to exploit the wealth of weaker peoples. The Indo-Europeans were undoubtedly warlike and they swept aside weaker nations, but they may have migrated for several reasons beyond the immediate gains of plunder. One possibility is that a change in climate around the Caspian and Black Seas region forced the Indo-Europeans to seek new lands for their survival. This possibility would explain the large numbers of migrating Indo-Europeans and why they populated the areas they acquired. Another possibility is that they expanded gradually following their trade with other peoples. Yet another explanation may be that they themselves were driven out of their homeland by yet more nomadic and fierce peoples to their east, which has historically produced such conquerors as the Huns, the Mongols, and the Turks.

The western Indo-Europeans are believed to have migrated from the Black Sea steppes down into what we now call the Balkans and up the Danube River valley into central Europe. Of these western migrants, one branch became known as the "Teutons" or "Germans." Another branch continued northward and eventually became the "Vikings" or "Norsemen." Yet a third branch continued westward into what the Romans called "Gaul" (France) and "Iberia" (Spain and Portugal). As early as the second millennium B.C., Indo-Europeans crossed the waters into the British Isles. The migrations into Briton and Ireland surely did not occur once, but many times, with different family groups and tribes arriving at different times up to the first century B.C., when the Romans invaded them. Many may have traveled by sea rather than by land and they may have come from both Gaul and Iberia.

Other Indo-Europeans colonized the rim of the Mediterranean Sea. The Greeks, Trojans, and Hittites of Asia Minor were Indo-Europeans. So, too, were the Romans. To their north and east, close to what was the "ground zero" of the migration, were the slavic peoples. To their east, other branches of the Indo-Europeans settled in Persia and the Indian sub-continent. Today's Iranians and many Indians are Indo-Europeans. Their languages are related to Greek, Latin, German, Russian, and Gaelic.

Through their common origin, the peoples of the British Isles were distantly related to the Romans. Even more distantly, the Scots had a dim memory, embedded in oral legends, of roots in "Scythia" and blood ties with the Greeks and Trojans.

By the time of the Roman Empire, the Celts of Indo-European stock inhabited most of western and northern Europe. The Celts of the British Isles were closely related to each other and to the Gauls on the mainland.

The Celts provided a cultural bridge from the pre-historic Indo-Europeans to contemporary Scots. They continued to live in small groups; the Celts were not builders of towns and cities. They were highly individualistic and difficult to organize. Just as Tacitus described, their great vulnerability was their lack of unity in the face of stronger invaders. They had a powerful social basis in extended families, but virtually no social or political affiliations beyond the clan unit. The Celts were primarily herdsmen, especially of cows, goats, and sheep. Secondarily, they were cultivators of grains, mostly barley and oats. They were very fierce warriors, as the Romans discovered. They were extremely proud people, easy to offend and difficult to placate. They were both curious to discover new ideas, but also very superstitious. The Celts believed in a parallel universe of supernatural beings and spirits. They loved ornamentation in clothing and jewelry. They may have worn garments of parallel lines, geometrical designs, and colors. They were a people of great generosity and hospitality among themselves, but also of great suspicion and even apprehension of foreigners. While they enjoyed an elaborate oral tradition of folklore, they had no written language.

Archeological evidence indicates that the Celts of the British Isles may have displaced, perhaps eliminated, earlier settlers. There certainly were peoples of Europe who were not Indo-Europeans and who were driven out of their homes by the apparently barbaric "Kurgans." These non-Indo-Europeans included pre-Celtic Spaniards (perhaps ancestors of today's Basques), Etruscans, and Phoenicians. Because of the known extent of very early Phoenician voyages throughout the Mediterranean Sea and the Atlantic coast, peoples of the Fertile Crescent may have explored and settled in the British Isles long before the Celts arrived. There were, for example, people called "the old ones," who were not Celts, known even to the Romans as late as the first century A.D. They are believed to have been small in stature with elongated features and black hair and dark complexions. In contrast, the Celts and the Gauls were generally tall, large boned with reddish-brown-sandy hair and light complexions. Perhaps today's dark Irish, Welsh, and Scots are genetic descendants of "the old ones." Whether by land or by sea, it is entirely possible that the British Isles were invaded by people from "Scythia the greater" as far back in time as Moses. Indeed, the story of Moses itself represents the symbolic history of many migratory peoples in this era.

During Roman times, several Celtic tribes lived north of Hadrian's Wall. Collectively, the Romans called them "Caladonians." These people were closely related to the Brigantes and other British tribes living in the Roman world south of the wall. By the time the Romans left Britannia, in A.D. 407, there were numerous tribes fighting with each other for their little kingdoms and defending themselves from invading Irish Scotti.

The Modern Scots

From the physical characteristics of Scotland and the nature of the migratory people who came to inhabit it emerged during the Middle Ages a people called the Scots. They were historically a blend of various Celtic tribes combined with strains of Anglo-Saxons, Norse, and Norman. The Scots were less homogeneous than the Irish, but more so than the English. In the modern history of Scottish emigration, during just the last four centuries, four particular types of Scots should be noted.

Highlanders. The first and most romanticized Scots were the Highlanders. They were the most "primitive" of the northerners, from the point of view of both Lowlanders and Englishmen, perhaps because they were the ones most unchanged from the ancient ways of the Indo-Europeans and the Celts. The Highlanders were the people of tartans, clans, kilts, bagpipes, and whisky. They lived in small, tightly knitted groups with strong blood bonds (clans). As they were fiercely loyal within their clan, they were highly suspicious of others. They took exceptional pride in their heritage, and too quickly took offense to insults. Feuds and fighting were frequent. Most of all, they were proudly independent and resistant to change imposed by outsiders.

The Highlanders were a mixture of different elements of the Celtic people. On the east side of Scotland, they were the descendants of Picts. The Picts spoke a different Celtic language, called P-Celtic, than the Irish Celts (Q-Celtic). They were a pre-literate people who have left many stone monuments but no manuscripts. Their name was given to them by the Romans, who allegedly called them "Picti" because of their tattoos or body paint worn into battle. They fought continuously with the Romans and later with the Anglo-Saxons, both to defend their homeland and to expand southward. They succeeded in penetrating as far south as the Tweed River, but not beyond Hadrian's Wall. On the western flank, the Picts were

21

challenged by the Britons of the Clyde and the Irish Scots. Relatively little is known in detail about Pictish culture before the union with the Scots in the 9th century.

The Picts had populated the east side of Scotland from the Forth River far to the north. They lived in large numbers in the northeast Lowlands from what later became Angus to Aberdeenshire. They maintained settlements in the mountains and islands on the west side, but their base was the rich agricultural lands on the North Sea. Although they frequently waged war with their Irish Celtic cousins on the west side after A.D. 500, they formed many commercial and personal connections with the Scots. By 843 the kingship of the Picts and Scots was united under Kenneth MacAlpine, who moved the seat of Scottish power to the east side. Despite this union, even as late as the 14th century, the east-west divisions between the Irish Scot and Pictish descendants were more profound than north-south or Highland-Lowland differences. In terms of Christian practices, the eastern Pictish customs, which were in conformity with Rome's, dominated over the Irish-style "Celtic church." In terms of language, the Scots imposed their Gaelic tongue (supported by a written language supplied by literate monks) upon the Picts, who had had no written language of their own. Indeed, the name "Scotland" obviously comes from the Irish Scots. The Pictish name would have been "Alba," "Albany," or "Albania."

On the west side of Scotland, the Highlanders were called Scots, from "Scotti," another Roman name for an Irish Celtic (Gaelic) tribe that lived in what became known as Ulster in northern Ireland. Significant numbers of Scots migrated into western Scotland during the 6th century. They founded their own land, which they called Dal Riada (later to be known as Argyll). The Scots apparently fought numerous wars with the Picts in the post-Roman era, but the Scots and Picts merged as one nation under a unifying monarch in the 9th century. The Scottish capital was then moved from Dunstaffnage, near Oban, on the west side to Scone, the inland heart of the Picts. Included in the move was the legendary Stone of Destiny, which had been carried by the Scots from Ireland to Dal Riada. After 843, the Scots intermarried extensively with the Picts so that both nations slowly merged into the Highlanders of the modern era.

It should be noted in passing that some of the most "Scottish" symbols came from Ireland and as late as the 15th century. The kilt originated as a large wool wrap (called a "plaid," meaning both the type of garment and its design) and likely had Celtic (perhaps Indo-European) origins. The "modern" kilt was at least partly an adaptation of a tunic popular in Ireland. The tartan kilts (and Gaelic tongue) of Highland clans were typically characterized as "Irish" by the Lowlanders. Likewise, the bagpipe came to Scotland from Ireland, although, again, its basic design goes back to very early times in the ancient civilizations of the Middle East. And whisky, now known popularly as "Scotch," may have also come to the Highlands from Ireland, where monks had distilled spirits from earliest times.

The Highland clan system traces its origins back to pre-historic Celtic family units, but its modern form dates back only to the late 12th and 13th centuries (with several major clans not emerging until as late as the 14th and 15th centuries). A few of the earliest clans came from the Pictish east side. When the first feudal earldoms were created from the mid-12th to the mid-13th centuries, the initial set of earls came exclusively from the ancient Pictish provinces of Moray, Mar, Buchan, Angus, Fife, Atholl, and Strathearn. Even as late as 1320, the Declaration of Arbroath, which was quoted in Chapter 1, presented the Pictish more than the Scottish version of the legendary origins of the Scottish nation.

The union of the Scots and Picts may have literally been forced upon them by the invading Vikings. The Scandinavians, primarily from Norway, invaded and settled along the northern and western coasts of the Highlands and upon many of the Scottish islands from about 700 to 1100. They also occupied parts of the southwest Lowlands, northern and eastern Ireland (Dublin was a Norse trading town), and western England. Earlier Norsemen had settled on the Seine Valley in France, where they were called "Normans." The Vikings interbred with the Scots, but perhaps not to the extent that they did in Ireland, England, and France. Some of the most powerful clans of the western Highlands and Islands were Norse-Celtic: MacDonald, MacLeod, and MacDougall.

A Gaelic revival in the 12th century led by the Gaelic-Norse warlord Somerled did much to reverse Norse influence in the west Highlands and islands. Many Norse names still remain in Scotland, especially on the outer islands, but the Vikings did not have as substantial a long-term cultural influence as did the Normans, who infiltrated rather than invaded Scotland.

The most notable foreign penetration of the Highlands came from the Normans more so than the Norsemen. Beginning in the 12th century, the Scottish crown actively encouraged Norman nobles and knights from England to settle in Scotland. David I, King of Scots (1124-1153), had been raised at the court established by force of arms in London by the Normans following the Battle of Hastings in 1066. He had made many friends among the Normans, and he established a semi-Norman feudal order in Scotland. From these Normans (and Britons, Flemmings, and other allied groups from the continent) sprang some of the greatest Highland clans and Lowland houses: Bruce, Buchanan, Cummings, Grant, Fraser, Graham, Gordon, Hamilton, Lindsay, Maxwell, Menzies, Montgomery, Ramsay, Sinclair, Stewart (Stuart), and Sutherland.

The economy and life style of the Highlanders was primarily pastoral, with particular emphasis on cattle and sheep. There were some cultivated fields in the valleys, especially the rich fields of the Strathspey, and some fishing, but cattle provided cash. For hundreds of years, the wealth of a clan chief or noble was measured in heads of cattle, which were annually driven across the drove roads of the Highlands to the Lowland marketplaces, where eager English buyers acquired them for export to beef-hungry London.

If wealth was often measured in cattle, then power was measured by the number of fighting men a clan chief could muster. Inter-clan battles could engage thousands of men. As long as power was measured in men, then the landowning clan chiefs, many of whom were also noblemen, encouraged large populations within their territories, even if the use of the land was inefficient and the support of the people merely marginal. Clan chiefs needed their own armies to exert their power within their lands and to defend their interests against other clans. But the jurisdictional authority of clan chiefs and inter-clan wars ended with the failure of the last Jacobite revolution and the Battle of Culloden in 1746.

After this date, both the wealth and power of clan chiefs and nobles were measured in pounds sterling, the best source of which became the use of pastures for Lowland sheep. Now the number of people on the land became a liability rather than an asset. By the end of the 18th century, impatient landowners in the Highlands were encouraging migration and army enlistment and even physically forcing tenants off of their land in an action termed the "clearances." From this time, the spirit of the Highlander was placed in the people apart from their land, much of which was given over to the comfort of wool.

Lowlanders. The most numerous group of Scots were the Lowlanders, who populated the eastern coast and the lands below the Glasgow-Edinburgh line but north of the English border. The principal cities of Scotland are all in the Lowlands: Aberdeen, Dundee, Perth, Edinburgh, and Glasgow. Inverness is the only population center of much size in the Highlands. While the Highlanders remained true to the Celtic tradition of small communities, the Lowlanders were sufficiently influenced by the Romans and English to discover the commercial advantages of cities. The Lowlanders, in contrast to the Highlanders, were less pastoral and more agricultural; they were also more vigorous in the trades and commerce. With opportunities to trade to the south and abroad, Lowlanders developed a diversified economy of finished goods as well as raw materials. Even as early as the 15th century, Lowlanders thought of themselves as further advanced culturally and materially than their cruder Highland kin.

Lowlanders were a blend of various Celtic tribes with infusions of invading Romans, Anglo-Saxons, and Anglo-Normans. In ancient times, the Picts occupied the rich agricultural lands of the northeastern Lowlands along the North Sea coast from as far north as Elgin to perhaps as far south as Edinburgh. The Celtic tribes south of the Clyde River-Forth River line had strong ties with southern British tribes, especially the Brigantes. They were exposed to Roman influences, although they resisted Roman domination. At one time the Romans constructed an earthen wall, the Antonine Wall, from the Clyde River to the Forth River. But the Romans failed to hold this line successfully and fell back to the stronger Hadrian's Wall. In the ebb and flow of Roman conquest, the ancestors of the Lowlanders had much exposure to Roman culture.

After the withdrawal of Roman armies in 407, the southwestern Lowlands, including what is now called Galloway, Ayr, Renfrew, and Lanark, became its own kingdom, known as Strathclyde. Its capital was the prehistoric fort of Dumbarton. Its people were Celts of the type known as Britons because of their close ties with the southern tribes. The Clyde kingdom may have been the power base of the legendary Arthur. It successfully defended itself against invading Anglo-Saxons and menacing Picts. It yielded some ground to the Vikings, but it was not annexed by them, as was Argyll and many of the islands. Over time, the people of Galloway acquired several Norse traits through cohabitation and intermarriage. By the 11th century, however, the Briton kingdom of Strathclyde had been annexed into the Scottish-Pictish Scotland.

The southeastern Lowlands provided a continual battlefield between contending influences. The Picts tried to dominate it from their strongholds north of the Forth, while the Anglo-Saxons tried to conquer it from their base in Bernicia (Northumbria). For about twelve hundred years the Celtic and the Anglo-Saxon peoples invaded each other across their boundary. While enormous property damage was done and thousands of people were killed or left homeless, neither side could prevail. The Picts and the Scots succeeded in holding the rich lands of the Lothians and the Borders from the Forth to Tweed Rivers, but failed to extend as far south as Hadrian's Wall and the Tyne River. The English seized the moors from the Tyne to the Tweed and the Scottish city of Berwick, but failed to expand farther, although they came very close to annexing all of Scotland in the troubled times of 1296 to 1314.

In particular, the Borders was a perpetual war zone of raids between Scots and English, between feuding clans, and between crown authorities and outlaws. The Borderers became known for their hardened character, their quickness to resort to violence, and their endurance in the face of hard adversity. The 16th century in particular saw long years of violence and lawlessness. The violence of the Borders was not ended until James VI, King of Scots, also became James I of England in 1603. Although Scotland and England remained separate countries until 1707, James used his powers on both sides of the boundary to maintain the King's peace.

By the 15th century, Lowlanders came to feel apart from, even superior to, their Highland brothers. They had more opportunities to trade with England and the continent and they were exposed to other cultures more than the Highlanders. Even as early as 1500, Lowlanders looked down on Highlanders as being crude, uncivilized, uneducated, and uncultured. As the Lowland economy grew while the Highlands remained poor, the Lowlanders rightly saw the Highlands as underdeveloped. Also by 1500 the Lowlanders were speaking a tongue called "Scots," which was a blend of Gaelic dialects and English. Mary, Queen of Scots, during her reign in the 1560s spoke French first and Scots second, but could not speak Gaelic. Language, manners, and standard of living had differentiated the Lowlander from the Highlander.

The Lowlanders accepted a very important custom from the Anglo-Saxons and Norsemen: living in towns and cities. The ancient Celts lived in small, widely dispersed communities, but did not aggregate into towns. This had once been true of all the British Isles. London was a Roman city and Dublin was a Viking port. In the Scottish Highlands, only one, rather small city emerged: Inverness. Otherwise, Highland towns are still infrequent and small (such as Campbelltown, Oban, Fort William, and Portree). But the Lowlanders created cities, and all the Scottish cities of any consequence (except Inverness) are in the Lowlands. These cities arose because of vigorous crafts, trade, and industry. The growing wealth and population of the cities were supported by an agricultural bounty unrealized in the Highlands.

Ulster Scots. Beginning in the early 1600s a significant number of Lowland Scots crossed the Irish Sea to resettle in Ulster. People had been moving back and forth from Scotland to Ireland for thousands of years. As mentioned earlier, the Scotti of northern Ireland occupied Dal Riada in the 6th century. Highland clans, especially the MacDonalds, extended their power into Ireland during the Middle Ages. Ireland had frequently been involved in the wars of Scotland, especially during the Wars of Independence in the 14th century. But the flood of Scottish people to Ulster did not begin until the political and religious turmoil that began with the reign of the English Queen Elizabeth.

In 1540 Elizabeth's father, the great Henry VIII, had assumed the title of king of Ireland. The extent of his power, however, extended little beyond Dublin. Elizabeth was determined to pacify, feudalize, and colonize the Emerald Isle. After the defeat of the Spanish Armada in 1588, the queen was determined to resettle Irish lands with loyal and Protestant subjects from Great Britain. Although two "plantations" were attempted but failed in Ulster during the 1570s, Elizabeth continued to attract British farmers, merchants, and craftsmen to Ireland.

In 1595 two powerful Ulster lords, Tyrone and Tyrconnel, rebelled against the authority of the English monarchy. The fighting had been bitter, but by 1603, the year of Elizabeth's death, the English had reasserted their control of northern Ireland. In 1606 Hugh Montgomery and other Ayrshire lairds from the Scottish Lowlands negotiated with the Irish to acquire peacefully legal claims to lands in County Antrim and County Down. Montgomery immediately attracted Lowland farmers to acquire and work on their own property in northern Ireland. By 1616, these private Scottish plantations had as many as 8,000 people with 2,000 fighting men.

In 1607, shortly after he ascended to the English throne, James I confiscated the titles and lands of the rebellious lords Tyrone and Tyrconnel that covered much of six of the nine counties of Ulster. James wanted to further "colonize" Ulster in order to increase the number of Protestants, isolate native Irish and Catholic opposition to the Crown, and stimulate further Irish economic development and trade with England. He may have also wanted to relocate contentious Lowlanders, especially Borderers, away from fighting with Englishmen and peaceable Lowlanders. During the 17th century, especially from about 1600 to the very serious Irish rebellion that began in 1641, perhaps as many as 200,000 Lowlanders resettled in Ulster. Further Scottish immigration into Ulster occurred from 1660 to 1688 and in the early 18th century. Ulster provided both economic opportunities and religious sanctuary to Lowland Presbyterians.

The Ulster plantation significantly changed the demographics and eco-nomics of northern Ireland. The power structure and propertied class became British and Protestant. But certainly not all of the new Ulstermen were Scots. The Scots dominated northern County Antrim (also called Colraine), but the

28

English dominated southern Antrim. Scottish Presbyterians also dominated Counties Down, Tyrone, Londonderry (or Derry), and Donegal; the English held most of Monaghan and Armagh. The city of Belfast was both Scottish and English. Of course, many of the native Irish remained, but intermarried very little with the British until well into the 19th century.

The Scots who resettled in Ulster were primarily Lowlanders and Presbyterians. The part of Scotland where most of them originated was the Southwest Lowlands (Ayr, Dumfries, Renfrew, Dumbarton, and Lanark). The next largest group came from the Lothians and the Borders. The third largest group came from Aberdeenshire. Relatively few came from the Highlands.

Much debate has raged whether the Ulstermen of Scottish extraction were "Scotch" or "Irish" or even a separate ethnic group. In British history, they are called "Ulster Scots" and in American history they are called "Scotch Irish." Up to the time of the American Revolution, the Ulster Scots had largely kept to themselves, both in Ulster and America, and they differentiated themselves from the Catholic Irish (whom they looked down upon, just as they denigrated Highlanders). They spoke Scots, observed Scottish customs, and followed the Kirk of Scotland. But after generations of living in Ulster, they came to think of themselves as Ulstermen separate from Scots, English, and Irish. With time, they grew apart from their Scottish origins, just as they grew apart from their Ulster origins after they came to America.

The categorization of Ulster Scots immigrating into America was very confused. Some records show all people emigrating from the island of Ireland as "Irish." This may be true in a geographic, not ethnic, sense. The Protestant Ulstermen, both Scottish and English, thought of themselves as being very different from the southern Irish. Just as it would be inaccurate to call all Ulstermen "Irish," it would also be incorrect to call all of them "Ulster Scots." The Ulstermen with Scottish names, family origins, and Presbyterian beliefs may be labeled "Ulster Scots." Ulstermen with Irish names, family origins, and the Catholic faith should be called "Irish", and those with English names, family origins, and Anglican (Episcopalian) beliefs should be categorized as English or Anglo-Irish.

Because of their Scottish origins and customs, the Ulster Scots, or Scotch-Irish, will be treated as the third of four Scottish groups who participated in the settlement of America.

Anglo-Scots. The fourth Scottish group was the Anglo-Scots who were living in England or Wales prior to emigration abroad. Scottish noblemen began to relocate to London in 1603 when James VI/I relocated the Scottish court from Edinburgh to London. After the Act of Union in 1707, many Scottish noblemen, gentry, members of parliament, civil servants, military men, merchants, and professionals and their families moved south, where opportunities for advancement were more abundant than in Scotland. An unknown number of Scots during the eighteenth and nineteenth centuries also migrated to the English factory cities to find work. It is very likely that this number was larger, perhaps considerably larger, than the number of Scots who migrated to Ireland. The flow of Scots southward was indeed so strong that Dr. Johnson quipped that the best road a Scotsman ever traveled was the one leading to London. These Scots adjusted to the English lifestyle and after a few generations became Anglo-Scots. Some migrated again to North America, and many more stayed in England. Dr. Johnson's disdain notwithstanding, London certainly was and still is the most popular location for Anglo-Scots.

As this brief ethnic history of Scotland has recounted, the Scots were a nation of mixed bloods: Celtic Scots, Picts, and Britons; Anglo-Saxons; Scandinavians; and Anglo-Normans. They had long been a migratory people. In the era of emigration from Scotland, there were the Scottish sub-groups of Highlanders, Lowlanders, Ulster Scots, and Anglo-Scots. What they shared in common was a geography, history, and culture from the northern British Isles that followed them wherever they roamed.

References

Accounts of the Indo-European peoples, the Celts, and the historical peoples of Scotland can be found in the following works:

Leslie Alcock, *Arthur's Britain. History and Archaeology, A.D. 367-634.* London: Penguin Books, 1989 (1971).

Nora Chadwick, *The Celts.* London: Penguin Books, 1987 (1971).

A. A. M. Duncan, *Scotland. The Making of the Kingdom.* The Edinburgh History of Scotland, Vol. I. Edinburgh: Mercat Press, 1992 (1975).

J. P. Mallory, *In Search of the Indo-Europeans.* Language, Archaeology and Myth. London: Thames and Hudson, 1989.

Robert O'Driscoll, ed., *The Celtic Consciousness.* New York: George Braziller, 1987 (1981).

Anna Ritchie, *Picts.* Edinburgh: Her Majesty's Stationary Office, 1989.

R. L. Graeme Ritchie, *The Normans in Scotland.* Edinburgh: Edinburgh University Press, 1954.

William F. Skene, *Celtic Scotland: A History of Ancient Albon.* 3 vols. Edinburgh: David Douglas, 1886-1890.

Alfred P. Smyth, *Warlords and Holy Men. Scotland, A.D. 80-1000.* London: Edward Arnold, 1984.

The quotation from Tacitus comes from "The Life of Cnaeus Julius Agricola," (A.D. 98), in *The Complete Works of Tacitus,* edited by Moses Hadas. New York: Modern Library, 1942, pp. 677-706; quotes on pp. 683, 684.

The legendary origins of the Scots and Picts are found in the following sources:

Bede, *A History of the English Church and People* (A.D. 731). Translated and with an introduction by Leo Sherley-Price. Revised by R. E. Latham. New York: Dorset Press, 1985 (1955).

Declaration of Arbroath (1320), in Gordon Donaldson, ed., *Scottish Historical Documents*. New York: Barnes & Noble, 1970, pp. 55-58.

John of Fordun, *Chronicles of the Scottish Nation (1384-1387)*. Translated by Felix J. H. Skene. Edited by William F. Skene. Edinburgh: Edmonston and Douglas, 1872.

The characteristics of Scottish Highlanders and Lowlanders have been discussed in countless histories, including those already cited in these references. Of particular interest for background information relative to Scottish social and economic conditions that contributed to emigration to America are

Frank Adam, *The Clans, Septs, and Regiments of the Scottish Highlands.* Revised by Sir Thomas Innes of Learney, Lord Lyon of Arms. 5th edition. Edinburgh: W. & A. K. Johnston & G. W. Bacon, Ltd., 1955 (1908).

J. M. Bumsted, *The People's Clearance. Highland Emigration to British North America.* Edinburgh: Edinburgh University Press, 1982.

William Ferguson, *Scotland. 1689 to the Present.* The Edinburgh History of Scotland, Vol. IV. Edinburgh: Oliver & Boyd, 1968.

George MacDonald Fraser, *The Steel Bonnets. The Story of the Anglo-Saxon Border Rievers.* London: Barrie & Jenkins, 1971.

I. F. Grant, *Highland Folk Ways.* London: Routledge, 1989 (1961).

Michael Hechter, *Internal Colonialism: The Celtic Fringe in British National Development, 1536-1966*. Berkeley, CA: University of California Press, 1977.

Andrew Hook, *Scotland and America: A Study of Cultural Relations, 1750-1835*. Glasgow: Blackie, 1975.

Bruce Lenman, *Integration, Enlightenment, and Industrialization. Scotland, 1746-1832*. The New History of Scotland, Vol. 6. London: Edward Arnold, 1981.

Rosalind Mitchison, *Lordship to Patronage. Scotland, 1603-1745*. The New.History of Scotland, Vol. 5. London: Edward Arnold, 1983.

Wallace Notestein, *The Scot in History. A Study of the Interplay of Character and History.* New Haven, CT: Yale University Press, 1952.

Marjorie Plant, *The Domestic Life of Scotland in the Eighteen Century.* Edinburgh: Edinburgh University Press, 1952.

T. C. Smout, *A History of the Scottish People, 1560-1830*. London: Fontana, 1972.

Col. David Stewart, *Sketches of the Character, Manners, and Present State of the Highlanders of Scotland*. 2 vols. Edinburgh: John Donald, 1 9 7 7 (reprint of 1822 edition).

John Watson, *The Scot of the Eighteenth Century*. London: Hodder and Stoughton, nd.

G. Whittington and I.D. Whyte, eds. *An Historical Geography of Scotland*. New York: Academic Press, 1983.

Among the numerous works on the Ulster Scots, see:

Charles Knowles Bolton, *Scotch Irish Pioneers in Ulster and America.* Boston: Bacon and Brown, 1910.

David Noel Doyle, *Ireland, Irishmen and Revolutionary America, 1760-1820.* Dublin: Mercier Press, 1981.

R. F. Foster, *Modern Ireland, 1600-1972.* London: Penguin Press, 1988.

Ian C. C. Graham, *Colonists from Scotland.* Ithaca, NY: Cornell University Press, 1956.

E. R. R. Green, ed. *Essays in Scotch-Irish History.* London: Routledge & Paul Kegan Paul, 1969.

James G. Leyburn, *The Scotch-Irish. A Social History.* Chapel Hill, NC: The University of North Carolina Press, 1962.

Kerby A. Miller, *Emigrants and Exiles. Ireland and the Irish Exodus to North America.* New York: Oxford University Press, 1985.

M. Perceval-Maxwell, *The Scottish Migration to Ulster in the Reign of James I.* London: Routledge & Kegan Paul, 1973.

Peter Roebuck, ed. *Plantation to Partition.* Essays in Ulster History in Honour of J. L. McCracken. Belfast: Blackstaff Press, 1981.

CHAPTER THREE:

SCOTTISH POPULATION
AND EMIGRATION

When compared with the Third World countries of the 20th century, Scotland has never been over populated in absolute numbers of people. But in terms relative to its meager natural resources and limited arable land, Scotland has been over populated for much of its history. The relief from crowding before the Industrial Revolution came principally from deaths due to famine, disease, and warfare. The relief from crowding since the Industrial Revolution has come largely from emigration. Because emigration relieved the population pressures on Scotland's very limited resources, the people who left Scotland did so, largely, to their own benefit as well as that of their homeland. Given the richer resources abroad, especially in the United States, the Scots found ways to exploit more fully their energy and talents for their own best gain. And the Scots who remained in Scotland by and large also benefitted by exploiting to their own advantage the human and technological opportunities of the Industrial Revolution without the stress of gross over population.

This chapter will review Scottish population growth and the pressures it created. Such demographic pressures combined with radical economic and social changes caused by agricultural and industrial progress caused dramatic demographic shifts, including emigration. This chapter will also provide the context for estimating how many Scots emigrated and how many found their way to America.

Population Growth

From the ancient accounts of the Romans, the lands north of Hadrian's Wall were fairly well populated by the first century A.D. The population density was likely not as great as it was in the rich southern Britannia, but it was greater than the Romans apparently expected. The Picts may have had a thriving population along the rich agricultural coasts of the North Sea. Agriculture was already well developed and sufficient to support a growing population. The Lowlands were peopled with Britons closely related to the tribes south of the wall. The northern and western Highlands and islands were apparently still thinly inhabited. While the Picts had a presence on the west side, they either lacked the ability or the interest to deny Argyll to the invading Scots from northern Ireland in the sixth century.

During the early Middle Ages, Scotland likely experienced a net population growth due to migrating groups. The Irish Scots occupied the western Highlands and islands. Their migration across the Irish Sea began in the fifth century and accelerated during the sixth. The Anglo-Saxons penetrated into the southeastern Lowlands during the sixth and seventh centuries. Beginning in the 790s, the Vikings from Norway conquered and settled the northern islands, the Hebrides, and the western Highlands, where they mingled with the established Picts and Scots. The Norsemen also occupied parts of the southwest Lowlands, as well as the Isle of Man and much of Ireland. Meanwhile, the Britons of the southwestern Lowlands and the Picts of the northeast likely continued to grow in population.

The population of Scotland by the year 1200 has been estimated at 250,000. With a territory of less than 30,000 square miles (78,784 square kilometers), this constituted a density of over eight people per square mile. However, the population was not in fact evenly distributed. Most of the population continued to reside where the subsistence was best: the northeastern coast and the southern Lowlands. If, at most, the arable portion of Scottish territory was 20% (and that figure may be high before the agricultural improvements of the 18th century), then the density of population by 1200 was about 42 people per arable square mile. Although the wars of the 13th century may have reduced Scottish population, it was increasing again by the end of the Middle Ages. If Scotland were not already over populated, it certainly was becoming crowded relative to the limited resources of a country that was widely considered as the backwater of Europe.

By the year 1707, when Scotland was joined with England and Wales by the Act of Union, the Scottish population had grown to an estimated 1,100,000. This figure might have been historically low, since the 1690s had been one of the worst decades in Scottish history for famine and disease. Nonetheless, the growth rate had been 440% over five centuries. The principal difference from the Middle Ages was the rise of the towns and cities, with Edinburgh, Glasgow, and Aberdeen becoming major population centers.

But the population of Scotland was small compared with that of the English. By the 18th century, the population of England and Wales was already about 5.5 million, or five times that of Scotland's, with London emerging as one of the largest metropolitan centers in the world with 675,000 people. On the other hand, Scotland had economically much less to offer than England. The English, lead by the likes of Dr. Samuel Johnson, typically degraded the Scots as poor and vulgar neighbors. Compared with the wealth of the south, many Scots did indeed seem like poor cousins from the hills.

The first systematic census of Scotland was performed by the Rev. Alexander Webster in 1755. By statistical standards of his day, Webster was remarkably precise. His estimate was 1,265,000 people. This figure has become the accepted baseline for understanding the subsequent population explosion in the second half of the 18th and the entire 19th centuries.

The first government census of Scotland occurred in 1801. The government figures for each ten-year census up to the 1930s appear in Table 1.

TABLE 1, THE CENSUS OF SCOTLAND
(from Michael Flinn, ed., *Scottish Population History from the 17th Century to the 1930's*, Cambridge: Cambridge University Press, 1977, pp. 58-64, 241, and 302.)

Year	Population	% Net Growth
1801	1,625,002	na
1811	1,824,434	12.3
1821	2,099,945	15.1
1831	2,373,561	13.0
1841	2,620,184	10.4
1851	2,888,742	10.3
1861	3,062,294	6.0
1871	3,360,018	9.7
1881	3,735,573	11.2
1891	4,025,647	7.8
1901	4,472,103	11.1
1911	4,760,904	6.5
1921	4,882,497	2.6
1931	4,842,554	-0.8
1939	5,006,700	3.4

In less than 200 years, from 1755 to 1939, the Scottish population increased about 400%, from about 1.3 million to just slightly over five million people. If earlier estimates are reasonably accurate, then the number of Scots increased almost as much in the modern era of 200 years as it had over about 500 years from the Middle Ages to the beginning of the 18th century.

Since World War II, the Scottish population has experienced about zero net growth. As late as 1984, it was estimated at 5,146,000, or just 140,000 more than it had been 45 years earlier (about 2.8% growth over 4.5 decades). The population of Scotland today comprises about 9% of the total population of the United Kingdom. Indeed, the Scottish population may be little more than about half the size of greater London.

Scotland saw a great population growth in conjunction with the early stages of industrialization, as most countries around the world have. What is there about the nature of technological and economic growth that stimulates greater reproduction? Probably nothing. There is no evidence that industrialization in Scotland led to more procreation, which has been a time honored activity among the Scots. The difference did not come so much in the birth rate as it did in the death rate, especially among young children. The birth rate has in fact steadily declined in recent times due to changes in family planning. In 1755, for example, the Scottish birthrate was an estimated 39 per 1,000; by 1950 it had fallen to just 18 per 1,000. The death rate, however, fell even more dramatically due to improved public sanitation, health care, and nutrition. As the death rate fell faster and sooner than the birth rate, Scotland had a booming population, which could barely be supported by the pre-industrial economic order. In many regards, what the Scots experienced centuries ago has been repeated by many Third World countries in this century.

Up to the 19th century, the leading causes of deaths in Scotland had been famine and epidemics, which too often came together. The principal victims were young children and the aged. Serious famines due to the failure of grain crops occurred during the 1620s and the 1690s. In fact, the famine of the 1690s, during which the population decline may have been as great as 15%, was the last great death-causing famine in Scotland. There were other famines to be sure, but they were mitigated by dietary supplements from potatoes and foods other than grains. After the 1690s there was malnutrition, but rarely starvation. During the potato famine of the 1840s, famine occurred in parts of the Highlands, although not in the Lowlands, but it certainly was not as horrible as the great hunger in Ireland.

Scotland likely experienced more deaths due to the bubonic plague in the 1640s than to the religious and political wars of that turbulent decade. During the plague, 50%-75% of all sick people died. It has been estimated that the city of Edinburgh lost one-third to one-half of its population to the plague. A century later, the plague was gone due to substantial improvements in public health and personal hygiene. The leading cause of death in the 18th century was smallpox, but it was largely eradicated due to vaccinations. By the year

41

1800, the leading causes of mass deaths, famine and epidemics, had been largely controlled. People generally lived healthier and longer lives, and hence the population grew, not because of more births but because of fewer deaths.

Wars and internal violence were certainly also causes for population decline, but they apparently did not have the sweeping effects that famines and diseases had. If Edinburgh had lost one-third to one-half of its population due to a siege, then such a massacre would have gone down in history as a dreaded day of national mourning. There were some terrible sieges and massacres in Ireland during the civil wars of the period 1641-1660 and 1688-1690, but such high levels of political violence were avoided in Scotland. The 16th century had been very violent and undoubtedly caused many deaths, but the casualties of the wars and rebellions of the 17th century were minor compared with those of Ireland and even England during the same period.

The population growth of Scotland in the 18th and 19th centuries would have undoubtedly created severe strains on natural resources had not profound economic and social changes caused massive population shifts, including emigration, as discussed below.

Population Shifts and Emigration

The tremendous economic and social changes in Scotland that began in the 18th century caused profound disruptions to age-old life styles and contributed to the migration of many people. These were not the political and religious disruptions, but more fundamental economic and social changes due to advancing technology, industrialization, and worldwide commerce. By the mid-18th century, there were too many Scots remaining on the land of subsistence agriculture and too few Scots in the labor markets of cities and factories. By the year 1755, fundamental changes had already started and by 1800 these changes had become clearly recognized. The collapse of the old order in Scotland had actually very little to do with Bonnie Prince Charlie's failed Jacobite rebellion of 1745 and a great deal to do with James Watt's patenting of the first commercially successful steam engine in 1769.

The first great shift of Scottish population in the 18th century was from rural to urban areas. This shift involved both rural Highlanders and Lowlanders

42

moving to the towns, which were located in the Lowlands. Jobs and money were to be found in the towns, not in the country. The chronic over population of many Highland areas relative to sparse productive land forced emigration by necessity. People had to leave their rural ways of life to find employment and a minimum standard of living in the towns. In the 18th century, far more Highlanders "self-cleared" their tenant lands than were "forced cleared." Agricultural improvements in the Lowlands likewise motivated tenant farmers to find new types of jobs in the towns.

The population of Edinburgh rose dramatically from 57,000 in 1755 to 81,600 in 1801 and 138,000 by 1821. It was the largest city in Scotland until 1801, when it was surpassed by Glasgow. After centuries of being a small market town on the Clyde River, Glasgow emerged in the 18th century as a great port of worldwide commerce and in the 19th century as a major industrial center. Its population grew from only 31,700 in 1755 to 83,700 in 1801 and 147,000 by 1821. The textile center of Paisley, not far from Glasgow grew from 6,800 in 1755 to 47,000 by 1821, surpassing Aberdeen, with 44,600 people, as the third largest city in Scotland. By the census of 1821, one quarter of all Scots lived in 13 cities of 10,000 or more people. By the 20th century, roughly half of all Scots lived in just the three greater metropolitan areas of Glasgow-Paisley, Edinburgh, and Aberdeen.

The second great shift paralleled the first: from the Highlands to the Lowlands, particularly the central industrial belt from Glasgow to Edinburgh and the northeast Lowlands port city of Aberdeen. Because of the rough terrain and land more suitable for pasturing of animals, especially sheep, than the cultivation of crops, the Highlanders and islanders felt forced to move, whether by self-initiation due to economic conditions beyond their control or by the forced evictions of the Clearances (which occurred approximately from the 1790s to the 1880s with the heaviest evictions from the 1820s to the 1860s). Highlanders faced with starvation or eviction had three general options: move to the Lowlands, where they sought work in the factories and mills of the towns and cities; move into England, especially cities like London, to find work as laborers; or move abroad, where they might not only find work but also might have the chance of owning land of their own. Of these three options, the largest number of migrating Highlanders chose the first -- to remain in Scotland, but to relocate from the Highlands to the Lowlands and from agricultural fields to city factories. But a large number also chose the third option: emigration abroad. This redistribution of the Scottish population is reflected in the data presented in Table 2.

TABLE 2, REDISTRIBUTION OF SCOTTISH POPULATION, 1755 TO 1821
(from T. C. Smout, *A History of the Scottish People 1560-1830,*London: Fantana Books, 1972, p. 242, and Central Office of Information, *Britain 1987*, London: Her Majest'ys Stationary Office, 1987, p. 8.)

Region	Land Area (sq. kilometers)	1755	1821
North Scotland (north of a line between the Tay and Clyde Rivers)	56,724 (72%)	652,000 (51%)	873,000 (41%)
Central Scotland (Glasgow-Dundee-Edinburgh triangle)	11,030 (14%)	464,000 (37%)	984,000 (47%)
South Scotland (south of the Glasgow-Edinburgh line)	11,030 (14%)	149,000 (11%)	234,000 (11%)
Totals	78,784	1,265,000	2,091,000

These figures show that in 1755 about 51% of the Scottish population of 1,265,000 lived in the Highlands and islands north of the Tay River-Clyde River line (including Aberdeen and the northeast Lowlands), which comprised about 72% of Scotland's territory. Conversely, about 49% of the people lived on about 28% of the land in central and south Scotland (the southern Lowlands). During the next 66 years, from 1755 to 1821, the total population increased by 835,000, from 1,265,000 in 1755 to about 2,100,000

44

in 1821. This was an increase of 66% spread over about six and one-half decades. But the distribution of that increased population changed. While the population of North Scotland increased by about 34%, by 1821 it comprised only 41% rather than 51% of the entire Scottish population. The population of Central Scotland increased by about 112% and rose from 37% to 47% of the total population. This reflected the rapid growth in the urban population of the Clyde Valley and of Edinburgh. And the population of South Scotland grew by about 57%, but remained at 11% of the total. In relative terms, Scots were becoming less rural, isolated, and agricultural and were becoming more urban, centralized, and industrial.

The figures for Scottish population, of course, reflect net population growth. Much of this growth came from births and some of it came from immigration into Scotland, largely from Ireland. As mentioned before, people have been moving from one side of the Irish Sea to the other for millennia. When times were particularly hard in Scotland, Scots moved over to Ireland, primarily for farming and trading; at least 200,000 Scots, largely Lowlanders, resettled in Ulster in the 17th and early 18th centuries. Likewise, when times were particularly hard in Ireland, Irish moved to Scotland to find work. This was particularly true in the 19th and 20th centuries, when Irish men came to Glasgow and other cities seeking jobs in factories, shipyards, and mills.

The population figures also show net growth after considerable population loses due to deaths and emigration. The figures in Table 3 indicate that natural growth was actually considerably higher than the net population growth.

TABLE 3, NATURAL AND NET SCOTTISH POPULATION GROWTH, 1861-1939
(from Flinn, *Scottish Population History,* pp. 304-305)

Years	% Natural Growth	% Net Growth	Years	% Natural Growth	% Net Growth
1861-1870	13.6	9.7	1901-1910	12.1	6.5
1871-1880	14.0	11.2	1911-1920	9.1	2.6
1881-1890	13.6	7.8	1921-1930	7.2	-0.8
1891-1900	12.4	11.1	1931-1939	4.4	3.4

For the census decades from 1861 to 1939, the natural growth rate was actually several percentage points higher than the net growth rate for every period except 1891-1900. The difference, the "lost population," was largely emigration out of Scotland. The effects of net immigration (or "out-migration") are seen in Table 4.

TABLE 4, SCOTTISH NET OUT-MIGRATION
(from Flinn, *Scottish Population History*, pp. 441, 442)

Years	Net Out-Migration	% Natural Growth
1861-1870	116,872	27.7
1871-1880	92,808	19.8
1881-1890	218,274	41.0
1891-1900	51,728	10.4
1901-1910	253,894	46.8
1911-1920	226,007	53.6
1921-1930	415,768	110.5
1931-1939	47,973	22.2

These figures reflect the third great movement of Scottish people, the emigration from Scotland to Ulster, England, and abroad (mainly the United States, Canada, Australia, New Zealand, and South Africa). Emigrants came from both rural and urban areas. Over half of the natural population growth for 1861-1939 emigrated. This figure includes out-migration to Ireland and to England and Wales as well as overseas. The only numbers available show that 748,577 Scots out-migrated to another part of the U.K. from 1841 to 1931. Therefore, it would be reasonable to conclude that generally two-to-three Scots left the U.K. altogether for every one Scot who resettled elsewhere in the U.K. from the early 19th through the early 20th centuries.

Statistics for Scottish emigration are fragmentary. We do not know exactly how many Scots left Scotland and how many came to the Thirteen Colonies and the United States. In the years 1825 to 1938, as many as 2.3 million Scots emigrated abroad, of which about one million went to the U.S. and another 750,000 entered Canada. These are estimates of direct emigration from Scotland, and they do not capture the numbers of Anglo-Scots, Ulster Scots, and Canadian Scots who eventually settled in the U.S. A reasonable guess is that at least two million Scots or people of Scottish origin came to the Thirteen Colonies or the United States since 1600s. Of these, at most 25% (and maybe closer to 20%) arrived before 1790 and at least 75% in the last 200 years.

The total of two million Scottish-American immigrants is just an approximation and may be in reality somewhat high. U.S. immigration and census data state the there were only about 750,000 Scottish immigrants from 1820 to 1950. This figure, however, seems too low. According to the same U.S. statistics, there were over 2.7 million immigrants from "England" and nearly 4.8 million from "Ireland" in the period of 1820 to 1900. Both of these group would have included ethnic Scots and Scottish descendants.

Just as the Scottish population growth was not evenly distributed, so, too, was the uneven pattern of emigration. In absolute terms, most Scottish emigrants were Lowlanders, since most Scots after 1600 were Lowlanders. In relative terms, however, more Highlanders emigrated among their set than Lowlanders. The figures in Table 5 show the percentages of actual and natural population growth in the regions of Scotland for three selected census decades. The difference in growth rates is the negative effect of emigration, so that these figures say that emigration significantly depopulated areas north of the Highland line and the Northeast Lowlands.

TABLE 5, SCOTTISH POPLUATION GROWTH BY REGIONS
(from Flinn, *Scottish Population History,* pp. 304-305)
(all figures are given as percentages)

Region	1861-1870 Actual	1861-1870 Natural	1891-1900 Actual	1891-1900 Natural	1921-1930 Actual	1921-1930 Natural
Far North	-2.2	11.1	-5.8	6.0	-11.3	0.7
Highlands	-1.9	8.9	-1.0	5.7	-13.8	1.0
Northeast	7.2	16.0	6.3	13.7	-1.4	7.9
West Lowlands	17.1	14.8	19.0	15.2	0.8	9.7
East Lowlands	10.1	13.0	10.1	11.2	-0.1	6.7
Borders	-0.1	12.9	-5.7	7.5	-1.5	4.2
Scotland	9.7	13.6	11.1	12.4	-0.8	7.2

According to these numbers, the natural population growth due to births in Scotland for the census decade of 1861-1870 was 13.6%, but the actual statistical population growth was only 9.7%. The difference of nearly four percentage points in population growth was the effect of emigration. And for all three sample decades, the natural population growth north of the Highland line was positive, but the actual statistical growth was negative. In a very broad sense, emigration replaced famine and disease as the great moderator of disaster-potential population growth in Scotland since the 19th century and perhaps even earlier. As it turned out, in most cases, the people who emigrated made the quality of life better for both themselves away from Scotland and for the Scots who remained home.

A data sample of Scottish emigrants to the U.S. appears to be roughly parallel to the above figures. Table 6 shows the distribution of Scottish origins of a sample set of 5,737 Scottish immigrants into the U.S. through the year 1854. These numbers, again, show that proportionately more immigrants came from the Highlands, but that in raw numbers most immigrants were Lowlanders, especially from the Glasgow and Edinburgh vicinities.

TABLE 6, REGION OF ORIGIN OF 5,737 SCOTTISH IMMIGRANTS
TO THE U.S. TO 1854
(from Stephen Thernstrom, ed., *Harvard Encyclopedia of American Ethnic Groups*, Cambridge, MA: Belknap Press of Harvard University, 1980, p. 910.)

Scottish Region	% Scottish Population	% of 5,737 Immigrants
Edinburgh and the Lothians	12.5	10.6
Borders	4.5	4.4
Lanark (including Glasgow), Renfrew, and Ayr	24.2	21.7
Galloway and Dumfries	7.2	8.9
Fife	6.8	4.5
Stirling and Dumbarton	4.7	3.1
Perth	6.9	8.7
Northeastern Lowlands: Kincardine, Angus, and Aberdeen	15.0	5.5
Sutherland, Caithnessand Orkney and Shetland Islands	5.3	0.1
Inverness	4.5	9.3
Ross and Cromarty	3.5	3.7
Argyl	4.9	13.9

Because the absolute population was greater in the Glasgow and Edinburgh vicinities, the largest number of Scottish immigrants to the U.S. came from these areas. The proportion of emigrants to the U.S. (10.6%) was similar to the proportion to the area's population relative to all of Scotland (12.5%). In the case of the northeast Lowlands, emigration to the U.S. was only 5.5% of the total number of emigrants counted, although this area had 15% of the Scottish population. Therefore, the northeast Lowlands, including the city and shire of Aberdeen, was under represented by the proportion of American immigrants. But the city and shire of Inverness and the western Highland shire of Argyll, including many of the islands of the Inner Hebrides, was over represented by the proportion of American immigrants. These numbers are consistent with the previous observation that in absolute terms, most Scottish immigrants to the U.S. came from the Lowlands, but in terms relative to the local population a higher percentage of Highlanders emigrated to America than the percentage of Lowlanders.

Exactly how many Scots came to America is very difficult to determine, especially before the first U.S. census in 1790. Very few came to America before 1718, when the pace of Scottish immigration increased to a noticeable level. One estimate (by Fischer) is that about 1,000,000 immigrants from Scotland, northern England, and northern Ireland came to America from 1718 to 1775. Of these, at least 150,000 came from northern Ireland and 75,000 came from Scotland. Another estimate (Bailyn) is that 150,000 immigrants came from Ulster alone in these same years. It is generally believed that the pace of immigration greatly increased from the end of the French and Indian War in 1763 to the beginning of the American Revolution in 1775. The low estimate (Graham) is that there were just 20,000 Scottish immigrants in the eight years of 1768-1775. Another estimate is that there were at least 40,000 Scottish immigrants from 1760-1775. Based on an analysis of the census of 1790, however, the number of Scottish settlers, their families, and descendants may have been as high as 250,000 Lowlander and Highlander Scots and as many as 225,000 Ulster Scots. By 1790, roughly 450,000 - 500,000 Americans were "Scottish," including the Scotch-Irish.

This chapter has provided an overview of Scottish population growth and the pressures it created for out-migration to other parts of the U.K. and abroad. In general, the principal reason why Scots emigrated to North America was to escape the over population and under opportunity of Scotland. The more specific circumstances for emigration will be further explored in the next chapter.

References

Of the many books on Scottish demographic and social history, these are particularly important:

Michael Flinn, *Scottish Population History from the 17th century to the 1930's*. Cambridge: Cambridge University Press, 1977.

D. F. MacDonald, *Scotland's Shifting Population, 1770-1850*. Philadelphia: Porcupine Press, 1978 (1937).

Eric Richards, *A History of the Highland Clearances. Agrarian Transformation and the Evictions, 1746-1886*. London: Croom Helm, 1982, and *A History of the Highland Clearances. Vol. II: Emigration, Protest, Reasons*. London: Croom Helm, 1985.

T. C. Smout, *A History of the Scottish People, 1560-1830*. London: Fontana Books, 1972.

G. Whittington and I. D. Whyte, ed., *An Historic Geography of Scotland*. London: Academic Press, 1983.

Works on the reasons for Scottish emigration will be fully listed in the forthcoming References for Chapter 4. The works specifically used for this chapter, in addition to the more general works already listed in the References for Chapter 2, were as follows:

Bernard Aspinwall, *Portable Utopia. Glasgow and the United States, 1820-1920*. Aberdeen: Aberdeen University Press, 1984.

Bernard Bailyn, *Voyagers to the West. A Passage in the Peopling of America on the Eve of the Revolution*. New York: Vintage Books, 1988.

Bernard Bailyn and Philip D. Morgan, eds., *Strangers within the Realm. Cultural Margins of the First British Empire.* Chapel Hill, NC: University of North Carolina Press, 1991.

William Brock, *Scotus Americanus.* Edinburgh: Edinburgh University Press, 1982.

T. M. Devine, ed. *Scottish Emigration and Scottish Society.* Edinburgh: John Donald, 1992.

David Hackett Fischer, *Albion's Seed. Four British Folkways in America.* New York: Oxford University Press, 1989.

Ian Charles Cargill Graham, *Colonists from Scotland: Emigration to North America, 1707-1783.* Ithaca, NY: Cornell University Press, 1956.

James G. Leyburn, *The Scotch-Irish. A Social History.* Chapel Hill, NC: The University of North Carolina Press, 1962.

Kerby A. Miller, *Emigrants and Exiles. Ireland and the Irish Exodus to North America.* New York: Oxford University Press, 1985.

Stephen Thernstrom, ed., *Harvard Encyclopedia of American Ethnic Groups.* Cambridge, MA: Belknap Press of Harvard University, 1980 (entries on Scots and Scotch-Irish).

Chapter Four:

The Push of Scottish Emigration

During good times as well as the bad times, some Scots decided to leave their homeland while others decided to remain in Scotland no matter how grim the prospects. Every emigrant had his or her own personal reasons for leaving. Generally, the reasons fell into two categories. One was the "push" out of Scotland, where conditions seemed so bad that the individual felt the need to leave in order to survive. The other category of reasons was the "pull" to other lands, where conditions seemed so much better that the attraction was too strong to resist. The single greatest "push" out of Scotland over the last four centuries has been population growth that threatened to exceed supporting resources. This theme was covered in the previous chapter. However, underneath the overpopulation of Scotland rested a more fundamental reason for emigration. This was the economic restructuring of Scotland resulting from the Industrial Revolution. This economic theme with closely associated social, political, and religious themes are covered in this chapter.

The fundamental cause of the Scottish diaspora, which peaked during the period from the end of the Seven Years War (1763) to the beginning of the Great Depression (1930) was economic: the Scots felt driven out of their homes by economic forces beyond their ability to control.

Economic Restructuring

To recount briefly the points made in Chapter 3, the population of Scotland virtually exploded during the 18th and 19th centuries. In 1707, the number of Scots was estimated to be 1.1 million. By 1901, it had grown to almost 4.5 million, despite heavy emigration. The population growth was primarily due to the declining death rate of children and the increasing life expectancy due to greatly improved nutrition and public health.

The population growth strained meager natural resources, especially as long as agriculture remained at the subsistence level (which it did until about the mid-18th century). At most, the arable land of Scotland was just 20% of the total territory, and the extent and fertility of Scottish land was very limited by primitive farming customs. The rich fields of the northeastern and southern Lowlands might have supported hundreds of people per square mile, but the mountains and barren lands that cover so much of Scotland could support only a few people per square mile, while they could maintain hundreds of grazing cattle or sheep. The Lowlands contained most of the rich land, but it also held most of the people, who placed strains even on the richest resources.

In response to the crowding conditions on the land, Lowlanders had three options. One was to stay on the land, but endure a likely decline in material well-being, particularly because of fluctuating produce prices but steadily increasing rents. The second choice was to relocate to the cities, particularly those of the Strathclyde, where jobs were available in factories and mills. While wages were often higher than the income from agriculture, the costs of urban living were typically higher than the costs of rural living and the quality of life was often poorer. The third choice was to emigrate to other opportunities beyond Scotland. The risks of starting over again in a new land were very high, but so too were the potential rewards.

Highlanders had the same basic choices, but more pressure to make them more quickly. The Highlands contained much of the grazing pastures that could support even fewer people per square mile than the Lowlands. Although the population of the Highlands was not as dense by the 17th century as it was in the Lowlands, relative to the available resources the

Highlands suffered more crowding than the Lowlands. After about the mid-17th century, the great value of the relatively mild and wet grasslands of the Highlands and islands was found in the grazing of cattle and sheep, not with the farming of men. Some Highlanders were given no choice: they were forced off of the land by the lairds, even their own clan chiefs, in the great clearances of the 19th century. Whether by choice or by force, many Highlanders shifted to the Lowlander cities for work, or to other parts of the U.K. (especially London), or they emigrated abroad.

In an immediate cause-and-effect relationship, the principal motivation for emigration abroad was overcrowding at home. But in a larger context, overpopulation was an effect of profound economic and social changes occurring in Scotland. Both the population boom and emigration were due to the fundamental restructuring of the Scottish economy.

During the 18th century, Scotland entered the Industrial Revolution, which changed national life from a largely rural, agrarian, and subsistence order to a primarily urban, technological, and industrial order. Many people could not make the transition within Scotland. Some were forced to change and others elected to make their own changes. One such change was emigration. Scottish emigrants left their homes in hopes of finding less crowded conditions and more material opportunities in new lands.

The push of emigration was also economics in the sense of business downturns, which we now call depressions and recessions. People who had made the vocational transition from farm hands to industrial workers now found themselves vulnerable to job layoffs. The new middle class of merchants, industrialists, and investors found themselves vulnerable to business failures. In response to lost jobs and failed enterprises, many emigrated to start over again.

The Industrial Revolution created enormous improvements in agriculture and the ability of Scotland to feed its people. It greatly improved public health. But it also created tremendous social disruptions, creating circumstances that forced people to make basic changes in where and how they lived. It changed occupations and lifestyles. The Industrial Revolution facilitated population growth; it also accelerated emigration.

Rack Rents and the Clearances

The Highlands were already experiencing a revolutionary change in the socio-economic order by the middle of the 18th century. While the politics of the Jacobite revolts captured people's attention at the time, the underlying economic changes were far more important than the superficial political turmoil.

One impact of the earlier Jacobite revolts had been the government's building of roads through the Highlands. They were meant to provide the means for the rapid movement of troops to quickly quell disturbances, just as the Romans had once built roads farther south for much the same strategic reasons. But the roads also provided a means for personal and commercial travel, and this means of transportation of people and goods did more to change the Highlands than the movement of Redcoats. The economic order of the Highlands became more integrated with the economic order of the Lowlands and even of England beyond. The result was that the economy of the Highlands became more dependent on the south for cash and capital investments. It also acquired southern ways of conducting business.

Another consequence of the last Jacobite rising of 1745 was the termination of the jurisdictional powers of clan chiefs. The chiefs lost much of their legal hold over their clansmen and tenants. In fact, the clan system of old was already disintegrating and the 1745 rebellion merely accelerated its demise. In addition to being the last Jacobite rebellion and the last political war within Great Britain, the Forty-Five was the last violent clan feud. After 1746 the power of a clan chief, who was also typically a titled and landed nobleman, was measured in cash from land rents and products rather than in fighting men. There was no longer a need for large numbers of men to call to arms by the symbol of the burned cross. There was no longer a need for men who contributed little to the value of the land and who paid historically nominal rents. On the contrary, after 1746 the surplus of fighting men working poor fields became an economic liability rather than a political asset. After 1746 the clan chiefs became businessmen who wanted money, not warlords who needed men.

After 1746, numerous Highland clan chiefs, nobles, and other land owners (the "lairds") significantly raised land rents. In some cases, the rent increases had begun modestly as early as the 1740s; elsewhere, the rents began to climb by the 1780s. The Highlands were experiencing a fundamental economic restructuring. Land was becoming more valuable due to technological improvements in the south and the rising prices for wool to be manufactured into cloth. The rich grazing lands of the Highlands had always been better suited for raising animals than for cultivating crops. Because of technological and agricultural improvements in the Lowlands, the value of land, and the rents charged for it, rose sharply across Scotland during the second half of the 18th century.

In general, in both the Highlands and Lowlands, land rents began climbing sharply after the Seven Years War (the French and Indian Wars in North America) ended in 1763. It has been estimated that rents doubled in just the 10 years of 1783-1793. They doubled yet again from 1794 to 1815, during the French wars. These dramatic increases reflected the appreciation of land values in Great Britain, in part due to significant agricultural improvements and growing industrial uses for land. But the escalating values created higher rents, which many tenants could not afford.

The practice of successive steep increases in rents became known as "rack rents." It placed a burden of productivity squarely on the land cultivators, the tenants. No longer needed as warriors, the farmers had to prove that their value-added to the land was greater than the sheeps'. The rising rents and the demand for cash rather than "rent in kind" placed severe hardships on many tenants, some of whom held only annual leases and some of whom had no binding arrangement at all. They typically had to pay their rents by May 25, which was called "flitting day." They either paid or they "flitted." If they could pay, they stayed; if they could not, they had to move on.

The first group to be hit hard by "rack rents" was the tacksmen. They were often related to the clan chief or land owner and a part of the socio-economic power circle. They held long-term leases from the land owner. They paid an annual rent to the laird and in turn collected rents from the individual tenants. In one sense, the tacksmen were middlemen; in another sense, they were the land managers, much as the merchant middle managers who were called "factors". Rarely did the lord ever deal directly with his own tenants; in most cases he relied upon the services of the tacksmen to manage the land, crops, animals, and people.

The tacksmen were uniformly hit hard by the increases in land rents. They felt betrayed and victimized by their lords. The tacksmen felt that successive increases in rents broke an age-old contract of mutual support between them and their superiors. It also put them in a tense squeeze between demanding lairds and indignant, and then too often indigent, tenants. But many tacksmen were resourceful enough to retaliate: they emigrated and took some of their tenants with them. From the mid-1760s, tacksmen led the emigration, especially from the Highlands and islands to America. We do not know the precise numbers, but the volume was in the thousands -- perhaps as high as 5,000 per year from the Highlands and islands prior to September 1775, when emigration to America was halted by British authorities. The emigration resumed after the peace of 1783, but again we do not know the exact numbers.

Once resettled in the New World, these tacksmen continued their roles as community leaders, business managers, and independent farmers. Most of them who had arrived by 1775 became Patriots rather than Loyalists and proponents of individual rights, including the protection of property, as expressed in the state constitutions.

One documented example of a particularly resourceful tacksman was James Hogg, who came from his native East Lothian, in the southeastern Lowlands, to lease and manage a part of an estate in Caithness in the far north in 1765. He tried to apply new methods of land improvements from the Lowlands, but he met continued resistance. After repeated unpleasant incidents, Hogg decided to emigrate to North Carolina, where his older brother, Robert Hogg, had preceded him and where he had become a wealthy colonial merchant. Hogg led his family of 16 members and another 280 tenants out of Thurso in June 1773. They encountered great hardships on stormy seas and turned back to Leith, the seaport of Edinburgh. A whole year later, Hogg's surviving party, now greatly reduced in numbers, departed again, this time from Greenock, the principal port of departure for American emigration on the Scottish west coast. His group arrived in North Carolina in August 1774 and relocated to Cross Creek (later Fayetteville, NC), where numerous Highlanders had already settled. Once in America, Hogg prospered as a merchant and land speculator. He played a leading role in the early settlements of Kentucky.

During their tour of the Highlands in August 1773, Dr. Samuel Johnson and James Boswell discussed the issue of "rack renting" with a Mr. McQueen, a tenant in Glenmorison (near Loch Ness). Mr. McQueen told them that the rent on his farm had been only five pounds sterling some 20 years previously, but that the current rent had risen to 20 pounds sterling. He claimed that he could live comfortably where he was at 10 pounds sterling per year. With little chance of increasing his income to cover increased costs, his plan was to emigrate to America, to which 70 from the same glen had already departed. According to Boswell's notes, "Dr. Johnson said, he wished M'Queen laird of Glenmorison, and the laird to go to America. M'Queen very generously answered, he should be sorry for it; for the laird could not shift for himself in America as he could do."

The emigration of resourceful and independent-minded Scots prior to about 1790 has been called "the people's clearance." They may have felt pressured, but they took the initiative to leave Scotland. They typically paid their families' fare aboard and resettled successfully.

By the 1790s, however, the lairds' forced clearances began in earnest. The bidding by Lowland enterprises for the use of Highland pastures for large numbers of sheep for commercial wool production rose too high for the Highland landowners to resist. The lairds could no longer wait for their tacksmen and tenants to make their own decision to leave; they began to evict all tenants to clear the land for sheep. The numbers of evicted people we, again, do not know for sure, but they would have been in the tens of thousands, perhaps as high as 100,000 or maybe one-third of the total population of the Highlands and islands. The volume of evictions was rather high during the 1820s through 1850s, although it declined in mid-century. When the clearances resumed in the 1880s serious violence occurred, particularly on the island of Skye. A government commission led by Lord Napier investigated the situation and recommended several reforms. In 1888 parliament passed legislation that protected tenant rights and long-term leases. The period of the clearances, which had lasted roughly 100 years, was over.

At the time of the clearances, in the late 18th and most of the 19th centuries, land tenants were generally identified as crofters or cotters. The crofters typically held by tradition or written lease the better infield lands. They were semi-independent farmers with social status just behind the tacksmen. They often supplied their own tools and equipment and marketed their own produce. They paid their rents in cash or in kind. During the 19th century, the lords often demanded cash, which was always in scarce supply in the Highlands and islands. The crofters were strong willed people, and they either fought back against rising rents and eviction or they emigrated abroad, where they could buy their own farms.

The cotters were generally less skilled, less advantaged, and less independent minded than the crofters. They held the poorer outfields. Or they supplied their labor to crofters or tacksmen. They were particularly hard hit by the clearances, as they had little wish to leave and very few resources to reinvest elsewhere. They were the true victims of the clearances because they were often left destitute and homeless. The worst cases of the clearances involved the burning of cotter shacks, sometimes with the cotters still inside of them. The lucky ones were those whose passage abroad was paid for them by the lairds or a benevolent group.

And what became of the evicted tacksmen, crofters, and cotters? None of them were restored by the reforms of 1888 and very few, if any, returned to their previous leases. What records were kept indicate that most of the "people's clearance" emigrants prior to about 1790 went to the thirteen colonies that became the United States. The people of the forced clearances after about 1790 scattered in several directions. Some moved to the Lowlands, where they sought jobs in the expanding factories and mills of the Industrial Revolution. Others moved on to England, especially to London, where there existed a strong demand for labor. Many emigrated. Of the emigrants caused by the clearances, most seem to have gone to Canada, Australia, and New Zealand, which were still within the British empire.

Rack rents also occurred in the Lowlands and Ulster during the 18th and first half of the 19th centuries, although forced clearances were rare. The value of land increased greatly in the Lowlands due to agricultural improvements of farm lands and the use of land for housing, factories, mills, and other capital improvements of the Industrial Revolution. Many farming families left the land for opportunities elsewhere. The mood of Lowland emigration, however, was generally more positive than that of the Highlands. Few Lowlanders were literally pushed off of the land. When rents got too high, many left more or less cheerfully in order to pursue opportunities for better employment in the cities or to own their own farms in America. In Scotland, the good land was already "taken" by landowners whose families held titles dating back hundreds of years. But in America excellent land was plentiful and cheap, just waiting to yield bounty to the experienced, hard-working Lowland farmer. The American pull was generally stronger than the Scottish push for Lowlander emigrants.

Rack rents were more of a problem in Ulster than in the Lowlands. Rising population was also creating social and economic problems in northern Ireland. So, too, were the socio-economic structural changes of land improvements and industrialization. Good land was limited in quantity and firmly held by the property-owning class. When the lairds raised their rents, many Ulster Scot tenants could not afford to remain. Alternative employment was more limited in Ireland than in Scotland. Some Ulster Scots returned to Great Britain; many more emigrated to America, especially the colony of Pennsylvania. Many of the Ulster Scots, like the Highlander tenants, emigrated with remorse if not bitterness because they felt pushed off the land their families had worked, but not owned, for generations. Also, many of the land-hungry Ulster Scots, who were called "Scotch Irish" or just "Irish" after they arrived in the colonies, were poorer than their Lowland cousins and prone to settle on good land whether or not they had a legal claim.

Economic Reverses

Another major economic push for emigration was periodic economic reverses, or what we call today "recessions." In the 18th century, they were generally called "panics," often created by a large bank failure or market collapse. A severe reversal was the collapse of the New Scotland Company and its colony at Darien in South America in 1699. One estimate has been that the amount of speculative investment lost equaled one-third of the entire Scottish gross domestic product. This reversal, however, contributed little to emigration abroad. Perhaps the Darien disaster even discouraged emigration. The economic ups and downs contributed little to emigration to North America before the 1770's.

After 1773, however, economic reverses became a major push for emigration to North America. In that year the large Ayr bank failed with a major contraction of the money market. Loans were called in and businesses failed. The new commercial and early industrial economic order had created sudden unemployment. Urban workers with no incomes had little means of survival. So many emigrated. Subsequently, economic downturns in the British economy stimulated emigration abroad. This was especially true for the 1920s, when Scotland suffered a major economic contraction following World War I. Almost 416,000 Scots, or about 8.5% of the entire Scottish population, emigrated during the 1920s, with almost 160,000 entering the U.S. directly from the U.K. Yet, when the Great Depression came in the 1930s, emigration dropped dramatically to less than 50,000. There were no more jobs to be had in the U.S. and Canada than in the U.K. Since World War II, emigration has been marginal with growing employment and housing in Scotland. So the period of emigration due to the push of economics lasted from about 1763 to 1930.

Religious and Political Repression

A popular misconception is that many Scots were exiled from their homeland due to religious and political reasons. Certainly some were, especially during the religious and political turmoil of Great Britain during the 17th century, but the number of emigrants due to exile was actually small relative to the much larger number of people who left for economic reasons. The religious and political reasons for emigration existed principally in the 17th and first half of the 18th centuries, whereas most Scottish emigrants left Scotland because of economic reasons from the mid-18th to the early 20th centuries.

Religious persecution drove some dissenting Scots to America during the 1600s. These emigrating Scots were largely Presbyterians from the Lowlands and Ulster from the 1620s until the early 1700s. Charles I, who reigned from 1625 to 1649, proved to be less astute than his father in dealing with the Scottish Calvinists. His repeated insistence upon an episcopal form of church government and his preference for the Church of England faith alienated the Calvinists, who rejected the authority of bishops and the "high church" ways of England. Dissenters in 1638 signed the Solemn League and Covenant as their protest against religious oppression. From this document, the Scottish dissenters took the name "Covenanters." In later times, we have simply labeled them as Presbyterians, although at the time Presbyterians were even more uncompromising in their insistence upon religious rigor than many Covenanters were.

Charles tried to suppress dissent in the 1640s, but rather than emigrate the Covenanters fought back in the First and Second Bishops Wars (1639-1641), which contributed to the outbreak of the English Civil War (1642-1646). During the 1640s and 1650s the entire British Isles were swept by wars among political factions (royalists, parliament, the army, and radicals), religious groups (Catholics, high church Anglicans, Puritans, Independents, Presbyterians, and Levelers), economic interests (nobles, gentry, merchants, and laborers), and nationalities (English, Scots, and Irish).

One major result of the English Civil War was the coming to power of General Oliver Cromwell and the Independents, whom we generally call Puritans. Although the Puritans shared Calvinist beliefs, they did not see eye-to-eye with the Presbyterians, both English and Scottish. More Presbyterians were driven from Great Britain under Cromwell than under Charles I. Some Scottish Covenanters, although they had opposed Charles I, rallied to the claim to the throne by Charles' exiled heir, Charles II, because of their differences with Cromwell and his assertion of English and parliament's authority over Scotland. Cromwell invaded Scotland in July 1750 and smashed all opposition more thoroughly than Edward I had in the early 14th century. Cromwell twice routed Scottish armies in support of Charles II. He destroyed a Scottish army near Dunbar in September 1750 and took an estimated 10,000 prisoners. While there was a plan to exile these prisoners to America, very few, perhaps just a few hundred, were actually sent to the New World due to the enormous logistical problems and expenses of shipping so many people so far away. Then in September 1651 Cromwell destroyed a second Scottish army at the Battle of Worcester, where as many as another 10,000 prisoners may have been taken. Again, a few were exiled to America, but not very many.

In terms of numbers, these exiled Scots from the battles of Dunbar and Worcester were insignificant, perhaps no more than 500 at most. In terms of importance, however, these Scots became early settlers in New England and the progenitors of some later famous families. For example, a Scot named Home or Hume was exiled to the Massachusetts Bay Colony in 1651 after Worcester. He was the founder of the very famous Boston family of Holmes, from which came Dr. Oliver Wendell Holmes, the physician and author, and the second Oliver Wendell Holmes, the legal genius and justice of the U.S. Supreme Court.

When Charles II was restored to the throne by parliament in 1660, he again, like his father, tried to impose a uniform church governance and faith in both England and Scotland. His repression of dissent in Scotland was even more brutal than that of either Charles I or Cromwell. The Covenanters were equally intolerant and violent in their response. The warfare that erupted in the Lowlands from 1681 to 1685 has been called the "Killing Time." Many Scots did emigrate, but more relocated to Ireland than to America. The level of political tension rose with the reign of Charles' brother, James II, from 1685 to 1688. James was a Catholic, which was even more unacceptable to most Scots than a high church Anglican. In 1688, James' second wife, an Italian Catholic, gave birth to a male heir (who became the "Old Pretender" and the father of Bonnie Prince Charlie in the next century). The English Protestants drove James from the throne and invited William, the Dutch Prince of Orange, and his wife Mary, both of whom were grandchildren of Charles I, to rule jointly. Stuart revolts against William and Mary were repressed in Scotland and Ireland.

Beginning with William and Mary in 1688, religious dissent declined as a major issue in Scotland, although it continued strongly in Ireland. Under the terms of the Act of Union of 1707, Scotland retained its national

Presbyterian church (kirk) and other forms of Protestant worship (the Episcopal church in Scotland parallel to the Anglican Church in England) were permitted.

The Ulster Scot Presbyterians felt more pressures to emigrate after 1688 because of religious reasons than either the Highlanders or Lowlanders. They were caught in the squeeze between native Irish Catholics and English Anglicans. A bloody revolt of Catholics in 1641 resulted in an Irish civil war that resulted in extensive loss of lives and properties in Protestant-dominated Ulster. Again in 1688-1689, during the Catholic support of the exiled James II against William III, Protestants were attacked in Ulster. The Ulster Scot responses were equally intolerant and bloody.

Ulster Scots did not enjoy the freedoms of religion that Scotland did, because Scotland had its own national kirk, but Presbyterians in Ulster continued to suffer the disciplines of an established Church of England in Ireland, much the same as the Catholics did. For example, the Test Act of 1704 excluded Presbyterians as well as Catholics from holding public offices in England and Ireland. While the Presbyterians were the established majority in Scotland, the Scottish Presbyterians were a discriminated minority in Ireland. In the early 1700s unsettled religious issues did create a push for emigration for Ulster Scots, many of whom sought religious freedoms as well as new economic opportunities in the American colonies.

Another misperception has been that numerous Scots emigrated abroad because of the Jacobite rebellions. After James II fled London in 1688, he and his heirs continued to claim the rightful title to the English and Scottish throne. They were called "Jacobites" after James. Revolts occurred in Scotland in 1689, 1708, 1715, and 1745. Support for the Scottish Jacobites lay largely in the Highlands among several clans that rebelled more in opposition to government clans, especially the Campbells, than they did against the Protestant succession. Most of them were not Catholics, which the Stuart heirs were, but Episcopalian or Presbyterian, although the Irish Jacobites were overwhelmingly Catholic. Their chief motivation, rather than religion, was the restoration of the Scottish line of the House of Stuart and even the reconstitution of the separate Scottish state. If Bonnie Prince Charlie had won his war in 1745-1746, he would have likely restored Catholicism as the established religion of a united kingdom of England, Scotland, and Ireland under the Jacobite Stuarts strongly supported by the French and Spanish. The Jacobites relied heavily upon French and Spanish assistance while they enjoyed very little popular support from the Lowlands and England.

After the collapse of each Jacobite revolt, some Jacobites were exiled abroad. Their number has been estimated to have been less than 1,000 from 1689 through 1746. Like the political and religious exiles of the previous century, the Jacobite emigrants have been highly romanticized because of their circumstances rather than their large numbers. More significantly, perhaps several thousand political refugees may have elected to emigrate from Scotland to avoid further trouble with British authorities.

Finally, it has been believed that in addition to religious persecution and political exile, there were significant numbers of common criminals expelled from Scotland to the New World. This is not supported by evidence. Again, there were indeed criminals sent abroad rather than jailed at home. But colonial officials objected to receiving colonists who would be a burden rather than an asset to the growing colonial society. The North American colonies had been founded as commercial enterprises, not as penal colonies.

In conclusion, the principal push for emigration out of Scotland since the 17th century has been economic. Insufficient and highly expensive land, food, housing, employment, and business opportunities to satisfy a rapidly growing population were the principal negative reasons for emigration. The positive reasons, or the pull for American immigration, will be reviewed in the next chapter.

References

Many of the same references used in Chapter 3 were also used for Chapter 4. Of particular value for this chapter were the following works:

Bernard Bailyn, *Voyagers to the West. A Passage in the Peopling of America on the Eve of the Revolution.* New York: Vintage Books, 1988. This analysis is based on real data: British government surveys of English and Scottish emigrants from 1773-1775. It is the only concrete evidence we have today for why emigrants left Great Britain. The account of James Hogg appears in Chapter 14, pp. 499-544.

Bernard Bailyn and Philip D. Morgan eds., *Strangers within the Realm. Cultural Margins of the First British Empire.* Chapel Hill, N.C.: University of North Carolina Press, 1991. While this volume contains several fine papers, of particular importance is the one by Eric Richards, "Scotland and the Uses of the Atlantic Empire," pp. 67-114.

J. M. Bumstead, *The People's Clearance: Highland Emigration to British North America, 1770-1815.* Edinburgh: Edinburgh University Press, 1982.

T. M. Devine, ed. *Scottish Emigration and Scottish Society.* Edinburgh: John Donald Publishers Ltd, 1992.

Charlotte Erikson, *Invisible Immigrants. The Adaptation of English and Scottish Immigrants in Nineteenth-Century America.* Coral Gables, FL: University of Miami Press, 1972.

Ian Charles Cargill Graham, *Colonists from Scotland: Emigration to North America, 1707-1783.* Ithaca, N.Y.: Cornell University Press, 1956.

James G. Leyburn, *The Scotch-Irish. A Social History.* Chapel Hill, N.C.: The University of North Carolina Press, 1962. The author explains Scottish immigration to Ireland as well as Ulster Scot emigration to America.

Kerby A. Miller, *Emigrants and Exiles. Ireland and the Irish Exodus to North America.* New York: Oxford University Press, 1985.

Eric Richards, *A History of the Highland Clearances. Agrarian Transformation and the Evictions, 1745-1886.* London: Croom Helm, 1982, and *A*

History of the Highland Clearances. Vol. II, *Emigration, Protest, Reasons.* London: Croom Helm, 1985.

T. C. Smout, *A History of the Scottish People, 1560-1830.* London: Fontana Books, 1972. Smout's social and economic analysis of the Scottish people during the Reformation and the early Industrial Revolution is a superb study, both highly readable and insightful.

Allan Wendt, ed., Samuel Johnson, *A Journey to the Western Islands of Scotland* [1775] and James Boswell, *The Journal of a Tour to the Hebrides with Samuel Johnson, LL.D.* [1785]. Boston: Houghton Mifflin Co., 1965; Boswell's account of the conversation with Mr. McQueen appears on p. 200.

For detailed discussions of Scottish demographics and the economics behind them, see:

Michael Flinn, ed., *Scottish Population History from the 17th Century to the 1930's.* Cambridge: Cambridge University Press, 1977.

D. F. MacDonald, *Scotland's Shifting Population, 1770-1850.* Philadelphia: Porcupine Press, 1978 (1937).

G. Whittington and I. D. Whyte, eds., *An Historic Geography of Scotland.* London: Academic Press, 1983.

CHAPTER FIVE:

THE PULL OF AMERICAN IMMIGRATION

As stated in the beginning of the previous chapter, each person who left Scotland did so because of some combination of push for emigration from home and pull for immigration abroad. The reasons for the push were discussed in Chapter 4. The reasons for the pull to America will be surveyed in this chapter.

In general, for every push, or negative quality, which the Scot encountered in Scotland, there was a corresponding pull, or positive quality, that attracted the Scot to America. The most important pull of American immigration was economic opportunity, the reverse of the push for Scottish emigration. For those who emigrated for religious freedoms or political refuge, America offered religious toleration and political asylum. In addition, there were some Scots prior to the American Revolution who came to America in the service of the Crown or one of the Scottish trading enterprises. One further attraction was the Scottish communities in America that called back to family in Scotland to come and join them in the New World.

Economic Opportunities

Clearly the single most important pull of American immigration was economic opportunity. However, the view of exactly what the opportunity was and the expectations of profit varied from person to person, group to group, and nation to nation. Each has had its own "American dream," but in virtually all cases it was to achieve greater material success and personal fulfillment.

The Early Quest for Gold. From the very beginning, the European interest in the New World was largely commercial. When Columbus sailed west from Spain in the summer of 1492, he was hoping to find an Atlantic route to the Orient. What he discovered was a whole new world of resources readily available for European exploitation. The Spanish quickly became more interested in American trade and wealth than the markets of the Far East. Their "American dream" was riches ready to be had. There were stories of fabulously wealthy native cities with streets paved in gold. Spanish conquistadors, led by such famous adventurers as Cortez and Pizzaro, conquered native empires merely to extract precious metals and stones to take back to Spain. The pillaging of Aztec and Inca cities were extremely lucrative. Other Spanish explorers penetrated the northern side of the Caribbean Sea to find magic wonders and riches. Most of these expeditions, however, ended in disappointment, disease, and disaster.

The Spanish, after the initial rush for gold, came to realize that their long-term exploitation of the New World could only be sustained and defended to the extent that they could colonize it with their own people. As early as 1512, just two decades after Columbus' initial discovery of the unknown West Indies, a Spanish settlement on the island of Hispaniola was producing for Spain $1 million a year worth of gold, sugar cane, cotton, and cattle. The enormous wealth of the New World lay ultimately in land, crops, and natural resources that could be transported and sold in the European market. The West Indian trade could be every bit as wealthy as the East Indian trade.

Spanish settlements spread from Hispaniola to neighboring islands of the Caribbean and all around its shores. On the north shore, after several failed attempts, they established in 1565 the fort and town of St. Augustine, facing the Atlantic Ocean, largely to block a French threat to their claims in Florida.

The French had their own version of the American dream. They imitated the Spanish in their initial exploration for easy wealth, but they found their "gold" in the form of animal furs. The French explorer Jacques Cartier in the

1530s and 1540s went looking for gold, like the Spanish, but he found instead animal furs and rich fishing, for which there was a high demand by European consumers. Cartier's voyages were followed by 11 different expeditions to North America by Samuel de Champlain. By the early 1600s the French had become vigorous investors in the North American fur trade and fishing industry. They penetrated the St. Lawrence river and founded the trading towns of Quebec and Montreal. They explored deeply inland through the Great Lakes and down the Mississippi and Ohio Rivers. They also probed the limits of Spanish penetration to the south.

English Trade Colonies. Like the Spanish and the French, the English also took an early interest in exploring North America. As early as 1497, Henry VII commissioned the Venetian explorer John Cabot to sail west. Cabot and his sons on repeated trips probed the North American coast from Newfoundland to the Chesapeake Bay. Further explorations for the English were undertaken by Martin Frobisher and Henry Hudson. Even as early as 1578 English investors tried to establish colonies in the vicinity of North Carolina. After several failed attempts, the first successful English settlement occurred at Jamestown in the colony of Virginia in 1607.

In the beginning, the value of the Virginian colony was not clear. There certainly was no gold in this area. But within only seven years, the early colonists cultivated their own "gold": tobacco. The first shipment of it went back to Europe in 1614. Europeans, especially the English, French, and Dutch, acquired the smoking and sniffing habit. A new commercial crop had been developed in the colonies for a growing market in Europe. Other crops and natural resources also could be sold in Europe, and so the economic development of the land by transplanted colonists, who could also defend themselves from the French and Spanish, became vitally important for English economic growth.

From the base in Virginia, the English settlers spread out in all directions. Additional colonies emerged to the north in Plymouth, Massachusetts Bay, Rhode Island, New Hampshire, and Connecticut. After 1660, the English acquired New York and New Jersey from the Dutch and established the colony of Pennsylvania. By the early 1700s, the English colonies along the eastern coast of North America from Maine to Florida were growing and flourishing as important parts of the worldwide English commercial empire

Scottish Trade Colonies. The Scots, too, wanted their own colonies in the New World. They wanted new lands that would be peopled by Scots producing goods to be carried to Scottish ports. They watched with envy the growing commercial wealth of the Spanish, French, and English, and they wanted their own trade colonies, too.

In the early 17th century, the Scots believed that they could have their own settlements under the protection of the joint Scottish and English Stuart monarchy. They soon discovered, however, that their interests would always be subordinated by both the Crown and parliament to English commercial interests. Beginning in the 1650s, the English parliament applied severe restrictions to trade with the English colonies. By the 1660s parliament barred ships from carrying goods from an English colony unless they were English ships that brought the goods into English ports. The Navigation Acts gave a virtual monopoly over the English colonial trade to English merchants. Legitimate Scottish trade was locked out, although Scottish smuggling thrived. The Scots, therefore, during the late 1600s made several attempts to found their own commercial colonies. All of them failed. The Act of Union of 1707 had the effect of reopening the expanding English colonial network to the Scots, so that the Scots gave up having their own colonies in favor of participating actively in the forming of the British (not just English) Empire.

The first Scottish "plantation" in the New World was in Nova Scotia in the 1620s. It was roughly based on the English and Scottish plantations in northern Ireland and on the English colony of Virginia. Its patron was Sir William Alexander, later Earl of Stirling, who was a Scottish favorite of James I. In 1621 Sir William received a charter for a Scottish colony in Nova Scotia ("New Scotland"). Settlements at Port Royal and Cape Breton began in 1629, but they fared poorly due to difficult living conditions and French harassment. In 1632, Charles I gave up Nova Scotia to the French. Of the few hundred remaining Scots, most returned to Scotland or relocated to the southern English colonies. The British did not regain Nova Scotia ("Acadia") until 1715, by which time nearly every original Scottish trace had vanished.

Several Scottish colonies were attempted in the 1680s, during the "Killing Times" of Crown repression of dissent in Scotland. Motivations of religious toleration and political escape mixed with economic motives for trade, land, and wealth. Following William Penn's proprietary charter for Pennsylvania in 1681, a business partnership of Scottish Quakers, largely from Aberdeen, founded a colony in East Jersey. A Scottish settlement was established at Perth Amboy in 1683. The colony did well at first and new settlements sprouted along the banks of the Raritan River into central New Jersey. But the turmoil of the 1680s eventually ruined the proprietary colony. It never fully recovered from the colonial "dictatorship" of Governor Edmund Andros and his consolidated Dominion of New England (which extended as far south as the East and West Jersey). In 1702 the Crown revoked the charters of both East and West Jersey and combined them into the Royal colony of New Jersey.

In 1684 a Covenanter colony was founded at Stewart's Town in the Port Royal Sound of present day South Carolina. It encountered the hostility of local Indians, the English at Charleston, and the Spanish in Florida. The Spanish eliminated this experiment in 1686.

The biggest Scottish colonial disaster occurred at Darien, near the Isthmus of Panama, in 1699-1700. A Scottish company raised significant funds to organize the colony of New Caledonia centered at the settlement of New Edinburgh. The first wave of settlers suffered badly from heat and disease. Subsequent settlers were driven off by the Spanish, who captured Fort Andrew on March 31, 1700. The Scottish survivors tried to find a haven in the English colonies, which were very unsympathetic to the Scottish "intruders." The financial loss to Scottish investors may have been so great that it amounted to one-fourth to one-third of the total Scottish national wealth. The Darien disaster was one important factor that led to the Act of Union in 1707.

Prior to 1707, the principal Scottish interest in the American colonies was the opportunity for trade and exploitation of the rich natural resources of the New World. It was an interest largely manifested by commercial groups, such as stock companies for proprietary charters. As seen by the above review, all of these efforts failed. Scotland as a separate sovereignty was too small to compete directly with the Spanish and English. But after 1707 Scotland became a component of Great Britain. Scottish merchants came into the British mercantile empire on a equal footing, at least legally, with the English merchants. Scottish individuals also gained free access to the colonies. Therefore, the rate of Scottish immigration into British North America significantly increased after 1707 and reached a peak between 1763 and 1775.

The Importance of Land. The most important economic attraction of the British colonies for Scots was the opportunity to own land, which was more dear to the hearts of Scots than gold. In the virgin wilderness, land could be acquired for a few pennies an acre. Under some conditions, the land was virtually free for the claiming. Individuals or groups came to America in the expectation of owning and farming their own land, which was an opportunity that did not exist at all for most Scots at home. Owning one's own land, farm, and home was beyond the reach of most Scots in Scotland, but in America one could acquire hundreds of acres of very rich farm land. The cost was not so much an issue of cash but of very hard work and personal risk. The risks included the hazardous voyage across the Atlantic, the often convoluted procedure to establish legal ownership of land, the dangers of wild animals, and the hostility of Indians. But for thousands of the brave and hearty, the opportunistic Scot could become in just one generation a wilderness baron. With land, a man and his family had status, tenure, and income.

The opportunity to own land was the single strongest American pull for Scots up to 1775. It appealed most to people who had been agricultural managers (tacksmen) and workers (crofters, cotters, and field hands) in Scotland who wanted to become independent farmers in America. This appeal resumed after the American Revolution concluded in 1783 and lasted for perhaps another 70 years.

By the time of the Civil War, however, the opportunity to own and operate land for farming had less appeal to Scots. Rather, the opportunity to own one's own house on a plat in a town or city became more attractive than having one's own farm. By the 1860s, most Scottish immigrants came to the U.S. seeking employment in factories or in their own businesses, which was more urban than rural. With the persistent housing shortage in Scotland, especially in towns and cities, people looked upon immigration as an avenue to live in one's own fine house.

Professions and Trade. Before 1776, the second most important economic pull for immigration was the opportunity to apply one's profession or trade for returns unobtainable in Scotland. Colonial America desperately needed skilled workers, for which pay was relatively high. There was more demand for their skills than there was supply. Men of skill and ambition could live very comfortably and acquire small fortunes in America. This was especially true for the upper middle class professionals: ministers, physicians, lawyers, and teachers. It was also true for skilled craftsmen, such as masons, carpenters, draftsmen, wrights, smiths, etc. In Scotland, the craftsmen were largely lower middle to lower class people, but in America they became solidly middle class. After 1776, these opportunities continued to have much attraction, but the shift for most Scottish immigrants was toward factory employment.

Jobs. The opportunity to find jobs, especially in American industries, had enormous appeal for working class Scots in the 19th and 20th centuries. The fantastic growth of the American economy provided many opportunities for jobs for all immigrants. When times were tough in Scotland and the factories laid people off, workers had few chances for alternative employment except abroad. An excellent example of this situation was the 1920s, when the Scottish economy declined but the U.S. economy continued to grow after World War I. During the 1920s, when the U.S. was better off than Scotland, nearly 160,000 Scots immigrated into the U.S. But in the Depression of the 1930s, when the U.S. economy was just as bad if not worse than the British economy, only about 16,000 Scots immigrated.

Business Ventures. In addition to owning land and finding work, America had the great attraction of providing entrepreneurial opportunities. From the earliest days, Scots looked upon America as a place to trade and invest for great wealth. The stockholders and proprietors of the early Scottish colonial adventures dreamed of lucrative trade on both sides of the ocean: to import into Europe the abundant and cheap resources of the New World and to export into the growing colonies the European finished goods that were yet unavailable to European settlers in their new homes.

Although the early Scottish commercial colonies failed, the Scots after 1707 did very well within the British mercantile system. The most successful were the so-called "tobacco lords" of Glasgow, who by 1775 had the lion's share of the Virginia tobacco trade. The Glasgow merchants set up a trading system that returned great profits on both sides of the ocean. They set up trading stations on the various Virginia rivers as far inland as ships could navigate. Some of these trading stations grew with settlements to become prosperous colonial towns, such as Alexandria on the Potomac, Fredericksburg on the Rappahannock, and Richmond on the James. They also used Norfolk as a principal tobacco port. The Scottish merchants bought tobacco directly from the planters, often in the form of credits. They also maintained retail stores, where the planters could use their credits to purchase fine English and Scottish goods, especially clothing, leather products, china, and luxury items. The merchants also dealt in other British colonial products, such as tea, coffee, sugar, and rum. From the colonies, the Scottish merchants carried their tobacco in their own ships to Glasgow. The end market for tobacco was principally France, where the merchants acquired either cash or fine French goods, especially wine, to sell for cash in Great Britain. From this system, some very wealthy Glasgow merchant families emerged, and with them came hundreds of prosperous middle managers in both Scotland and Virginia.

Many Scots came to America to seek their fortune. This fortune was not necessarily the gold that the Spanish originally sought in the New World, but rather the fabulous investment opportunities of British colonial trade and the American Industrial Revolution. Most Scots did well, even if only modestly well, and a few did very well.

To give just a few famous examples, Robert Livingston emigrated from the Scottish Lowlands to the English colonies in 1673. He became a very wealthy merchant and land owner in New York and began one of the most powerful and respected families in the colonial and early Federal periods.

Duncan Phyfe, who was born Duncan Fife in the northern Highlands in 1768, came to Albany, New York, in 1784. He learned the cabinet making trade and moved to New York City in 1792. He founded a very successful furniture-making business based on the neo-classical and Empire "Duncan Phyfe style."

Andrew Carnegie was 13 years old when his family moved from Dunfermline to Pittsburgh in 1848. He became the builder of the American steel industry and founded the U.S. Steel Company. He amassed a huge fortune, much of which he donated to libraries and educational institutions.

Finally, Alexander Graham Bell, who was born at Edinburgh in 1847, resettled in 1872 at Boston, where he managed a school for teaching the teachers to the deaf and invented the telephone in 1876. Bell held numerous patents and participated in the creation of the Bell telephone system, which made him a very wealthy man.

These examples are in fact the extraordinary rarities, but they illustrate well the aspirations of many enterprising Scots who came to America.

As one Scot in America before the Revolution wrote to his relatives back home, America was the best poor man's country in the world. Although most Scottish immigrants were not truly poor, they had ambition to become richer than they were in Scotland. The economic pulls of America included the opportunities to acquire one's own land, farms, and homes; to practice profitably one's own profession or trade; to find jobs; and to seek fortunes through business enterprises.

Religious and Political Toleration

While the economic motives were primary for most Scottish immigrants into America, other motives also existed. One important consideration in the early years was religious and political toleration. During the turmoil of the 17th century, a few Scottish Calvinists came to Massachusetts Bay Colony and Puritan New England to escape Anglican repression. They grew as uncomfortable with New England as they had been with old Great Britain. As mentioned earlier, Scottish Quakers led the proprietary enterprise of East Jersey from 1682 to 1702. Scottish Covenanters sought their own colonial refuge in South Carolina in the 1680s during the "Killing Times", although many more escaping Covenanters relocated to Ulster rather than America. After 1707, when Scotland politically merged with England but retained a separate Presbyterian Kirk (Church) of Scotland, religious toleration became less an issue for immigration to America than it had been in the previous century. In the U.S., under the Bill of Rights, all people were assured the freedom of worship and this had a further appeal to Scottish immigrants, although freedom of religion was not as important a pull as the freedom of economic pursuit.

Religious freedom was more of a pull for Ulster Scots than for Highlanders or Lowlanders in the 18th century. The majority of them were Presbyterians, but in Ireland they were outside of the established Church. Many Ulster Scots left northern Ireland for both the reasons of seeking better economic opportunities and freedom of worship in the American colonies.

Likewise, a few Scots came to America for political toleration. In the 17th century, religious and political toleration was much the same issue. In the 18th century, periodic Jacobite rebellions caused some Scots to flee Britain to escape the penalties of treason. As mentioned in the previous chapter, it has been estimated that no more than 1,000 Jacobites were exiled to America, although more may have elected to emigrate to escape political repression. In the 19th century, some Scots seeking social and democratic reforms may have immigrated to the U.S. to enjoy the rights of the Constitution. Even so, the number of Scottish immigrants due primarily to political reasons would have been far fewer than those due to economic motivations.

Family and Friends in America

Once Scottish individuals or families settled in America, they often called for other family members and friends to join them. James Boswell in his account of Dr. Johnson's and his tour of Scotland in 1773 recalled that when the earliest Scottish emigrants departed their families cried hysterically when they saw the emigrants embark for America. But after a while, the flow of emigration became so strong that when emigrants departed their families calmly waved farewell and said that they would join them later in America. The parting for many emigrating Scottish families and friends became merely temporary.

The largest Scottish communities in the British colonies were located in New York, New Jersey, Pennsylvania, North Carolina, South Carolina, and Georgia. After the French and Indian War, many veterans of the three Scottish regiments that served in North America chose to remain on land offered to them. Several hundred of these soldiers settled in upstate New York in the vicinities of Albany, Lake George, and Johnstown. Indeed, Sir William Johnson actively recruited Highlander soldiers to settle in the Mohawk Valley. These veterans, naturally, sent for their families and established Scottish communities that lasted through the Revolution. Ulster Scots were also coming to the New York frontier along the Mohawk Valley.

In addition to upstate New York, New York City attracted many Scots, especially merchants, craftsmen, and professionals. Once established, they sent for families to rejoin them. With the earlier Lowlander colony of East Jersey close by, the New York City and eastern New Jersey area attracted many more Scottish immigrants to settle there.

Pennsylvania also attracted the Scots, especially the Ulster Scots. Because of the economic opportunities provided by the city of Philadelphia and the extraordinarily rich farm land of rural Pennsylvania and the guarantees of religious toleration under the Quakers, this colony became very popular with Scots. With the Germans firmly established in Lancaster, many Scotch-Irish moved on to the wilder frontier. By 1775 the Scots and Scotch-Irish dominated central and western Pennsylvania.

The Pennsylvania Scottish professionals, tradesmen, and merchants were typically well networked with their counterparts in New York and New Jersey.

Lowlanders were numerous in the trading towns of tidewater Virginia. By the Revolution, there were more Scots in Virginia than any other colony. Scottish communities existed in Alexandria, Fredericksburg, Richmond, Petersburg, and Norfolk. The Scotch-Irish were attracted to the farm lands of the frontier, especially the Shenandoah Valley, which they could reach by way of the Great Wagon Trail from York, Pennsylvania, to South Carolina.

A large Highlander community grew in the vicinity of Cross Creek, or Campbelltown (now Fayetteville) on the Cape Fear River valley of North Carolina. It became a magnet for thousands of Highlanders and islanders during the 1760s and 1770s. Lowlander farmers found plentiful and rich land for very modest prices in North Carolina. Gabriel Johnston, the colonial governor from 1734 to 1752, was himself a Scot and actively recruited Scots to settle in North Carolina. In addition, by the 1760s significant numbers of Scotch-Irish farmers were coming into western North Carolina and South Carolina by way of the Great Wagon Trail.

Charleston, South Carolina, had a Scottish community, largely Lowlander merchants, tradesmen, and professions. Further south, Proprietor James Oglethorpe of Georgia recruited Highlanders to settle in his colony and to help him defend it from the Spanish. A Highlander community grew up at Darien on Altahama River.

From these colonial settlements, the Scots after the Revolution spread into Ohio, Kentucky, Tennessee, and Alabama. By 1820, these Scottish-Americans were moving further west and south to Michigan, Indiana, Illinois, Missouri, and Texas. Wherever the Scots became established, they became a pull for new Scottish immigrants to co-locate with them.

Duty and Assignment

Finally, one pull of America before the Revolution was duty in the service of the Crown or on assignment with a Scottish-based enterprise. At the upper end of the social system, men of noble birth, particularly the younger sons of nobles and the sons of cadet branches of noble families, served as colonial authorities and military officers. Some served in North America and then returned to Great Britain. Others, however, stayed in America and integrated into colonial society.

One famous example was Alexander Spotswood, a career army officer who served as the resident governor of Virginia from 1710-1722. He owned and operated his own plantation of 83,000 acres and became a leader of the emerging iron industry along the Rappahannock River in what became Spotsylvania County, Virginia.

Spotswood was but one of at least a dozen Scottish-born senior colonial administrators in the colonies of New York (Cadwallader Colden and Robert Hunter), New Jersey (Andrew Hamilton and Robert Hunter), Pennsylvania

(James Logan and Andrew Hamilton), Virginia (Spotswood, Robert Dinwiddie, Robert Hunter, and Lord Dunmore), North Carolina (Arthur Dobbs, Gabriel Johnston, and Thomas Pollock), and South Carolina (James Glen) prior to the Revolution. These men generally came from fine families, if not always the British aristocracy, and took the places at the head of colonial society.

Below the top civil and military officers of the Crown were the lesser officers and common soldiers who were sent to North America for duty. Three Highland regiments saw action in the French and Indian War (1754-1763). Many of the survivors remained in America, especially New York and Pennsylvania. In addition, many Scots served as officers and men in predominantly English and colonial regiments. Many of them, like the veterans of the Highland regiments, decided to remain in America after 1763. One famous example was Arthur St. Clair, a native of northern Scotland who had served as an officer in an Anglo-colonial regiment. After 1763, he became a prominent land owner in western Pennsylvania. During the Revolution, he served as a general officer under Washington and later became the first governor of the Northwest Territory.

Also among the upper social strata were ministers sent to America as agents of the church. Both the Church of England and the Church of Scotland supplied ministers to parishes in America. The most famous example was James Blair, a Scottish Episcopalian raised in Edinburgh and educated in Aberdeen. In 1685, at the age of 30, he was sent by the Church of England to Virginia. Four years later he was appointed the Commissary (resident representative) of the Bishop of London, who held church authority for Virginia. Blair remained the chief voice of the Church of England in this colony for the next 54 years, until he died in 1743. He became extremely influential in colonial politics by marrying into the Harrisons, one of the elite families of Virginia (also intermarried with the Carters and the Birds), and by serving on the governor's council. He was so powerful that he undid several resident governors, including his fellow Scot Spotswood.

As mentioned earlier, the tobacco lords of Glasgow maintained many business agents ("factors," the social equals of the agricultural tacksmen) in the colonies. Some of these became very wealthy merchants, land owners, and political leaders. One was Robert Henderson, a tobacco merchant in

Virginia who later became a Patriot in the Revolution. Another was Neil Jamieson, who rose to become a partner in the great tobacco firm of Glassford, Gordon, and Monteath. Besides becoming extremely wealthy in the tobacco trade, he diversified into distilling (Jamieson, Campbell, Calvert & Company). He remained loyal to the Crown and fled to Nova Scotia when the Patriots overran his base at Norfolk.

In summary, the principal pull of Scottish immigration into America, from earliest times but particularly after 1707, was economic. The allure was the opportunities to acquire one's own land, farm, and home; to start one's own trade or business; to find jobs that were more appealing and paid better than jobs, if they were at all available, at home; and to fulfill one's own pursuit of material happiness.

Reasons of political and religious freedom existed for some immigrants, especially in the 17th century, but more often they were secondary to the economic motivations. Others came because of duty or assignment, but even they did so for material reasons rather than altruism.

The Scottish immigrants largely sought an American dream of self-fulfillment through material success. As the next chapter will explain, many of them already had the education, resources, and status of the middle class, and they became more firmly middle class and sometimes upper class in American socio-economic terms.

References

The attractions of the New World are usually discussed in the same sources as the distresses of the Old World. Therefore, much of the information for this chapter was drawn from the same works cited in Chapter 4. Of particular significance for the magnetic pull of the American colonies, see the following references:

Bernard Aspinwall. *Portable Utopia. Glasgow and the United States, 1820-1920.* Aberdeen: Aberdeen University Press, 1984.

Bernard Bailyn. *Voyages to the West. A Passage in the Peopling of America on the Eve of the Revolution.* New York: Vintage Books, 1988.

William R. Brock. *Scotus Americanus.* Edinburgh: Edinburgh University Press, 1982.

R. A. Cage, ed. *The Scots Abroad. Labour, Capital, Enterprise, 1750-1914.* London: Croom Helm, 1985.

Ian Charles Cargill. *Colonists from Scotland: Emigration to North America, 1707-1783.* Ithaca, NY: Cornell University Press, 1956.

Linda Colley. *Britons. Forging the Nation, 1707-1837.* New Haven: Yale University Press, 1992.

Roger Daniels. *Coming to America. A History of Immigration and Ethnicity in American Life.* New York: Harper Collins, 1990.

Charlotte Erickson. *Invisible Immigrants: The Adaptation of English and Scottish Immigrants in Nineteenth-Century America.* Coral Gables, FL: University of Miami Press, 1972.

John H. Finley. *The Coming of the Scot.* New York: Charles Scribner's Sons, 1940.

David Hackett Fischer. *Albion's Seed. Four British Folkways in America.* New York: Oxford University Press, 1989.

Ned C. Landsman. *Scotland and Its First American Colony, 1683-1765.* Princeton, NJ: Princeton University Press, 1985.

James G. Leyburn. *The Scotch-Irish. A Social History.* Chapel Hill, NC: University of North Carolina Press, 1962.

Duane Meyer. *The Highland Scots of North Carolina, 1732-1776.* Chapel Hill, NC: University of North Carolina Press, 1961 (1957).

CHAPTER SIX:

PROFILES OF THE SCOTTISH IMMIGRANTS

Just as every Scottish immigrant to the U.S. had his or her own "push" and "pull" reasons for leaving Scotland and coming to America, each was unique individual. But just as there were general patterns of push and pull for immigration, there were general characteristics of the ones who came to the U.S. This chapter will review the general profile for the Scottish immigrants to this country in regard to socio-economic class, age, gender, and marital status.

Socio-Economic Classes

Very few statistics were kept on early Scottish immigrants, but the few that do exist are largely consistent with each other and with anecdotal material. In general terms at least half, and more likely two out of three, Scots who came to the U.S. were middle class by American standards and upper-lower to middle class by the British standards of their own day. Most of the Scottish immigrants came to this country because they wanted to do so; most paid their own way; most had a little money, some skill, and a lot of ambition to invest in a new life. Very few Scots who relocated to America were from the noble or landed class; the very upper strata of British society had little reason to leave Great Britain and less reason to go to America, especially after

91

1775. Likewise, very few of the poor made their way to America; they had little means to escape their poverty. In general, the people who came to America were the ones most likely to make a go of a new situation because they had some assets (material, mental, and emotional) to put into it.

One set of data was collected on 9,868 emigrants from December 1773 to March 1776 (all but 44 by September 1775). Of this set, 3,884 (39%) departed from Scottish ports, especially Greenock. Yet the figure of 3,884 seems low in relation to evidence of substantial Highlander, Ulster Scot, Anglo-Scot, and Scottish-Canadian emigration at this time that was likely missed in the official British statistics. Of these Scottish emigrants, nearly 93% went to the thirteen American colonies (with 71% going to just the two colonies of New York and North Carolina).

The self-declared socio-economic class status for that time was reported as the following:

Gentle [nobles, lairds, gentlemen, and professionals]	1.5%
Merchants	5.2%
Agriculturalists	24.0%
Craftsmen and artisans	37.7%
Laborers	31.9%

A second set of data was derived from Scottish genealogical records on 2,664 Scottish emigrants to the U.S. up to the year 1854. According to this study, the distribution of socio-economic classes is shown in the following table:

Gentlemen, Landowners, Planters		6.0%
Professionals		11.5%
Ministers	4.1	
Physicians/surgeons	3.0	
Teachers	1.8	
Civil authorities	1.6	
Lawyers	1.0	
Merchants		9.2%
Farmers		22.0%
Craftsmen		22.9%
Weavers	5.0	
Construction	3.8	
Tailors	2.4	
Wrights	2.3	
Smiths	1.5	
Mariners	1.5	
Shoemakers	1.4	
Others	5.0	
Unskilled Laborers		16.4%
Servants, fieldhands	11.1	
Laborers	5.3	
Others/Unknown		12.0%

These two sets of data are remarkably similar in showing that relatively few Scots of the higher social status emigrated to America. The bulk of Scottish emigrants were middle class professionals, merchants, managers, and independent farmers (who may not have owned land in Scotland but who acquired and worked their own farms in America). Alternatively, they were skilled workmen and craftsmen. In Great Britain, they would have been considered the lower middle class or the upper lower class -- somewhere below merchants and independent, land-owning farmers but higher than factory workers, farm hands, and unskilled labor. Most of these Scots quickly became middle class in America, where their skills were more highly valued than in Scotland.

A discussion of the socio-economic classes of the 17th and 18th centuries will provide more background on the status of Scottish emigrants to America. The following remarks focus on Lowland and Highland Scots, although many observations will likewise apply to Ulster Scots and Anglo-Scots. In general terms, the Lowland Scots were the most advantaged. Many of the Scottish professionals, merchants, managers, and land-owning farmers came from the Lowlands. Fewer came from the Highlands, which supplied more farmers than professionals and merchants and more common laborers than skilled workmen. Most of the Ulster Scots were somewhat less well off than the Lowlanders and more like the Highlanders in socio-economic status. In general, the Ulster Scots were farmers with less resources than most Lowlander or Highlander emigrants to America before 1800.

Upper Classes. In British society the pinnacle of the socio-economic pyramid has been the titled and landed nobles (known as the "peers"). According to the Union Roll of 1707, Scotland had 154 peers. Of these, 19 lost their titles due to their participation in the Jacobite revolt of 1715 and one permanently lost his title due to the last Jacobite revolt of 1745. A few new titles were created by the Crown, but the size of the peerage in Scotland by 1800 would have been about 130 or so. These ranged from the very top, the dukes (Hamilton, Queensbury, Buccleuch, Argyll, Atholl, and Huntley) to the barons who were peers.

The chiefs of major Highland clans and the heads of extended Lowland families were generally noblemen. As examples, the chief of Clan Campbell was the Duke of Argyll; the Duke of Buccleuch was the head of the Lowlands Scotts. Lesser clan and family heads were often lesser nobles, or barons outside of the peerage. Virtually no clan chief or family head emigrated from Scotland before 1800, unless he was taking up residence in London.

Very few members of the upper class ever left Scotland permanently. If one were to have come to America, it would have been as a civil or military officer of the Crown before 1775. One famous example was John Murray, the Earl of Dunmore, Viscount Fincastle, and Baron of Blair, Moulin, and Tillymont. After serving as a Scottish peer in the House of Lords, Lord Dunmore served as governor of New York in 1770 and the resident governor of Virginia from 1771 to 1775. He alienated many Virginians and stood firmly for the king, but failed to hold his colony for the Crown against the rebelling Patriots in 1775. He returned to London and served once again as a colonial governor, for the Bahamas in 1787-1796.

Below the peers were the lesser barons, knights, and untitled landowners, who were generally known as "lairds." They included barons who were not also peers and landowners who were not even knights. Some were chiefs of minor clans. Others were cadet branches of powerful families. Many were wealthy merchants and professionals who purchased their land, often from the great families who continuously needed cash to support their peerage lifestyles. The upper end of the Scottish lairds included men who in England were called the gentry (or squires): rural landowners, many of whom lived on and managed their own estates, who enjoyed the right to a family coat of arms but not to a noble title. The lower end of the Scottish lairds also included men corresponding to the lesser English class of yeomen, who owned and worked their own farms without a coat of arms or a title and who were less affluent and influential than the gentry.

Included in the upper class, but barely, were the "gentlemen," the younger brothers and younger sons of the nobility. They enjoyed the higher social status of their families, but they largely had to make their own way in the world. Many became military and naval officers and colonial agents of the Crown. Some became career estate managers, usually for their peer relatives. Because their families could afford to support their education, some gentlemen went to college and became professionals, primarily ministers, physicians, lawyers, and educators. They enjoyed academic titles and ranks in lieu of aristocratic, landed titles. A few became merchants, but the merchant class emerged more from the agricultural middle class and the craftsman strata than from the upper class.

As the data show, there were a few Scottish lairds and gentlemen who came to America, most of whom likely arrived before 1775. They would have sought large tracts of land in America upon which to build considerable estates. Examples include Lachlan Campbell, the founder of the Argyll Patent in upstate New York in 1737-1739; Neill Campbell, the younger brother of the Duke of Argyll who founded the estate of "Raritan River" in Somerset County, New Jersey in 1685; and Arthur Dobbs, an Ulster Scottish

95

laird with large land holdings in County Antrim who became an investor in and colonial governor of North Carolina, 1754-1765. When these gentlemen came to America, they hoped to establish estates and semi-feudal titles of their own. Not surprisingly, the few Scottish lairds and gentlemen in the colonies by 1775 were largely Loyalists during the Revolution.

In the United Kingdom prior to the 20th century, buying land and becoming a landowner was difficult. Social mobility into the landowning class existed, but only to the extent that the entrenched landowners, mostly the nobility, had to or were willing to sell off their holdings (or transfer land through marriages). In contrast, in America buying land was relatively easy. Land, in some instances, was virtually free to the risk taker. The barrier was not a feudal social system in which all the land was already taken; the barrier was the ordeal of immigrating to and surviving in the colonial wilderness. Social mobility existed in America for those people who successfully crossed the ocean, found a suitable place to start a new life, employed tremendous hard labor, and defended their stake against hostile elements, including Indians.

Middle Classes. The emerging middle classes of the 18th century ranged broadly from professionals at the upper end through various levels of merchants and businessmen to small shopkeepers, tradesmen, and craftsmen at the lower end. Middle class status in Great Britain typically rested more on occupational respect, education, and money than titles and lands. The middle classes in colonial America, likewise, were also based on respect and money, as well as landholdings (but no titles, which were prohibited after 1775 by many state constitutions and forbidden by the Federal constitution of 1787). The American middle class has been historically much broader and more cohesive than the middle classes of Europe. Even if some Scottish emigrants were not considered to enjoy middle class status at home, most qualified as middle class soon after they arrived in America. As mentioned above, most Scottish immigrants to the U.S. could be labeled middle class.

At the top end of the middle class were the professionals. Many of them were younger sons of large landowners or of cadet branches of major families. Their status largely depended upon some element of social privilege and money to gain the necessary education. It also depended upon the knowledge and skills of the individual regardless of social status by birth. There was more social mobility into the professional ranks than into the upper class, because the sons of well-to-do merchants and early industrial tradesmen could also obtain a professional education, which was unusually plentiful in Scotland with excellent universities at Glasgow, Edinburgh, St. Andrews, and Aberdeen.

Army and navy officers and civil authorities, who were respected as professionals, were largely drawn from noble or cadet families. Many of them came to America in service of the Crown before 1783, when American independence was formally recognized, but relatively few remained. Attorneys came from both landed and merchant families. While undoubtedly several came to America, we do not have adequate records for them. Presbyterian and Episcopalian ministers, likewise, originated from both landed and merchant families. They played particularly important roles in colonial society. Physicians, surgeons, scholars, and teachers largely came from the lesser lairds and merchants. They came in significant numbers and were as influential as the ministers. Of course, once a man was established in his profession, he could use his position to bring his sons into it, too. By the 19th century, an increasingly high percentage of people in the professions came from professional families.

Several British military officers and civil authorities served and settled in America before the Revolution. Alexander Spotswood, in contrast to Lord Dunmore, became the resident governor of Virginia (1710-1722) due to his distinguished army career rather than his status as an aristocrat. Spotswood's father came from a lesser branch of a noble family and had become a professional man serving as an army surgeon; Spotswood followed his father's lead, but as a army field officer rather than as a surgeon.

Another example was Robert Hunter, a native of Ayrshire and a professional army officer. He served in America as the resident governor of Virginia from 1707 to 1710 and as the Governor of both New York and New Jersey from 1710 to 1719.

Numerous ministers came to America to serve the growing number of Scots and other people in the New World. The most famous of these, as mentioned earlier, was James Blair, the resident representative of the Bishop of London in Virginia from 1689 to 1743. Another notable Episcopalian minister was William Smith, who came to New York in 1751, resettled in Philadelphia in 1754, and became a founder of the University of Pennsylvania.

Among the outstanding Presbyterian ministers was Francis Makemie, an Ulster Scot who emigrated to Virginia in 1698 and helped to establish the first American presbytery in Philadelphia in 1706. A very famous minister was John Witherspoon, who left his Presbyterian ministry in Paisley to become the President of the College of New Jersey (Princeton University) in 1768. In addition to serving as Moderator of the First General Assembly of the Presbyterian Church in America, he served in the Continental Congress. Witherspoon was an influential Patriot and a signer of the Declaration of Independence.

Several Scottish physicians came to America before the Revolution and became prominent colonial figures. Because of its excellent medical colleges, Scotland was unusually rich in medical talent in the 18th century (for example, from 1750-1850, Oxford and Cambridge universities produced 500 physicians while Aberdeen, Edinburgh, and Glasgow universities produced 10,000). One famous example of a Scottish physician in the colonies was Cadwallader Colden, who was an Ulster Scot and Edinburgh University graduate. In addition to being a physician, he was also a respected botanist and mathematician. After initial settlement in Philadelphia in 1710, Colden relocated to New York in 1718, became a large land owner (29,000 acres) and colonial Lt. Governor (1760-1775).

Another famous Scottish physician was Hugh Mercer, a native of Aberdeenshire. He sided with Prince Charlie in 1745 and served as a Jacobite field surgeon through the Battle of Culloden. He emigrated to Philadelphia in 1746 or 1747. During the French and Indian War, he served with a colonial regiment as a field officer rather than as a doctor. After 1763 he relocated to Fredericksburg, Virginia, where he became a prominent citizen and friend of George Washington. He sided with the Patriots and became a Brig. General in the Continental Army under Washington. Mercer was killed in action during the Battle of Princeton on January 3, 1777. In addition to his own fame, he is remembered as an ancestor of an even more famous general, George S. Patton, Jr.

Although the Scottish professionals typically found success in America and played leading roles in colonial society prior to 1776, their number was not large. They certainly enjoyed an influence in colonial affairs far beyond their numbers.

About as numerous, and as difficult to count, as the professionals were the merchants and businessmen who came to America. In Great Britain, some merchants came from the younger sons of the nobility, but not many. Most of the Scottish merchant class came from well-to-do craftsmen and minor lairds, especially the Scottish squires of the Lowlands. During the 18th century, this segment of society grew rapidly, particularly after Scotland gained commercial access to worldwide British trade after 1707. Once established, the wealthy merchants often bought land, married their daughters into the noble class, and raised their sons to be either merchants or professionals. Many lesser merchants thoroughly enjoyed a middle class life style in Scottish cities and towns. A few prosprous merchants emigrated, but not many. They may have traveled widely, but they most often returned to Scotland, where their wealth was invested. More commonly, lesser merchants went to America to find the opportunities to become wealthy.

Prior to 1776, the Scottish merchants played an important role in the British imperial trading system. The most influential Scottish merchants were the factors (the middle managers of trade much as the tacksmen were the agricultural middle managers) of the Glasgow tobacco lords in Virginia. They operated the trading stores at the fall line of the rivers, where they bought bulk tobacco from planters for shipment to Glasgow and where they sold European finished goods (many made in Scotland) to the same planters. The most famous factors were Robert Henderson, Neil Jamieson, and Francis Jerdone.

In addition to the trading factors were the young men who came to America to start up their own businesses. The most famous was young Robert Livingston, the son of a Lowland Presbyterian minister who emigrated alone to Boston in 1673 at the age of 19. He began as an employee of a Puritan merchant, but he soon relocated to Albany, New York. Because he had lived in Holland as a boy and spoke fluent Dutch as well as English, he was quickly accepted as a secretary to the Dutch landowners of the Hudson valley. He married the widow of his employer, Van Rensselaer. With great energy, business talent, and ambition, Livingston became one of the wealthiest and most influential merchants in colonial New York. He also became the patriarch of a very distinguished family in colonial and early Federal affairs that included a signer of the Declaration of Independence (Philip Livingston), a governor of New Jersey (William Livingston), a very famous Chancellor of New York (Robert R. Livingston), two U.S. Ministers to France (Robert R. and Edward Livingston), a Secretary of State (Edward Livingston), as well as numerous successful merchants, businessmen, and lawyers.

Another ambitious Scottish merchant in New York and a friend of Robert Livingston was William Kidd, who came from Greenock, the principal port for emigration on the Clyde River. Having had training as a seaman and merchant, Kidd became a legalized English privateer against French shipping. His base of operations in the 1690s was New York City, where he enjoyed the life style and influence of a wealthy merchant. But by the end of the decade, he was accused of crossing the thin line between privateering and piracy. The notorious "Captain Kidd" was tried, found guilty, and hanged for piracy in London in 1701.

The largest group of Scottish emigrants were categorized as "agriculturalists." Many of them were part of the American middle class by virtue of their owning even small plots of land. They numbered more than the professionals and merchants, but slightly less than the tradesmen.

This category varied greatly in wealth and status. At the upper end were the rural tacksmen, who were the agricultural middle managers between the lairds and their tenants. In the rural society of the Highlands, the tacksmen were substantially middle class. They typically held long-term leases from the lairds, but they rarely owned land in a legal sense; they often directly managed and worked on their leases; and they sub-leased the land to the working tenants and collected their rents. They usually were related to the lairds and up to 1746 had rendered martial as well as managerial services to their clan chiefs. With the rising of land rents after 1746, a substantial number of Highland tacksmen emigrated to America to find land of their own. Their election to emigrate has been called "the people's clearances."

Similarly, many agricultural middle managers of the Lowlands, whether called tacksmen or not, emigrated to own and manage their own farms. This group of husbandrymen had abundant farming and money management skills and often a small grub stake with which to invest; but they were certainly not well-to-do and they did not enjoy as much influence, either in Scottish or colonial society, as did the professionals and merchants.

Below the tacksmen where the crofters and cotters. In 18th century Scotland, some of the crofters might have been middle class, while cotters were definitely working class. Generally, the crofters held leases of one type or another and lived toward the center of the laird's lands. They worked the better fields and stood just behind the tacksmen in social standing. The cotters, however, held the shifting ground between rural middle and lower classes. They typically held no leases, lived in poorer housing on the periphery of the estate, and worked the poorer land.

Before the 1790s, some crofters and cotters had emigrated to America, often in groups with their tacksmen. The flow was greater from the Lowlands than from the Highlands, partly because there were simply more Lowlanders than Highlanders, but also because agricultural improvements and the restructuring of rural society began earlier in the Lowlands than in the Highlands. As it turned out, too few elected to emigrate from the Highlands. With rising land values and rents, many Highland lairds made the decision for their tenants that they would do better off the land. These were the clearances. Many crofters and cotters were literally evicted from the land. Some moved on to Lowland cities to work in factories and mills. Others emigrated. The principal attraction of America for them was the abundance of land. If they had the choice of where to go, they liked America, where they sought their own farms or to work on the spreads of the Scots who had already gotten established on this side of the ocean.

Working Classes. The term "working class" comes from 19th century political rhetoric. In 18th century Scotland, the majority of people were considered "common people" or "labourers," rather than "working class." Whatever the term, they were the ones who lived near the subsistence level and owned few personal possessions and virtually no property (only rarely their own home). At the upper end of the laboring classes were the craftsmen and

101

tradesmen. Many of them became middle class when they relocated to America. At the lower end were many cotters, itinerate farm hands, unskilled and semi-skilled factory workers, and many so-called "day laborers." They comprised the lower classes of both Great Britain and America.

The largest single group of Scottish immigrants to the U.S. was the craftsmen, artisans, and tradesmen. They were skilled workers who found many rewarding applications for their talents in this country. In Scotland by the 18th century the gilds asserted firm control of trades. The rules for apprentice and journeyman status were very stringent and achieving master status was highly prized but difficult and rare. Consequently, due to the harsh rules of trade, many apprentices and journeymen sought new opportunities to practice their trade and perhaps even begin their own businesses in the New World.

In the same sense of seeking new opportunities, some craftsmen found their livelihoods threatened by the mechanization of the Industrial Revolution. By the middle of the 18th century, Scotland had entered a period of profound economic and social restructuring due primarily to the technologies of agricultural improvements and industrial production. Where mechanization was a push for emigration, the great demand for craftsmen of all sorts in a rapidly growing economy supplied a powerful pull for emigration to the U.S.

In the past two centuries, the periodic economic depressions in Scotland caused many unemployed or underemployed craftsmen to emigrate just to find work. Many came to the U.S., where work opportunities were typically more abundant than in the U.K., at least before the Great Depression of the 1930s.

Of all the various kinds of crafts and trades practiced, the two dominating among Scottish immigrants into the U.S. concerned clothing and construction. In the general category of clothing were the weavers, tailors, shoemakers, and other trades applied in Scotland in the production of cotton, wool, and leather products. Scotland became a major producer of cotton cloth from imported (largely American) cottons. Paisley, near Glasgow, was particularly famous for its cotton mills; its name was given to a pattern from India that was applied to many cotton products. The wool cloth and clothes, obviously, came from the growing herds of Scottish sheep, often owned by large Lowland lairds and grazed on the depopulated estates of Highland chiefs. The wools were woven into various tweeds and plaids for export around the world. And the leather products came from cattle, which had long been the principal "cash crop" of the Highlands. Scotland had had an historical tradition of thousands of years in cattle and sheep and an honored tradition in the crafting of textiles, clothes, shoes, and other animal-based products.

The other principal trade of Scottish immigrants was the various construction skills, broadly defined to include masons, carpenters, and materials wrights, and a wide variety of related tradesmen. In more recent years, mechanical draftsmen have found abundant employment opportunities in the U.S.

Lastly, a relatively small number of common laborers made their way to America. They were largely unskilled field hands and urban workers. In Scotland, their numbers were declining in the countryside, but increasing in the urban environment of the Industrial Revolution. Their status was below that of the craftsmen and the skilled laborers, but above the indigent and desperately poor. They immigrated if they had sufficient money and ambition to do so, especially when they could find no work in Scotland. Many did pay their own passage; others came as indentured servants before the Revolution or as laborers already sponsored by an American employer. In either case, the immigrant agreed in writing to serve the sponsoring employer for a fixed number of years (four being the average) and at a rate that included the expenses of voyage immigration. Relatively few of the total number of indentured who came to America were Scots, and relatively few Scots (certainly less than 15%) came as indentured laborers. Most of the Scottish indentured servants -- and exiled prisoners, too -- came in the 17th rather than the 18th century.

Ages

Less information exists on the age distribution of Scottish immigrants than on the socio-economic profile. Of the Scottish emigrants in the British Register of Emigrants from December 1773 to March 1776, the age distribution was as follows:

age	%
1-9	16.1
10-14	8.6
15-19	16.4
20-24	19.4
25-29	15.1
30-34	8.9
35-39	6.0
40-44	4.3
45-49	2.7
50-54	1.0
55-59	0.7
60-64	0.5
65-69	0.2
70+	0.1

These figures show that emigration was a young adult enterprise. More than one-third (35.8%) of all emigrants from Scotland were young adults from age 15 through 24. Another almost one-third (30.0%) ranged from ages 25 through 39. Less than 10% were age 40 or more. The 24.7% that were children must have been brought to America by their parents. It is most likely that at least half, if not more, of all Scottish immigrants to the U.S. were 25 to 39 years old or the children of parents in that age range. Over 90% of all Scottish immigrants were 15 to 39 years old or the children of parents in that age range.

Genders and Martial Status

Again, data are scarce on gender. The British Register of Emigrants from December 1773 to March 1776 showed a distribution of 60% males and 40% females among the Scottish emigrants to America. Many family histories show that the Scottish emigrants before the Revolution tended to be young married couples, sometimes with small children, or young singles who married within two years of settling in America. More single men immigrated to the U.S. than single women. A young Scottish adult male was more likely to take the risk of emigrating alone than a young Scottish adult female. The young adult females tended to emigrate with husbands or within a social group, which provided financial support and physical security. Female children typically emigrated only with parents or close relatives. Older females may have emigrated alone, especially the poor ones who came as indentured servants.

In the 19th century, the ratio of males to females may have increased beyond 3:2. A common pattern was for a young adult male to come to the U.S. alone to find a job and a place to live. He typically spent two to five years alone establishing himself. If he failed to take root in America, or if he never intended to stay longer than it took to earn a "small fortune," he returned to Scotland or emigrated to yet another country. If he did take root, which most did, then he paid the passage of family left in Scotland. This family might include a wife and small children. It might also include brothers and sisters, perhaps even cousins. It did not typically include older parents; the older one became, the less likely he or she would emigrate.

By the 20th century, the gender ratio may have shifted back to a closer balance. The Scottish immigrant into the U.S. was most typically a young adult male, sometimes alone but more often as part of some group traveling as a family or community unit. Second most likely was the young adult male traveling with his young adult wife, either as a couple or as a family with children.

Conclusions

The purpose of this chapter has been to profile typical Scottish immigrants to the U.S. by socio-economic status and occupation, age, and gender and marital status. The data are admittedly sparse and the profile is largely based on just two statistical samplings. However, the data are significantly consistent with known family histories and anecdotal accounts. Until better information emerges, the typical Scottish immigrant to the U.S. was a middle or upper-lower class person engaged in a profession, business, farming, or a skilled trade; the immigrant was a young adult between the ages of 15 and 39 or the child of such a young adult; the immigrant was more likely, but almost equally, male than female traveling with a social unit, often the family. The following chapter will elaborate on where in the U.S. the Scots settled.

References

The study of 9,868 British emigrants to North America in 1773-1776 can be found in Bernard Bailyn, *Voyages to the West. A Passage in the Peopling of America on the Eve of the Revolution*. New York: Vintage Books, 1988. The study of 2,664 Scottish emigrants to the U.S. through 1854 can be found in Gordon Donaldson, "Scots," in Stephan Thernstrom, ed., *Harvard Encyclopedia of American Ethnic Groups*. (Cambridge, MA: Belknap Press of Harvard University, 1980), pp. 908-916, based largely on data from Donald Whyte, *Dictionary of Scottish Emigrants to the U.S.A.* Baltimore: Magna Carta, 1972. Whyte published a second volume of emigrant data in 1986. Additional lists of Scottish emigrants to the Thirteen Colonies and the U.S. can be found in the published works of David Dobson. In particular, see David Dobson, *The Original Scots Colonists of Early America, 1612-1783*. Baltimore: Genealogy Publishing Co., 1989.

Background material on the Scottish socio-economic classes can be found in the following:

J. M. Bumsted, *The People's Clearance. Highland Emigration to British North America.* Edinburgh: Edinburgh University Press, 1982.

Linda Colley, *Britons. Forging the Nation, 1707-1837.* New Haven: Yale University Press, 1992.

Bruce Lenman, *Integration, Enlightenment, and Industrialization. Scotland, 1746-1832.* London: Edward Arnold, 1981.

John B. Owen, *The Eighteenth Century. 1714-1815.* The Norton Library History of England. New York: Norton, 1976 (especially pp. 139-151).

T. C. Smout, *A History of the Scottish People, 1560-1830.* London: Fontana, 1972.

An excellent account of American colonial life and its attractions for the Scots can be found in David Hackett Fisher, *Albion's Seed. Four British Folkways in America.* New York: Oxford University Press, 1989.

CHAPTER SEVEN:

THE SCOTTISH COLONIES BEFORE 1707

Previous chapters have addressed the questions of why Scottish emigrants left Scotland, why many of them came to America, and who they were, at least as a general profile. The next several chapters will discuss where in America they chose to settle and why. The current chapter will specifically address Scottish colonies attempted apart from the British empire before the union of Scotland and England occurred in 1707. Later chapters will cover Scottish immigration into the Thirteen Colonies from the Act of Union to the Revolution.

Scottish Imperialism

As mentioned previously, the Scots of the 17th century were envious of the Spanish, French, and English colonies. They wanted their own colonies, too. But like the Dutch and the Swedes, the Scots learned that establishing and defending colonies were very expensive enterprises, both in money and lives. By the beginning of the 18th century, the Scots learned that they would be further ahead inside of the expanding English colonial trade network than outside of it.

Prior to 1707, to review just briefly the main contours of British history, Scotland was outside of the English mercantile system. Since 1603, when

James VI of Scotland also became James I of England and Ireland, Scotland and England shared the same monarchy, but they had remained separate countries. The two kingdoms had separate parliaments, legal establishments, education systems, and established churches. Although Scots technically shared equal rights with Englishmen and enjoyed free trade with the south, they were increasingly cut out of the growing English trade empire by the English merchants who commanded great influence in the English parliament. In addition, despite their Scottish origins, the Stuarts were often willing to subordinate Scottish interests to more pressing English interests. Whether the Stuarts, the Puritans, or the Whigs dominated Westminster, Scottish economic interests typically came second to English economic interests.

During the same year as the Stuart restoration to the British throne, the English parliament passed the Navigation Act of 1660, in which Scotland was systematically excluded from direct access to English colonies. While Scottish merchants continued their direct access to English markets, they were legally excluded from the colonial trade unless they first passed their goods through English ports and on English ships before reaching Scotland or the continent. Consequently, Scottish smuggling became a major industry, but it was a poor second to the profits of direct colonial trade.

During the 17th century, the Scots had dreams of their own colonies in the New World, separate from the English colonies. These Scottish settlements would be peopled with Scots and they would trade directly with Scotland through Scottish merchants. They would be "plantations" in the same general sense of that term used when James I encouraged Scottish and English settlements in northern Ireland. More than 100,000 Protestant Scots, perhaps as many as twice that number, had relocated, primarily from the southern Lowlands, to Ulster from the 1590s to the 1720s (with the heaviest flow roughly from 1610 to 1625 and from 1680 to 1720). These Ulster Scots had acquired land, survived hardships, endured local hostilities, and even fought in civil wars, but they succeeded in acquiring their own wealth and trade with Scotland and England. It was widely believed that the Ulster "plantation" experience could be repeated in North America.

But it was not to be. The Scots attempted four major colonies and settlements: Nova Scotia (1621-1632); Stewart's Town, Port Royal Sound,

South Carolina (1682-1686); East Jersey (1682-1702); and New Caledonia at the Gulf of Darien (1699-1700). Each collapsed as colonial enterprises. The East Jersey experience was the most successful; the settlers prospered under the reorganized Crown colony of New Jersey. The other three were failures, and the Darien attempt was a major national disaster and ended Scottish national colonial ambitions.

This chapter will briefly recount the stories of these four Scottish colonies prior to the Act of Union, which merged Scotland into the British empire, in 1707.

Nova Scotia

James I was a vigorous champion of overseas colonization, both English and Scottish. He promoted the English and Scottish "plantations" in northern Ireland. He had granted a charter to the English company that founded the settlement of Jamestown (named for the king) in the colony of Virginia in 1607. By 1624, the same year that James died, that company failed and Virginia became the first Royal Colony, which meant that the responsibility for the colony passed for the first time from private hands to the Crown and parliament. James had also granted the charter for the company that founded the colony of Plymouth in 1620.

The initiative in most cases had come from merchants and investors who had petitioned for and received charters from the Crown as private companies to conduct trade. In other cases, individuals could receive charters as proprietary owners of land and businesses, including colonies. These proprietary charters, obviously, went to particular favorites of the king. One such favorite from Scotland was Sir William Alexander of Menstrie, who became the Earl of Stirling. In 1621 Alexander received a charter from the king's Privy Council for the Scottish colony of Nova Scotia (New Scotland) on the North American coast farther north than Plymouth. Alexander in turn organized a company of settlers and investors with the intention of relocating Scots to Nova Scotia to live, to work (primarily fur trapping and fishing), and to engage in trade with both Scotland and England, which was still open to any colonial trade prior to 1660. Alexander acquired not only what is known today as Nova Scotia and Cape Breton Island but also much of New Brunswick, Gaspe, and the upper St. Lawrence River valley, including an English monopoly on the fur trade of these lands.

Scottish settlers founded the first settlement of Nova Scotia at Port Royal in 1628 or 1629. The second settlement went up at Port Baleine on Cape Breton Island. It included James Stewart of Killeith; Andrew Stewart, Lord Ochiltree; Alexander's own son; and about 50 people. It lasted all of three months before the French seized it. Indeed, the French took a very dim view of the Scottish colonial effort, which they saw as an encroachment upon their own claim over what is now eastern Canada.

The fatal blow to the Nova Scotia colony came not directly from the French but from the hand of Charles I. He had no intention of letting Scottish colonial schemes interfere with Anglo-French relations. In the Treaty of St Germain-en-Laye of 1632, the Crown officially recognized the French claim to lands called Acadia, or Nova Scotia. Most of the Scots returned to Scotland or relocated to the English colonies to the south. The French repopulated their Acadia with their own people, who soon greatly outnumbered the few remaining Scots. By 1755, however, the British were back in control of Acadia, and fearing local French support for the French armies at war with the English in the French and Indian War, the British exiled most of the French Acadians, some of whom became the ancestors of today's Louisiana Cajuns.

In the 18th and 19th centuries, Nova Scotia once again became a land of Scottish immigrants, but long after the passing of Sir William Alexander's first Scottish colonists. Scottish Highlanders began to repopulate Nova Scotia after the end of the French and Indian War in 1763. At the end of the American Revolution in 1783, Nova Scotia also received a large number of resettled Loyalists who fled the U.S. It has been estimated that as many as 60,000 Loyalists fled the thirteen states and perhaps as many as one-third of these were Scots. Of the Scottish Loyalists, a significant number, perhaps half, eventually relocated to Nova Scotia. An undetermined number of Scots and Scottish descendants from Nova Scotia have re-immigrated into the U.S. over the last 200 years.

After the Restoration of the Stuarts to the Crowns of England and Ireland and Scotland in 1660, Charles II tried to impose a greater degree of religious uniformity upon his realms. The result of imposed Anglican-style uniformity in Scotland was a religious and social conflict that grew into virtual civil war, culminating in the violence called "killing times" of the 1680s. Tension was so high in the Lowlands that many uncompromising Covenanters emigrated to Holland, Ulster, and America from the Restoration of 1660 to the Glorious Revolution of 1688.

One group of Lowlander Covenanters (principally from Galloway, Dumfries, Lanarkshire, and the Borders) founded the American settlement of Stewart's Town (or Stuart's Town) at Port Royal Sound, in the general vicinity of today's Beaufort, South Carolina. This area had once been settled by another persecuted religious sect, the French Huguenots. The Huguenots had built Fort Caroline, but it had been destroyed by the Spanish in 1564. During the 1680s Port Royal Sound was still a zone of contention, between the English colony of the Carolinas, with a major settlement at Charleston, and the Spanish Floridas, with a major town at St. Augustine.

In 1665 Charles II had granted a second charter to the Carolina proprietors, one of whom was Sir Anthony Ashley Cooper (who in 1672 became Earl of Shaftesbury). Cooper worked with Henry Erskine, Lord Cardross, to establish a Scottish colony south of Charleston that would provide a colonial haven for Covenanters. The principal motivation behind the colony was religious, with economic ambitions a close second. Lord Cardross' dream was to create with Scottish Covenanters a righteous and prosperous southern colony much as the English Puritans had made a success of the northern colony of Massachusetts Bay.

In 1682 the Carolina proprietors granted a charter to Lord Cardross to form within the Carolinas an independent Scottish settlement, which became in 1684 the tenuous Scottish settlement at Stewart's Town not far from the site of the former French Huguenot colony. About 140 Scots led by Lord Cardross himself constituted the first settlers.

113

Stewart's Town, however, soon attracted the hostility of both the English and the Spanish. The English at Charleston petitioned colonial authorities in London for the arrest of Lord Cardross for intruding upon the English claim to Port Royal Sound. The Carolina proprietors, however, supported Lord Cardross and won English acquiescence for the Scottish colony.

During the troubles with the Carolina colonists, the Stewart's Town Scots formed an alliance with the Yamasee Indians against the Spanish. It was the Spanish, not the English, that terminated the Scottish experiment, just as they had ended the Huguenot colony. In September 1686 a Spanish expedition of only about 150 troops and three galleys from St. Augustine attacked and totally destroyed Stewart's Town. The Spaniards might have also attacked Charleston, but they were prevented by a storm from doing so.

The hero of the Scottish evacuation from Stewart's Town was William Dunlop, a Covenanter minister who relocated the survivors to Charleston, where the people were not very sympathetic or friendly to the distressed Scots, despite the fact that the Scots rather than the English had suffered the recent wrath of the Spanish. Dunlop himself returned to Scotland after the Glorious Revolution of 1688 and became the minister of Ochiltree and later Principal of the University of Glasgow.

East Jersey

The most successful Scottish colony was East Jersey, principally the town of Perth Amboy and the Raritan River valley of today's state of New Jersey. It began as both a commercial enterprise and a religious experiment among English and Scottish Quakers. The colony as a proprietary grant lasted only about 20 years, but the settlements were successful to the extent that the earliest Scottish settlers established businesses, estates, and influence that lasted at least up through the Revolution.

What is New Jersey today began as an extension of the Dutch colony of New Amsterdam, centered on Manhattan, in the 1640s and 1650s. After years of conflicts between the Dutch and neighboring English colonists, an English military and naval expedition seized New Amsterdam in 1664. Charles II granted much of the former Dutch colony to his brother, the Duke of York (who in 1680 became James II). The center of this new colony, called New York, was the settlement on Manhattan (New York City), Long Island, and the Hudson River Valley.

The Duke of York in turn granted proprietary rights to lands on the west side of the Hudson River to his loyal friends. In 1664 he gave a proprietary right to the lands between the Hudson and Delaware Rivers, roughly what became the state of New Jersey, to John Lord Berkeley and Sir George Carteret. Lord Berkeley, in turn, sold his interests to a group of English Quakers, including William Penn (who acquired by 1681 his own colony west of the Delaware River). Lord Berkeley's territory became West Jersey and Sir George Carteret's lands became East Jersey. After Lord Carteret died in 1680, his interests were sold to a group of proprietors (initially 12, but expanded to 24 in 1682) led by Penn. These East Jersey proprietors included six Scottish Quakers. By 1684, half of the 24 proprietors of East Jersey were Scots, both Quaker and Episcopalian, largely from the Aberdeen area. These Scots played a leadership role in settling East Jersey as a Scottish dominated colony.

The principal Scottish proprietor was Robert Barclay, a Quaker from Urie. He acted as the official governor of East Jersey. His Scottish associates included his brother David Barclay; his cousin James, Earl of Perth; Perth's brother John Drummond, later the Viscount Melfort; Barclay's uncle Robert Gordon of Cluny; and the Dutch-born Scottish Quaker Arend Sonmans. All were politically acceptable to the Duke of York (in fact, after 1688 three of them became Jacobites regardless of the religious issues).

In 1685 more proprietors (now known as "fractioners") were admitted. One was Neil Campbell, the younger brother of the Earl of Argyll, from a Presbyterian family. Another proprietor was George Scot of Pitlocy. These men, who generally were the younger sons of titled families, wished to create large land holdings in East Jersey that would approximate the social and economic order of Scotland in the 1680s. In other words, they would have liked to have seen themselves become the de facto nobility of colonial East Jersey. To achieve this, in part, required the relocation of Scottish crofters, laborers, craftsmen, and servants to America.

By 1683 the first successful Scottish settlement in the New World began at Perth Amboy on Ambo Point at the mouth of the Raritan River. Amboy had been a name known to the local Indians and the Dutch. "Perth" came in honor of the proprietor, the Earl of Perth. During the 1680s Perth Amboy was a distinctly Scottish town populated with people with surnames including Alexander, Barclay, Cameron, Campbell, Drummond, Forbes, Fullerton, Gordon, Haige, Hamilton, Hardie, Henrie, Johnstone, Macgregor, Mackenzie, Riddel, Robertson, and Scot. An estimated total of 700 Scots came to East Jersey by 1685. Among these were the titled Lord Minevard and "gentlemen" Neil Campbell, George Lockhart, George Gordon. Perhaps fully half of the first 700 were indentured servants recruited by the proprietors. Most of them were young and single; maybe one-fourth immigrated with their families.

The Scots of East Jersey had come from several different places in Scotland, and the regional differences created problems for social harmony along with religious and economic differences. The initial proprietors and their followers were largely Quakers from Aberdeen and the northern Lowlands. Also, the early settlers included Episcopalians from this same area. With the addition of Neil Campbell to the list of proprietors came a small number of Highland settlers from Argyll, on the west side. Although some Highlanders settled in New Jersey, most Scots were probably Lowlanders.

In 1685 a ship carrying 100 or more prisoners left Scotland for East Jersey. About one-third died in route. Although there had been some interest in Scotland and England in exiling prisoners to America, the practice did not become popular. Exiling prisoners was expensive and inconvenient. Too many died en route, even when capital punishment was not intended. Settlers and colonial officials did not want criminals compromising the economic and social attractiveness of their colonial investments. From an economic point of view, the best settlers were people who worked hard and had skills to offer. The character and economic value of the people building new communities turned out to be far more important than issues of class, politics, and religion.

From the established town of Perth Amboy, the Scots founded large farms (plantations or estates) up the Raritan River valley. John Barclay founded "Plainefield" and James Johnstone founded "Spoteswood." One of the largest estates, "Raritan River" belonged to Neil Campbell. It covered about 8,000 acres in what became Somerset County. Another great estate was at Basking Ridge. It was owned by James Alexander, a relative of the Sir William Alexander who had founded Nova Scotia in 1621. Alexander came to East Jersey from New York and became a late colonial proprietor. James Alexander's son, William Alexander, developed a fine estate at Basking Ridge, returned to New York, claimed the vacant British title "Lord Stirling," and served as a general in the Continental Army under George Washington.

But colonial America suffered from its own version of political turmoil in reflection of the English disorders of the 1680s. The Duke of York became James II in 1685 and his proprietary colony of New York became a Royal colony. A year later, the king appointed Sir Edmund Andros as governor of the newly created Dominion of New England, which embraced the separate English colonies of Massachusetts Bay, Plymouth, Maine, New Hampshire, Rhode Island, Connecticut, New York, the Jerseys, and Pennsylvania. As governor of just New York, Andros had had several conflicts with the Jersey proprietors. In March 1688, the king supported Andros in revoking the royal charters for both West Jersey and East Jersey. Although the king fell from power that same year, Andros retained his authority until 1692.

The proprietors tried to reassert their authority in East Jersey in 1692, and they called upon Andrew Hamilton, a Scot, to be governor. Hamilton served as governor of both West Jersey and East Jersey, although they were again separate colonies, from 1692 until he died in 1703 (at which time he was also the deputy governor of Pennsylvania).

But the proprietors never fully recovered their powers after 1692. The original proprietors who had championed East Jersey were largely gone. Robert Barclay had died in 1690. Several, who had been political friends of Charles II and James II, continued to support the Stuart king after he was driven out of London in 1688. Under William and Mary, these Jacobites became outlaws, and several (including Perth and Melfort) fled to the continent. Another driving force of East Jersey, Neil Campbell, returned to Scotland to play an active role in clan affairs and Scottish politics.

Furthermore, the population of East Jersey experienced strong growth, but with English immigrants rather than Scots. During the 1680s the Scots had experienced the tensions stemming from social, regional, and religious differences brought from the homeland. In the following decade, the Scots tended to bond together in the face of growing tensions with English settlers. The Englishmen resented the domination of the Scottish proprietors, especially their attempt to set themselves up as the aristocracy of a mini-Scotland in the New World. The anti-proprietor riots that broke out in 1700 seriously undercut the credibility of the proprietors to manage the colony.

Back in London, the Board of Trade in 1701 recommended to the Crown that private colonies become Royal. In the case of the Jersies, the proprietors did not strongly oppose this change. In April 1702 the proprietors of both West and East Jersey transferred governmental authority to the Crown, although they retained all of their individual property rights. The two Jersies were combined into one colony, New Jersey. From 1703 to 1738 the governor of New Jersey was the same person as the governor of New York, but after 1738 New Jersey was governed separately, although New Jersey and New York continued to have close economic and social ties.

One person who illustrated the close social and commercial ties between Perth Amboy and New York City was John Johnstone. He had been a druggist in Edinburgh before emigrating to East Jersey. He was married to the daughter of George Scot, and Johnstone became in time a major proprietor. He not only enjoyed considerable influence in East Jersey, he also became the mayor of New York City.

One of the joint governors of New York and New Jersey was Robert Hunter, a native of Ayrshire in the southwest Lowlands. Hunter had been a British army officer until he was appointed the resident governor of Virginia from 1707 to 1710, when he was shifted over to become governor of New York and governor of New Jersey, a post which he held for nine years.

The Scots of East Jersey continued to exert much influence in New Jersey up to the time of the Revolution, if not into the nineteenth century. The initial Scottish immigration of the 1680s declined in the 1690s and remained low until the 1720s, when another wave of Scottish and Ulster Scot immigration occurred. By 1750, there were an estimated 4,000 Scottish born or descendant people in New Jersey, perhaps as many as 20% of the colony's total population. The first settlement at Perth Amboy had led to further settlements up the Raritan River as far as today's Bridgewater. Scots also spread out across central New Jersey. For example, on the Delaware River a Scottish Quaker, William Trent, founded in 1714 a ferry and resting place for travelers from Philadelphia to New York. Trent's town became Trenton.

Another Scottish enclave lay less than 20 miles away from Trenton. In Princeton, English and Scottish Presbyterians established the College of New Jersey, which later became Princeton University. The president of the college from 1768 to 1798 was John Witherspoon, an already influential minister from Paisley. Witherspoon exerted enormous influence, both religious and political, in New Jersey affairs. He was a Patriot, led the New Jersey Patriots against the Loyalists (led by the governor, Benjamin Franklin's son), and signed the Declaration of Independence. The university attracted many Scots and Scottish Americans because of its Presbyterian seminary and the strong Scottish presence among faculty and administrators.

By 1790, the state population of New Jersey was counted at 184,00 of which an estimated 7.7% were Scottish (immigrants and descendants) and another 6.3% were Ulster Scot.

Darien

The worst Scottish colonial disaster was Darien in 1698-1700. It was not just a blow to Scottish pride, it was also a huge financial loss for Scottish investors. In terms of national disasters, the failure of Darien ranks closely with the catastrophic military defeat of the Scots by the English at Flodden in 1515.

The principal champion of Darien was William Paterson, a financial wizard who was a founder of both the Bank of Scotland and the Bank of England. In 1695 he and fellow investors put together the Company of Scotland Trading to Africa and the Indies. Over 200,000 pounds sterling worth of stock was sold in Scotland alone. The largest single investor was the Earl of Argyll, whose younger brother had been a proprietor in the Scottish colony of East Jersey. The company received from the Crown a 31-year monopoly on Scottish trade with America, Africa, and Asia. The investors had dreams of great wealth. As part of their dream, they wanted to establish Scottish colonial outposts. The initial site selected for a colony was the Gulf of Darien on the coast of South America near the isthmus of Panama.

In July 1698 some 1,200 colonists, including William Paterson himself, sailed from Scotland for Darien. They arrived by November 4. The first settlement was called New St Andrews and the second called New Edinburgh. The colony was called New Caledonia (as opposed to New Scotland, or Nova Scotia). Conditions could not have been worse: oppressive heat and humidity, insufficient fresh water and food, disease, and unfriendly Indians and Spanish. The Spanish in particular were very hostile to the intruding Scots, just as the Spanish had been to Stewart's Town in South Carolina in the previous decade. Even the English turned hostile, as London merchants and English colonial authorities took a dim view of the Scottish adventure. By mid-June 1699 the remaining Darien colonists were ready to abandon New Caledonia.

Three ships with a total of about 900 of the original colonists left Darien during June 1699. The *Caledonia* arrived at Sandy Hook, New York, on August 8. It lost 115 passengers, and even then New York authorities tried to keep the unwanted Scottish refugees from remaining in the English colony of New York. The *Unicorn* arrived in New York City just five days later and experienced the same troubles, despite having lost 150 at sea. The third ship, *St. Andrew*, was not even allowed in port at Jamaica.

A second expedition from Scotland arrived at the abandoned Darien colony after the 900 original colonists had departed on the three above named ships. The Spanish seized one of two Scottish ships and harried the colonists. A third Scottish expedition arrived with 1,300 new colonists on three ships. They erected Fort Andrew with the intention of defending themselves against the hostile Spanish. Even though a fourth, and final, Scottish expedition arrived at Darien in February 1700, the Scots could not muster the resources to resist the Spanish. Although the Scots routed the inept Spanish troops in the field, they could not hold up against an overwhelming Spanish siege. On March 18, 1700, Fort Andrew surrendered. The surviving Scots were allowed to depart on two ships, which eventually took them to the Carolinas.

One of these Scottish refugees from Darien who remained in the Carolinas was the Rev. Archibald Stobo. His daughter Jean married another

Scot, James Bulloch, who had immigrated to Charleston in about 1728. Their son, Archibald Bulloch, became a Patriot leader and the first governor of the independent State of Georgia in 1776. His son, James Bulloch, married Ann Irvine, who was a Scottish descendant on both her father's and mother's side of the family. They eventually had a granddaughter who was an Atlanta belle and married a wealthy New York City businessman (whose mother was an Ulster Scot descendant, although his name was old New York Dutch). Their second son, born in New York City in 1858, was Theodore Roosevelt, President of the United States from 1901 to 1909.

The Darien settlement collapsed upon Spanish capture of Fort Andrew in March 1700, and with it the Company of Scotland Trading to Africa and the Indies failed. It was an enormous financial loss and national embarrassment. The Darien disaster may not have caused the Act of Union in 1707, but it contributed to the reasons for Scottish and English union when promises were made in London to provide relief to the Company of Scotland investors and to open English colonies to direct trade with Scotland. From the English perspective, it was wiser to have the troublesome Scots (both Jacobites and Whigs) within the British system, and under its control, than to endure them as a continuous sore on the English outer skin. From the Scottish perspective, it was wiser, at least economically, to be within the British colonial system than excluded from it. The 1690s had been a very difficult decade for Scotland, and the Darien fiasco occurred close behind several years of agricultural failures and serious famine. Scotland was depressed, in many respects, entering the eighteenth century. With the Act of Union of 1707, no reason remained for independent Scottish colonies. After 1707, Scottish merchants and immigrants blended, more or less, into the British colonies of America, typically to the material advantage of the Scots.

Conclusions

Scottish attempts to found Scottish colonies in the New World during the 17th century failed. Scotland did not have the resources to compete with the

Spanish, French, and English. From the perspective of Scottish trade and settlements, the Act of Union created new opportunities that had been closed to the Scots. After 1707, numerous Scots (including merchants, army and navy officers and men, civil servants, and colonists) were far better off inside the British empire than they had been outside of it.

Although the four Scottish colonies failed, they established important precedents for much heavier Scottish immigration during the 18th century. Nova Scotia became a magnet for Scottish colonists, especially from the west Highlands and islands, during the second half of the 18th century and the 19th century. Because of the prior East Jersey experiment, New Jersey attracted numerous Scottish settlers before the Revolution. Despite the failed Stewart's Town, South Carolina also continued to attract Scots. The one exception was the failed colony of Darien: no Scots wished to return to Panama. There were Scots in Jamaica and the Caribbean islands, but they stayed away from the Spanish colonies. The name "Darien," however, continued to be used for Scottish settlements in the U.S.

References

William R. Brock, *Scotus Americanus.* Edinburgh: Edinburgh University Press, 1982.

Andrew Hill Clark, *Acadia. The Geography of Early Nova Scotia to 1760.* Madison, WI: The University of Wisconsin Press, 1968.

John T. Cunningham, *The East of Jersey. A History of the General Board of Proprietors of the Eastern Division of New Jersey.* Newark, NJ: New Jersey Historical Society, 1992.

Ian Charles Cargill Graham, *Colonists from Scotland: Emigration to North America, 1707-1783*. Ithaca, NY: Cornell University Press, 1956.

George Pratt Insh, *Scottish Colonial Schemes, 1620-1686*. Glasgow: Maclehose, Jackson & Co., 1922.

Ned C. Landsman, *Scotland and Its First American Colony, 1683-1765*. Princeton, NJ: Princeton University Press, 1985. [a scholarly history of the Scots of East Jersey]

D. MacDougall, ed. *Scots and Scots' Descendants in America*. Baltimore: Genealogical Publishing Co, 1992 (1917).

J. P. MacLean, *An Historical Account of the Settlements of Scotch Highlanders in America Prior to the Peace of 1783*. Baltimore: Genealogical Publishing Co., 1978 (1900).

John Prebble, *The Darien Disaster*. Edinburgh: Mainstream Publishing, 1978 (1968).

John G. Reid, *Acadia, Maine, and New Scotland. Marginal Colonies in the Seventeenth Century*. Toronto: University of Toronto Press, 1981.

CHAPTER EIGHT:

SCOTTISH SETTLEMENTS OF
THE CHESAPEAKE BAY

As discussed in the previous chapter, the union of Scottish and English governments in 1707 eliminated the need for the Scots to have their own colonies. After 1707, with new access to the British colonies, Scottish merchants and emigrants were free to go anywhere within the British empire that they wished. Subsequently, Scots played a prominent role in the settlement of the thirteen colonies, Canada, and the British West Indies through the 18th century. Yet, despite their freedom of choice, the Scots favored some areas more than others. The patterns of Scottish settlement in the American thirteen colonies from 1707 to the Revolution is the focus of the next four chapters. Chapter 8 will begin with the Chesapeake Bay colonies of Virginia and Maryland.

Overview of Scottish Immigration

In general terms, the Scots during the 18th century favored the thirteen colonies more than any other British area. For example, of the 3,884 Scots recorded in the British Register of Emigrants from 1773 to 1776, 92.7% went to the thirteen colonies (with only 4.2% going to Canada and 3.0% going to the West Indies). Much of Canada had been under French control until the British acquired it in 1763 as a result of the French and Indian War. Scots began to emigrate to Canada after 1763, but not in the same numbers as those immigrating further south. After the Revolution, more Scots emigrated to Canada than before 1775. In very simple terms, the thirteen colonies offered the most attractive economic "pulls" for immigration as well as a temperate climate.

In this same data set, 71.0% of the 3,884 Scottish emigrants departed for just two colonies: New York and North Carolina. Certainly by the 1770s, these were the two most favored colonies, especially for the large number of Highlanders emigrating at that time. However, other evidence shows that earlier a preference had been shown for Virginia, Pennsylvania, New Jersey, and South Carolina. Lowlander professionals, merchants, and craftsmen favored the cosmopolitan society of New York, New Jersey, Pennsylvania, and Virginia. Lowlander farmers preferred New Jersey, Pennsylvania, Virginia, and North Carolina. Highlanders gravitated to upstate New York, central North Carolina, and tidewater Georgia. And Ulster Scots, most of whom were farmers and craftsmen, liked Pennsylvania and the frontier backwaters of Maryland, Virginia, North Carolina, and South Carolina. Few of them cared for the homogeneous English and Puritan society of New England, and the New England colonies contained the fewest number of Scots of any American region by 1790.

By the first Federal census of 1790, the state with the single most number of Scottish-Americans was Virginia. With a total population of nearly 700,000 (of whom about 250,000 were blacks and slaves), Virginia was the most populated state in the U.S. in 1790. Of the white population of 442,000, about 113,500, or 26%, were Scots or Americans of Scottish extraction (Lowlanders, Highlanders, and Ulster Scots). In neighboring Maryland, there were about 28,000 Scots out of a total white population of 209,000. Virginia and Maryland, the colonies of the Chesapeake Bay, were the early target of Scottish settlers. In addition, by the time of the Revolution, they enjoyed the most trade with Scotland -- largely tobacco going to the great port of Glasgow.

The Scottish presence in Virginia and Maryland before the Revolution is the topic of this chapter.

Early Virginia and Maryland

The first successful English colony in America took root at Jamestown, Virginia, in 1607. The settlement was named for a Scot, James VI, King of Scots, who just three years earlier had also become James I of England. The early colonists of Virginia struggled through the first decades until they grew strong enough to weather hostile enemies and elements. The foundation of Virginia's economic growth was tobacco, the first cash crop raised for European consumers. Cultivating and shipping tobacco was not as easy as discovering gold, but it was the next best thing to it. For many Scots, Virginia and Maryland tobacco was their New World "gold."

Among the earliest settlers of Jamestown was a Thomas Henderson, who is believed to have been an Anglo-Scot. If so, he may have been the first Scottish settler in America, but he certainly attracted no followers. The first Scot directly from Scotland to settle in Virginia may have been Thomas Crawford, who appeared in the Chesapeake area by 1643. Prior to that date, a few Scots from Nova Scotia and the West Indies may have come into New England and the Chesapeake Bay area. Certainly the number of them was insignificant and they blended immediately into English colonial society without establishing uniquely Scottish communities.

More Scots appeared in the colonies after 1660 and especially after 1707. During the 1660s a Scottish merchant named Patrick Fleming entered the Virginia tobacco trade. Because of the Navigation Act of 1660, Scottish tobacco merchants must have been trading legally only between the colonies and England or trading illegally directly with Scotland. Either way, trade attracted Scottish interest. By 1680 there were enough Scots in Norfolk, the principal Virginia port for tobacco headed for Europe, to constitute a Scottish Presbyterian congregation.

Early Scottish settlers appeared on the east side of the Potomac River as early as 1670. By 1690, perhaps as many as 200 Scots lived in the area between the Potomac and Patuxent rivers in the colony of Maryland. During the last decades of the 17th century, Scottish settlements appeared in Accomac, Dorchester, Somerset, Wicumico, and Worchester counties on the East Bank.

The Scots came to the Chesapeake Bay to find employment and to work their own land. As the early Scots prospered, they attracted other Scots, especially their immediate families and friends. Among the Scots were some men of particular influence, not just among the Scots, but throughout the Chesapeake Bay colonies. These individuals were primarily ministers, colonial governors, and the powerful tobacco merchants.

The Ministers

The Scots included among their numbers their own ministers, primarily Presbyterian and Episcopalian (the Scottish parallel of the Anglican Church). As the Scottish communities grew, they called for more ministers to join them to tend to their congregations. Among the many Scottish ministers in the Chesapeake colonies, two exercised great influence: Francis Makemie and James Blair.

Francis Makemie. The most influencial Presbyterian minister in the early period of the colonies was the Rev. Francis Makemie, an Ulster Scot who came to Maryland in 1683. He had been born in c.1658 in County Donegal and had been educated at the University of Glasgow. He had just been ordained when he emigrated to America. He traveled widely, first having established Presbyterian churches in Maryland and in Virginia. He was banished from the colony of Massachusetts, where he challenged the rigid beliefs of the Puritans, and he had been imprisoned in New York. He founded the first presbytery in America at Philadelphia (where he was easily tolerated by the Quakers) in 1706, two years before his death at his last home, in Virginia. In recognition of his pioneering work, Makemie is often called "the father of American Presbyterianism."

James Blair. The most influential Scottish pastor in America, certainly in early Virginia and perhaps in all of colonial history, was the Commissary James Blair. A native of Edinburgh and a graduate of Marischal College in Aberdeen, Blair immigrated as a young man to Virginia in 1685 as an Episcopalian minister. Four years later Blair was selected by the Bishop of

London, who had spiritual authority over Virginia, as the bishop's official representative ("commissary") in the colony. He held the position as the virtual resident bishop in Virginia for the rest of his life, which lasted to the age of 88 before he died in 1743. Blair became a very powerful man. In addition to his church leadership, he served on the governor's council, where he fought with several governors and had a few removed by exerting his considerable influence in London. Blair also married a Harrison, and thereby entered the Virginia gentry class of Harrisons, Carters, and Byrds. As an educated man himself, Blair helped organize and became the first president of the colonial college William and Mary in Williamsburg. He held the presidency of the college for about half a century.

Blair fully integrated into colonial Virginia society. He became the patriarch of a large family that proliferated through the colonies. He also encouraged his Scottish relatives to relocate to Virginia. One who did so was a younger brother, Dr. Archibald Blair, a graduate of the University of Edinburgh and a physician. He came to Jamestown in 1690 and practiced medicine in Virginia for the next 43 years. Furthermore, Blair recruited many Scots to come to Virginia as ministers. Because of his power, Blair had many opportunities to offend colonists. One of the major complaints against him by the English was that he exploited his church position to further the interests of Scots in the Chesapeake Bay area.

The Scottish Resident Governors

Among all authorities in the colonies, the representatives of the Crown exercised the greatest power in the colonies before the Revolution began in the spring of 1775. In the case of Virginia, the colonial governor remained in Great Britain, where he exercised great influence at Court but not so much direct power over the colonists. At least one Scot, Lord George Hamilton Douglas, the Earl of Orkney, served as an absentee Governor of Virginia, in the early 18th century. With the governor over 3,000 miles away, the chief executive authority in the colony was exercised by the resident Lieutenant Governor, who for all practical purposes was the actual governor. Four of Virginia's Lieutenant Governors, or resident Governors, were Scots: Robert

Hunter (1707-1710), Alexander Spotswood (1710-1722), Robert Dinwiddie (1751-1758), and John Murray, Lord Dunmore (1771-1775). Two of them were Anglo-Scot career British army officers (Hunter and Spotswood), one was an accountant and business manager in the service of the Crown (Dinwiddie), and one was a Scottish nobleman (Lord Dunmore). Three were Lowlanders and only one, Lord Dunmore, was a Highlander. All four were powerful and wealthy men who channeled the course of Virginia growth and encouraged other Scots to settle in their colony.

Robert Hunter. The first Scot, a Lowlander, to serve as a colonial governor in America was Robert Hunter. He had been born at Hunterston, Ayrshire, in the western Lowlands. Although a Scot, he had served as an officer in the English army even before the Act of Union in 1707. As a major, he was wounded at the Battle of Blenheim, the Duke of Marlborough's great victory over the French in Flanders in 1704. In large part due to his military expertise as well as his political connections, Hunter was made the resident Governor of Virginia in 1707 during Queen Anne's War (1702-1713) between the English on one side and the French, Indians, and Spanish on the other. He had the bad luck of being captured at sea by the French, but he was released to assume his post in the colonies. Hunter undoubtedly provided the professional military leadership in Virginia that London felt was vital to the defense of its largest colony. Just three years later, in 1710, Hunter was shifted to the governorship of New York and the recently created Crown colony of New Jersey, including what had been the Scottish proprietary colony of East Jersey. He retained the joint governorships of New York and New Jersey until he returned to Great Britain in 1719. Before his death in 1734, Hunter served the Crown one more time as the colonial governor of Jamaica from 1727 until 1734.

Alexander Spotswood. When Hunter left Virginia in 1710, he was replaced by another professional English army officer of Scottish origin, Alexander Spotswood. The son of an army surgeon from a minor branch of the distinguished Scottish family of Spottiswoode from Berwickshire (in the southeast Lowlands), Spotswood was born and raised in the English army.

130

He had been born at the English garrison in north Africa in 1676 and had grown up within the army. He had entered the army as an officer in 1693 and served under the Duke of Marlborough in Flanders during the wars with Louis XIV. He was wounded at Blenheim, as was Robert Hunter, and taken prisoner at Oudenaarde. Having left the army in 1709, he received the post as lieutenant governor of Virginia due to his outstanding military service and the confidence of Marlborough and Lord George Hamilton Douglas, the Earl of Orkney, who was the titular Governor of Virginia. Having already had the experience of being a French prisoner, he luckily got to Virginia without having repeating the same bad luck at sea that his predecessor had.

Spotswood, age 34 and still unmarried, assumed his responsibilities in Williamsburg in 1710. The colony of Virginia was already over a century old and contained 80,000 people (of whom 25% were black slaves). Its principal natural resource was land. Because of the large quantity of wilderness but relatively few Europeans, Virginia offered "headrights" of 50 acres to any settler or any individual who brought a settler to the land. For example, for an indentured servant, Virginia gave 50 acres to the ship's captain who transported the servant, 50 acres to the transactional agent, 50 acres to a sponsoring planter, and yet another 50 acres to the indentured servant when he or she had served out four years of service. In addition to headrights, one could buy land at the usual rate of 50 acres for five shillings (a quarter of an English pound sterling). Either way, acquiring land in Virginia was easy, and so many English and Scots came to this colony to own their own farm land. However, as easy as the land was to claim, it was often too difficult to legally document ownership. Easy land meant difficult legal claims to settle. In addition, there were disputes over quasi-feudal quitrents to the Crown, which the colonial government tried to collect but landowners tried to avoid.

The principal income of Virginia, its own form of "American gold," was tobacco. By 1710, Virginia was exporting to England 30 million pounds of tobacco per year. This trade was dominated by the English merchants of London and Bristol until later in the 18th century when the Glasgow merchants captured much of this market. Yet the trade had many irregularities that favored some colonial planters and English merchants over others.

Spotswood did well leading the colony in defense against hostile Indians, French, and pirates. He was a professional soldier with skill and dedication to duty. He also tried to reform land laws and regulate the tobacco trade. On this matter, Spotswood alienated the strongest planters, including William Byrd II. He even tried to subordinate the governance of the Anglican Church to civil authority. On this score, he alienated the Commissary Blair. After 12 years of service, Spotswood was replaced in 1722 by authorities in London highly influenced by Byrd and Blair.

Although relieved of his post, Spotswood remained in Virginia as a planter. As early as 1714 he had sponsored the settlement of Palatinate Germans in the vicinity of the Rappahannock and Rapidan rivers. Their town became known as Germanna, in the area of what later became Fredericksburg (in Spotsylvania County, named for Alexander Spotswood.) He actively encouraged, and invested, in iron mines and forges. In 1722 he changed roles from government to business leader. He acquired, and successfully defended his legal claim, to 83,000 acres extending from the Rappahannock west to the Shenandoah Valley, which he had first explored in 1716. In 1723 he exported 20 tons of pig iron back to England. He left Virginia in 1724 to settle his claims in London, and returned to his secured frontier estates in 1729. He brought with him a wife, children, and his extended family. He personally managed his business affairs along with a Scottish cousin, John Graeme, and another Scottish factor (or tacksman) named Robert Rose. By the year 1740, when he died at the age of 64, Alexander Spotswood had become a powerful Virginia planter and businessman, an early Scottish transplant who built his fortune in the New World.

Robert Dinwiddie. The third Scot to serve as the resident Governor of Virginia was Robert Dinwiddie. He had been born near Glasgow and had apprenticed as an accountant and merchant. From 1727 to 1738 he served as the British customs collector for Bermuda and from 1738 to 1751 he occupied the very powerful position as Surveyor General of Customs for the Southern Part of America, including Virginia, Maryland, Pennsylvania, the Carolinas, Bahamas, and Jamaica. With a strong reputation for honest and effective business management, he served as the Lieutenant Governor of

Virginia from 1751 to 1758, in the heat of the French and Indian War. He was not the professional soldier that Hunter and Spotswood had been, but he shared many other values with them. He championed the vigorous economic development of the colony and its westward expansion. He was willing to press Virginia's claim to the Ohio Valley even at the risk of war with the French and their Indian allies. Like Spotswood before him, the governor was a large investor in land. In Dinwiddie's case, he became a principal in the Ohio Company. He found a young, ambitious native-born Virginian to carry out his imperial designs in the trans-Appalachian frontier: George Washington. Despite the early disasters of the war, Dinwiddie supported the careers of men like the squire from Mount Vernon.

Lord Dunmore. The fourth and last Scottish resident Governor of Virginia was John Murray, Lord Dunmore. He was an example of Highland nobility tainted by Jacobitism who would go considerably out of his way to demonstrate his loyalty to the Crown after 1746. His father had "gone out" with his Murray kinsmen for Bonnie Prince Charlie in the Jacobite rebellion of 1745. As a consequence, his father had been stripped of all lands and titles. In 1756, however, John Murray, at the age of 24, inherited his father's claims and had his family lands and titles restored to him by the Crown. He became the Earl of Dunmore, the Viscount Fincastle, Baron of Blair, Moulin, and Tillymont. He returned the favor of the Crown by serving as a reliable Whig peer in the House of Lords from 1761 to 1770. In 1770 he was appointed the Governor of New York, where he relocated happily for just one year. In 1771 he was appointed the Lieutenant Governor of Virginia, the most prestigious colonial post.

Lord Dunmore's tenure in Virginia, however, proved much less pleasant than his stay in New York. He staunchly defended the prerogatives of the Crown and the authority of Parliament. Lord Dunmore was absolutely unyielding in his position and damaged the Loyalist cause by alienating so many Virginians. About the only issue on which he had popular support was pressing the Virginian claim to the Ohio Valley (as had his two Scottish predecessors, Spotswood and Dinwiddie). He personally led an expedition of Virginia militia to the Ohio River during "Lord Dunmore's War" with the

Indians in 1774-1775. Yet his uncompromising position against the Virginians, including his personal enmity for the radical Patrick Henry, the Virginia-born son of a Scottish immigrant, made him extremely unpopular. When Dunmore fled the capital, his successor as the first governor of the independent state of Virginia was Henry himself.

Lord Dunmore led a British naval and military assault on Patriot forces at Norfolk on New Year's Day, 1776. Although his attack destroyed much of the town, it failed to dislodge the Patriots. Dunmore's career in Virginia was over, although he received another Crown post as governor of the Bahamas from 1787 to 1796.

Scottish Tobacco Merchants

Lord Dunmore was one, but not the only reason, why Scots had become rather unpopular in Virginia by the time the Revolution began in New England in April 1775. Other reasons included the powerful Scottish tobacco merchants. Although they had started trade before 1700, they became increasingly powerful during the 18th century until they dominated the Virginia tobacco trade by the early 1770s. The Scottish merchants grew rich due to efficient use of trading posts and ships. They carried the trade both ways, to and from the tidewater planters.

Scottish merchants established their stores as far inland as the rivers were navigable. In Maryland, they planted themselves at Blandensburg on the Anacosta River (today an eastern suburb of Washington, D.C.), as well as other posts. In Virginia, the Scots placed themselves at Alexandria and Dumfries on the south bank of the Potomac River; at Fredericksburg (near Spotswood's estates) and Falmouth on the Rappahannock River; and Richmond on the James River. For example, the Glasgow firm of William Cunnighame and Company maintained 14 stores throughout Virginia (perhaps the 18th century version of chain stores). The hub of the Scottish merchant network was the principal ocean port of Norfolk.

The Scottish merchants bought tobacco directly from the planters. They often paid the best price, but the exchange was typically in credit rather than currency. The planters used their credits from tobacco to buy goods from the

British Caribbean and fine finished products from Scotland, England, and the continent, which was provided at good retail prices by the same local Scottish merchants. Too often the planters bought more on credit than they sold in tobacco, so that they fell into substantial debt to the Glasgow tobacco houses. The Scots, meanwhile, were making huge fortunes. They always carried full ships (tobacco to Glasgow and finished goods back to Virginia, often by way of the Caribbean) and they made profits both buying and selling to the colonial planters. They also made large profits reselling colonial tobacco from Glasgow to the Europeans, especially the French.

The Scottish "store system" in Virginia and Maryland (and North Carolina, to a lesser extent) worked very well as long as the credit held out. John Glassford, perhaps the greatest of the multi-millionaire tobacco giants of Glasgow, estimated in the 1760s that American planters owned as much as 500,000 pounds sterling to Scottish merchants. A later estimate, made in 1778, put the debt as over 1.3 million pounds sterling. But during the colonial political tensions of the early 1770s, the Glasgow merchants began to call in their debts, and the planters resisted. By 1775, the Scottish merchants were caught in a terrible dilemma: they risked alienating their planter supplier-buyer-debtors or risked the interruption of their profitable trade by British warships. The merchants who cleared most of their assets in the colonies and warehoused tobacco in Glasgow before 1775 did very well financially; those who had not lost everything. In 1776 the Patriot-controlled Virginia legislature expelled all "foreign" merchants from the state. Some Scottish merchants declared themselves to be "Virginians," but most fled. Two years later, in 1788, the legislature confiscated the property of "Tories" and nullified all debts to Britons loyal to the Crown. The Scottish tobacco barons and their agents went out of business almost entirely in Virginia, as well as in other states.

The height of the Scottish tobacco trade with all of the colonies was about 1773 with 47.2 million pounds of tobacco from America imported into Scotland. Most of the trade was with the Chesapeake Bay colonies of Virginia and Maryland, with lesser amounts with North Carolina. By 1775 the volume had declined slightly to 45.9 million pounds and then collapsed during the Revolution. By 1780, Scottish imports of tobacco amounted to just

135

about 5.0 million tons. The trade started to return in the 1780s, but fell again in the 1790s due to the turmoil of the wars of the French Revolution. By 1795, Scotland was importing only 2.7 million pounds of tobacco from the U.S.

The Scottish merchants who got their tobacco and collected planter debts before 1775 made windfall profits. For example, in the period 1770-1775 the buying price for Virginia tobacco was about two pence per pound; by 1776 the buying price, either from Virginia or Scottish warehouses, ranged from a low of eight pence per pound for the lowest quality leaf up to as much as one shilling, eight pence for the best quality leaf. In the early 1770s, the selling price of a pound of Virginia tobacco offered by Scottish merchants to French buyers was about 2.5 pence for pound, but by 1781 that price had risen to as high as two shillings, ten pence per pound. Unfortunately, by 1781, the Scottish merchants had exhausted their pre-war supplies and lost both their supply and their demand markets (with French trade cut off when the French came into the Revolution on the side of the Patriots in 1778).

The giants of the Glasgow tobacco trade were John Glassford, Alexander Spiers, William Cunninghame, Andrew Buchanan, James Jamieson, Andrew Thomson, and Thomas Donald. Their relationships with one another were intertwined by marriages, blood relations, and numerous business partnerships. Among them they formed six principal groups of trading companies and partnerships: the Cunninghame group (a network of several stock companies dominated by William Cunninghame), the Spiers group, the Glassford group (perhaps the most complicated and richest network of companies), the Buchanan-Jamieson group, the Thomson-McCall group, and the Donald group. Just three of these men -- Cunninghame, Spiers, and Glassford -- controlled over half of all the Clyde trade in colonial tobacco. In addition, each had other major investments, in such manufacturing enterprises as textiles, brewing, tanning, iron, rope, hats, silk, cotton, sugar, etc (all of which produced some goods to be sold to colonial planters as the trading stations). Most of all, these merchants bought Scottish land and became lairds of great estates. Typical of the emerging Scottish merchant middle class, the great businessmen of the 18th century arose from families of Lowland agricultural managers (tacksmen), craftsmen, ministers, and tradesmen, but not the aristocracy or landed gentry. However, having made their fortunes in commerce, the merchant barons were quick to buy what they had not been born to: land, titles, mansions, and manners.

One distinguishing business trait of the Scottish merchants was that they liked to manage their own investments. The Glasgow tobacco barons had their own business managers, called factors, operating in the colonies. When times were good, these local Scottish factors were popular with the planters; but with the tensions that led to the Revolution in 1775, the Scottish factors became very unpopular. Even though Virginia had many Scottish settlers, some of whom had been in the colonies for several generations, Scots became the object of scorn and contempt in part due to the unpopularity of the Scottish tobacco factors (especially when they were collecting on planter debts).

Some of the colonial factors became wealthy in their own right and became full partners-in-residence. These included Matthew Blair, John Campbell, John Craig (son of James Craig, the laird of Braidland in Ayrshire), David Walker, and James Robinson.

The most famous of all the Scottish tobacco merchants of Virginia was Neil Jamieson. He was the resident partner of Glassford, Gordon, and Monteath in Norfolk. In addition to the tobacco trade, he invested in many enterprises, including distilling. When the Revolution broke out, he tried to salvage as much as he could for his Glasgow partners. His base of operations, Norfolk, was vastly destroyed early in 1776 when Lord Dunmore tried to recapture the town from the Patriots. Jamieson remained loyal to the Crown and relocated to Nova Scotia. His numerous attempts to recover confiscated property in Virginia failed.

After the Revolution, the Scottish tobacco merchants lost their hold on the Chesapeake Bay tobacco trade. The Glasgow merchants tried numerous times to recover their lost stores and debts in Virginia, but they always failed to achieve restitution. The Revolution had disastrously interrupted the Scottish tobacco trade, and the Scots never recovered. By 1800, the tobacco era of Glasgow was over, with the Scots losing to the English and the Dutch.

Likewise, the Loyalist Scots of Virginia and Maryland never recovered their confiscated properties or their prior power. Most simply returned to the British Isles or resettled in Canada. The ones who had been patriots, however, continued their businesses, but without the power of the Glasgow millionaires behind them. Because of lingering hatreds, the Scots who remained in Virginia assimilated very quickly into mainstream Commonwealth Virginia.

Conclusions

Scottish settlers began to arrive in Virginia and Maryland during the 17th century. Their chief interests were in land and trade, largely tobacco. During the 18th century, more Scots and their families settled in Virginia than in any other colony. Not only did they greatly influence the colony by their numbers, they also enjoyed much authority through such powerful men as James Blair and the four Scottish resident Governors. But by 1775, the Scottish community was as badly divided in their loyalties as the rest of the colony. As a general rule, the Scottish colonists who had arrived early tended to be Patriots, while the more recent immigrants tended to be Loyalists. Farmers and planters were largely Patriots; merchants, particularly the Glasgow store system managers, remained Loyalists. Those who had come to the colony by their own resources were primarily Patriots, but those who came to serve the Crown stayed loyal to King George. Many Scots, most famous of whom was Patrick Henry, played prominant roles in the Revolution and the founding of the new republic. Their stories will be told in later chapters.

References

Bernard Bailyn, *Voyages to the West. A Passage in the Peopling of America on the Eve of the Revolution.* New York: Vintage Books, 1988.

William R. Brock, *Scotus Americanus.* Edinburgh: Edinburgh University Press, 1982.

T. M. Devine, *The Tobacco Lords. A Study of the Tobacco Merchants of Glasgow and Their Trading Activities, c.1740-90.* Edinburgh: Edinburgh University Press, 1990 (1975).

David Hackett Fischer, *Albion's Seed. Four British Folkways in America.* New York: Oxford University Press, 1989.

Ian Charles Cargill Graham, *Colonists from Scotland: Emigration to North America, 1707-1783.* Ithaca, NY: Cornell University Press, 1956.

Walter Havighurst, *Alexander Spotswood. Portrait of a Governor.* Williamsburg, VA: Colonial Williamsburg, 1967.

Charles Haws, *Scots in Old Dominion, 1685-1800.* Edinburgh: John Dunlap, 1980.

D. MacDougall, ed., *Scots and Scots' Descendants in America.* Baltimore, Md: Clearfield Co., 1992 (reprint of 1917 edition).

Alf J. Mapp, Jr., *The Virginia Experiment: The Old Dominion's Role in the Making of America, 1607-1787.* Lanham, Md: Hamilton Press, 1985 (reprint of 1957 edition).

Eric Richards, "Scotland and the Uses of the Atlantic Empire," in Bernard Bailyn and Philip D. Morgan, eds., *Strangers Within the Realm. Cultural Margins of the First British Empire.* Chapel Hill, NC: The University of North Carolina Press, 1991, pp. 67-114.

Stephen Thernstrom, ed. *Harvard Encyclopedia of American Ethnic Groups.* Cambridge, MA: Belknap Press of Harvard University Press, 1980.

In addition, biographical sketches of James Blair, Robert Dinwiddie, and John Murray Dunmore may be found in *The Dictionary of American Biography (DAB).*

CHAPTER NINE:

SCOTTISH SETTLEMENTS OF
THE CAROLINAS AND GEORGIA

In general, the Scottish settlers of America before the Revolution preferred the southern rather than the northern colonies. One reason may have been the weather: many Scots found the winter cold of the northern colonies more uncomfortable than the summer heat of the south. A second reason may have been the enormous quantity of available land and the richness of economic opportunities that were available to the Scots in the southern colonies. The cash crop of tobacco attracted many Scottish farmers and merchants to Virginia, Maryland, and North Carolina. After 1707, colonial investors actively recruited Scottish settlers in North Carolina, South Carolina, and Georgia. In addition, there were more Scottish governors, military officers, and colonial officials in the southern colonies, and they attracted families and friends to join them.

Of the estimated 479,000 Scots (Highlanders, Lowlanders, and Ulster Scots) and their descendants in the U.S. by the census of 1790, over half (about 249,000, or 52%) lived in the five states of Virginia, Maryland, North Carolina, South Carolina, and Georgia. As discussed in the previous chapter, Virginia had the largest number of Scots and North Carolina ranked close behind it. Only four states had 10% or more of their population of Scottish origin, and all four were in the South (Virginia, North Carolina, South Carolina, and Georgia). Georgia had the highest percentage of Scots (27%)

141

of any state in the U.S. The distribution of Scots in the South, as determined by the American Historical Association analysis of the 1790 census, is seen in Table 1.

Of course, no demographic statistics should be accepted uncritically, now or 200 years ago. The percentages given above are only of the states' white population, excluding blacks and slaves. The American Historical Association analysis was based largely on surnames rather than on immigration records or even self-declared reporting of people surveyed. Some scholars have objected to these numbers as exaggerating the numbers of Highlanders and Lowlanders and understating the number of Scotch-Irish. In addition, the figures include American-born Scots as well as immigrants, so that the numbers may be misleading in representing too many immigrants. On the other hand, these figures may be low because they missed people of Scottish descent without having Scottish surnames. Nonetheless, these figures are the best available, and they seem reasonable approximations when supplemented by historical accounts of the colonial peoples. While some scholars have raised objections to these percentages, none has offered better data, and some researchers have confirmed that the statistics for 1790 were actually quite accurate.

This chapter will survey the Scottish settlers of the Carolinas, North and South, and the southern most colony of Georgia.

TABLE 1, DISTRIBUTION OF SCOTTTIH POPULATION IN THE SOUTH
(from: Richard B. Morris, ed., *Encyclopedia of American History*, New York: Harper & Row, 1976, p. 653; and Bureau of the Census, *Historical Statistics*, Washington: Government Printing Office, 1976, I, pp. 24-37 and II, p. 1168.)

State	Scots	Scotch-Irish	Total Scots	Scots
Virginia	10.2%	6.2%	16.4%	113,488
Maryland	7.6	5.8	13.4	28,006
North Carolina	14.8	5.7	20.5	59,040
South Carolina	15.1	9.4	24.5	34,300
Georgia	15.5	11.5	27.0	14,310
Average	12.6	7.7	20.4	
Total				249,144

North Carolina

In many respects, North Carolina was an outgrowth of Virginia. As the Virginia tobacco lands became crowded with people and depleted in richness, colonists from the Chesapeake region looked for new fields farther south. As early as 1653, Virginians had settled the area north of Albemarle Sound between the Chowan River and the Atlantic. The Virginian assembly encouraged settlements to the south as a buffer against hostile Indians.

In 1663, the restored Stuart monarch Charles II granted a proprietary charter to create a new colony of "Albemarle." Originally, there were eight proprietors, all nobles loyal to the Stuarts. In 1691 the new colony adopted the name of North Carolina. Land was plentiful and immigration strong, but personal and political rivalries continuously disrupted economic growth. In 1729 the Crown revoked the proprietors' charter and reconstituted North Carolina as a royal colony with a governor selected by the Crown.

The earliest attraction for settlers was tobacco. Farmers came to own their own land and to raise this crop for export to Europe. They also raised other crops and animals. From Albemarle Sound they spread south and inland. Merchants came to deal in tobacco and other goods. The growth of agriculture and trade further attracted craftsmen, who were in demand throughout the colonies.

Following the general pattern of settlements, Lowlander Scots were attracted to the Tidewater and Piedmont of North Carolina. Scottish merchants, primarily Lowlanders, located in the towns, especially Wilmington, the principal port of the colony. Highlanders did not come in large numbers until after 1763, and they settled mostly inland from Wilmington. The Ulster Scots, or Scotch-Irish, settled primarily in the mountains and the upper Piedmont.

During the 18th century, the chief port of entry for the Scottish immigrants was Wilmington, which grew into the chief commercial center of the colony by the Revolution. Scottish merchants, craftsmen, and professionals took a prominent role here, just as they did in Alexandria, Richmond, and Norfolk, Virginia. From Wilmington, many Scots settled inland along the Cape Fear River. As early as 1732 Scots, primarily Highlanders from the west Highlands and islands, began populating the region about 100 miles up river from Wilmington. Under the leadership of John Innes, Hugh Campbell, and William Forbes, they founded a trading town that was first named "New Campbelltown," for the village on the Kintyre peninsula of Argyll. By 1775 the community was better known as Cross Creek, and after the Revolution the town was renamed Fayetteville in honor of the French Patriot LaFayette. By 1775, Cross Creek had one of the largest, if not the largest, population of Highlanders in the Thirteen Colonies.

While the Scots came to prominence in Wilmington, they were not always a popular minority. For example, in 1739 a Neil McNeill brought some 350 Highlanders to Wilmington, where they were "made fun of" by the locals. Lowlander professionals, merchants, craftsmen, and farmers likely had little or no difficulty blending in with the English settlers, but the Highlanders were noticeably different, to both the Lowlanders and the English. Many of the Highlanders still spoke only Scottish Gaelic, while the Lowlanders quickly shifted from their Scots dialect to English. Before the Proscription Laws of 1746, the Highlanders may have arrived in North Carolina in their native attire, including kilts. If they did, they would have certainly posed an odd figure in colonial society. Lowlanders, on the other hand, had already adopted English-style dress, and so were visually indistinguishable from the English. In the face of social ridicule and torrid summer temperatures, it is most likely that the Highlanders of Wilmington and Cross Creek quickly changed from wool kilts and hose to pants, although they may have retained their tartan regalia for special occasions.

The great flood of Scottish immigrants into North Carolina came after the successful conclusion of the French and Indian War in America. One estimate is that by 1753 there were 4,000 to 5,000 Highlanders in the Cape River valley. Another estimate is that by 1775 the number may have risen to as many as 20,000. In the years 1768-1771 alone, some 1,600 Highlanders immigrated into the area. A large number of these Highlanders came from the islands of the Inner and Outer Hebrides. The island of Skye feared severe depopulation in the early 1770s because of the flood of emigrants to America, principally North Carolina. In disputes over rents, more than one MacDonald tacksman moved whole communities of crofters and cotters to the colonies.

It is possible that in the 10 years before the summer of 1775, as much as one-fifth of the entire population of Skye emigrated to America. Whatever the actual figure may have been, both Dr. Samuel Johnson and James Boswell in their recollections of their tour of 1773 commented with great distress about the large number of islanders who shipped off to the New World.

In addition to farming, the Highlanders of Cross Creek are credited with having introduced a Highland economic activity to North Carolina: the raising and droving of cattle. For hundreds of years, the Highland drovers, not too dissimilar to the later American cowboys of the great Western cattle drives, had directed herds of cattle from the island and Highland pastures to the markets, called trysts, of the Lowlands. In North Carolina, the Highlanders raised cattle locally and drove them to the markets of the Tidewater towns, especially those in Virginia. Herds of 200 to 300 head were not unusual; some were actually as large as 1,200. During the 1760s, some 30,000 cattle a year were driven from North Carolina to Virginia. Wilmington was an alternative market. The colonial drovers, like their Scottish counterparts, typically walked and employed dogs as their assistants. To control their animals and to also defend them from wild animals, the drovers typically used bull whips, and from the snap of these whips the drovers may have acquired the name "Crackers," which became an uncomplimentary term for rough Southern farmers and herdsmen (as, indeed, the drovers of Scotland were often held in both fear and contempt as "loners" and "broken men," although the same traits of the later Western cowboys were glorified as virtues rather than vices).

Also like Virginia, North Carolina had several Scottish governors and Crown agents. The most notable was Gabriel Johnston, who was born in the Scottish Borders in about 1698. The son of a minister, he attended the university at St. Andrews, where he received a Master's degree in 1720 and where he taught Hebrew for the next five years. Politically reliable and well connected, he received an appointment as the colonial governor of North Carolina in 1734. He served the Crown well for the next 18 years. During his tenure, Johnston was an enthusiastic colonist, and he actively recruited Scots, particularly Highlanders, to settle in his colony. In 1740 he encouraged the colonial assembly to exempt new settlers in the Cape Fear region from all taxation for 10 years. The colony also offered tax exemptions to settlers who came in groups of 40 or more. Johnston encouraged former Jacobites after the collapse of the Stuart rebellion in 1746 to relocate in North Carolina. For this gesture, however, he received much criticism from colonists loyal to the Crown.

Johnston sponsored the immigration of his own nephew, Samuel Johnston, in 1736. The younger Johnston became a successful lawyer and planter in the eastern Tidewater. Like his uncle before him, Samuel Johnston played an important role in the development of North Carolina, but as a Patriot rather than a Loyalist. When the revolution broke out in 1775, he sided against the Crown and became the first chief executive of the independent State of North Carolina. He later served in the Congress and became governor for the years 1787-1789. Johnston was a Federalist and a supporter of the ratification of the Constitution. He served as a Federalist Senator from North Carolina from 1789 to 1795.

Another Scottish colonial governor was Arthur Dobbs, who was born a Lowlander in Ayrshire in 1689 and became a prominent Ulster laird in County Antrim. Having served as a politically reliable member of the Irish parliament, he received the Crown appointment as governor of North Carolina in 1754, two years after the departure of Gabriel Johnston. Dobbs held his position until 1765. During his service, he was an enthusiastic champion of Ulster Scottish immigration into North Carolina as Johnston had been for the Highlanders.

North Carolina experienced much social and political tensions before the Revolution. In 1771 the so-called "Regulators," largely Piedmont and mountain farmers, violently contested the domination of colonial affairs by the Tidewater elite. Many Scotch-Irish participated in the Regulator revolt. The Highlanders of Cross Creek, however, sided with the colonial authorities, and a prominent Cross Creek leader, Farquhar Campbell, raised a company of men to fight against the Regulators. The governor's forces defeated the Regulators near Hillsboro and crushed the revolt.

Four years later, many of the Regulators took up arms again in support of the Patriots against the colonial governor. Once again, many of the Ulster Scots came out for the rebels while the Cross Creek Highlanders generally stayed loyal. At first Farquhar Campbell favored the Patriots, but he switched to the Loyalists by early 1776. The Cross Creek Loyalists were vocal in their support of the King, while the local Patriots remained quiet. Having suffered the turmoil of earlier Jacobite revolts in the Highlands and having felt the sometimes brutal reprisals of the Crown, many colonial Highlanders were very reluctant to "go out" against the King's colonial government in 1775, especially if they already owed gratitude to the Crown for past favors and pardons following the collapse of the Jacobite rebellion in Scotland in 1746.

One example to illustrate the point was Allan MacDonald of Kingsburgh. His father, Alexander MacDonald, had been a Jacobite on the island of Skye. His wife was the illustrious Flora MacDonald, who had assisted Bonnie Prince Charlie in his escape from pursuing Redcoats after the Battle of Culloden. Arrested and threatened with trial for treason, the MacDonald family had received amnesty from the King. Nearly three decades later, Allan MacDonald, who had become a disgruntled tacksman, led his extended family to North Carolina in 1774. His wife was generously received by both the Lowlander Scots of Wilmington and the Highlanders of Cross Creek. By early 1776, he had acquired a 475 acre estate of his own. Faced with unpleasant choices, he sided with the Loyalist Highlander MacDonalds of Cross Creek. He served as a major until the Battle of Moore's Creek Bridge. With his lands confiscated by the Patriots, he and his family returned to Skye in 1779. Flora MacDonald had suffered the pains of having been on the losing side of two revolts, as a Scottish Jacobite in a failed revolt against George III and as an American colonial Loyalist on the wrong side of a successful revolution against the Crown.

In the summer of 1775 the colonial governor Josiah Martin believed that he could hold North Carolina for the Crown by raising local Loyalist regiments, including as many as 3,000 Highlanders, and supplementing them with 2,000 British regular troops moved from Boston to Wilmington. In July he commissioned two Cape Fear Highlanders, Lt. Col. Donald McDonald and Capt. Alexander McLeod (both very likely from Skye) to raise a battalion of the Royal Highland Emigrant Regiment. The governor offered an incentive of 200 acres of free land and generous tax exemptions to recruits. Between these incentives and their own forceful leadership, which in some cases undoubtedly constituted coercion, McDonald and McLeod gathered no more than 1,300 fighting Highlanders at Cross Creek by February 18, 1776. Led by pipers and perhaps attired in native kilts, they marched on Patriot-controlled Wilmington, but never reached their target. On February 27, the Highlanders were ambushed by the Patriots (undoubtedly including numerous Scots) at Moore's Creek Bridge, some 18 miles up river from Wilmington. Some 70 Loyalists were killed and wounded; among the dead was Capt. McLeod. Another 850 Highlanders, including Major Allan MacDonald, were taken prisoner. The Patriots, on the other hand, suffered only one killed and one wounded. In a follow-up action, many more Highlanders were taken prisoner.

After the disaster of Moore's Creek, the Highlander Tories of Cross Creek largely kept quiet and stayed out of the war. The Patriots ran the state virtually unchallenged until the British offensive came to the Carolinas in the spring of 1780. When Charleston fell to the British, much of North Carolina was exposed. The British army and navy took Wilmington and held it until the war ended. In the meanwhile, local Tories in both North Carolina and South Carolina rallied to the support of the British troops. Even so, Cross Creek remained remarkably quiet and unresponsive to British calls for assistance. Even when the British army marched through the Cross Creek area, very few Highlanders welcomed it.

The Scotch-Irish of the Southern frontier largely supported the Patriot cause. They turned out to be the backbone of local resistance to the British when the Continental Army failed to repel the invaders. A relatively small battle won by Virginia and North Carolina militia with many Scotch-Irish frontiersmen rallied Patriots to the cause that led to their final victory. The key battle was King's Mountain, fought near the North and South Carolina border on October 7, 1780. About 900 Patriots were led that day by a Virginian Scotch-Irishman named William Campbell. They surprised an encampment of about 1,100 Loyalists under the command of Col. Patrick Ferguson, a native-born Scot. The withering fire of the frontiersmen cut the Loyalists to ribbons. By the end of the fight, Ferguson and about 120 other Tories had been killed, another 123 had been wounded, and 664 more captured. The Patriots lost only 28 killed and 62 wounded.

The victory yielded surprising strategic dividends for the Patriots, as it cautioned the British army to pull back from North Carolina and to go into winter camp early rather than risk an exposed left flank if it continued its march north. The further delay only helped the Patriots prepare better to meet the spring 1781 invasion through North Carolina and into Virginia, where the final Patriot victory under Washington at Yorktown in October 1781 ended the war.

South Carolina

South Carolina originated as part of the proprietary grants of the Carolinas in the 1660s. The first attempted English settlement in this region occurred at Port Royal Sound in 1670. It lasted only months before the settlers relocated up the coast to the Ashley River, where they built at Albemarle Point a settlement which they called Charles Town in honor of Charles II. A decade later, the community relocated again to the junction of the Ashley and Cooper Rivers, where they renamed their city Charleston. It grew into a major port that rivaled Boston, New York, and Philadelphia for triangular trade among English ports, the Caribbean, and the Thirteen Colonies.

As discussed in Chapter 7 (*U.S. Scots*, No. 8, Summer 1994, pp. 29-30), a Scottish colony was attempted at Port Royal Sound, near the present city of Beaufort from 1684 to 1686. A charter had been granted by Carolina proprietors to Henry Erskine, Lord Cardross, who recruited repressed Lowland Covenanters to populate his new colony. Only some 140 came to settle Stewart's Town. The colony immediately drew the fire of hostile Spanish and the English at Charleston. The Spanish destroyed it in September 1686, while the English refused any assistance and even drove off the desperate Scottish survivors. Likewise, the Charleston settlers refused aid to the dislocated Scots of the Darien colony in what is today Panama -- another Scottish colony wiped out by the Spanish.

Despite early hostility, many Scots came to Charleston after the Act of Union in 1707. Attracted by the trade, several Lowland Scottish merchants conducted their business there. They in turn attracted Scottish professionals and tradesmen. With the growth of the new colony of South Carolina, created

149

in 1729, fertile and inexpensive land attracted Scottish, predominantly Lowlanders and Ulster Scots, farmers.

As the figures presented at the top of this chapter show, there were fewer Scots in South Carolina than in North Carolina, but more Scots as a percentage of the state's population by 1790. Most of the Lowlanders were located in Charleston and the Tidewater. The number of Highlanders in South Carolina seems to have been quite small and they were much less noticeable than the Highlanders of either the Cape Fear River valley of North Carolina or the Altamaha River valley of Georgia. The state had numerous Ulster Scots, again, as in Virginia and North Carolina, primarily in the upstate frontier.

The Scottish community of Charleston was well enough established by 1729 to organize the first St. Andrews Society in America. The expressed intent of the group was to raise money to send to the needy back home. Less obvious, but likely more importantly, the St. Andrews Society was a social and material support group for Scottish immigrants. They existed for their own enjoyment of Scottish social traditions and to help each other out in times of need. Just like other groups of Scots, the loyalties of the St. Andrews Society of Charleston were divided during the Revolution. The organization discontinued meetings during the British occupation, but resumed them after the war with both Patriots and former Loyalists.

South Carolina had Scottish officials, although not as many or as powerful as those in North Carolina. One of particular importance was James Glen, who served as the Royal governor from 1738 to 1765.

The Scotch-Irish of the upstate frontier of North Carolina and South Carolina produced an extraordinary number of military and political leaders of the new American republic. The most famous was "Old Hickory," Gen. Andrew Jackson. Jackson's parents had emigrated from Carrickfergus, County Antrum, to North Carolina in 1765. They were Presbyterians with a Lowlander heritage. Jackson was born at Waxhaw, near the current border between North and South Carolina, in 1767 and grew up on the Carolina frontier. His family were staunch Patriots and Jackson himself was captured and mistreated by British soldiers -- an episode that left Jackson a bitter Anglophobe. As a young adult he studied the law and was admitted to the

North Carolina bar. In 1788 he relocated to Nashville, Tennessee, which at that time was a western extension of North Carolina that attracted numerous Scottish and Scotch-Irish frontiersmen from western Virginia and South Carolina as well as North Carolina. After Tennessee became a state in 1793, Jackson rose to prominence in state politics as a Jefferson loyalist. Like so many Scotch-Irish, he was quick to anger and slow to forgive. He held strong views of what was right and what was wrong, and he was not above killing a man in a dual to defend his and his wife's honor. He was a man of the law, but he was also the two-fisted descendant of generations of belligerent Borderers and Ulstermen. Jackson rose to national fame as a general in the War of 1812 and the hero of the American victory over the British at the Battle of New Orleans. In 1828 he was elected the seventh President of the United States and he was re-elected, amid great controversy, in 1832. Jackson stood for the democratic rights of the "common man," national unity, and Western expansion -- all solidly Scottish-American virtues.

Yet another Scotch-Irish political leader of Jackson's generation from Ulster Scottish origins in South Carolina was John C. Calhoun, who was born at Abbeville in upstate South Carolina in 1782. Calhoun's grandfather, James Calhoun, had emigrated from Ulster to Pennsylvania in about 1733. Like many Scotch-Irish, the Calhouns came down the Great Wagon Road in search of new land and settled in frontier upstate South Carolina. Calhoun's father was a Patriot during the Revolution, but opposed the ratification of the Constitution, which he viewed (as did the Scottish-American Patrick Henry of Virginia) as an infringement upon the sovereign rights of the states and upon individual liberties by a strong, central government. John C. Calhoun was educated in the North (he was graduated from Yale in 1804) and returned to South Carolina to practice law and engage in state politics as a Jeffersonian. He was elected to Congress, where he was a bellicose proponent of the war with Great Britain in 1812. He served as the Secretary of War under Scottish-American James Monroe and as Vice President under John Quincy Adams. Calhoun broke with Adams in 1824 and allied himself with Jackson as his Vice Presidential running mate. But during his second term, Calhoun experienced both personal and political problems with Jackson. Both of Ulster Scot extraction, both uncompromisingly held to their beliefs. Calhoun resigned and opposed Jackson in favor of his own native state in the South Carolina Nullification Crisis (in which the state nullified an act of Congress and asserted the ultimate right of secession). As a Senator from South Carolina from 1832 until his death in 1850 (except for one year, 1844-1845, when he served as Secretary of State under Polk), Calhoun became the political and ideological leader of Southern states' rights and slave interests.

Georgia

Georgia, the last of the Thirteen Colonies, had the highest proportion of Scots and Scotch-Irish of any state by 1790 with 27% of the state's population. But because the total population of Georgia was small, the absolute number of Scots, about 14,000, was less than that of any other Southern state. The Georgia Scots were largely Highlanders specifically recruited by the colony as the frontline defenders against the Spanish in Florida. They were recruited by James Edward Oglethorpe, a distinguished English army office and Member of Parliament who founded the colony. In 1732 he and his group of proprietors received a royal charter to organize a new colony south of the Savannah River in lands that had been in dispute between English South Carolina and Spanish Florida. Oglethorpe himself led the expedition that founded the town of Savannah in 1733. For the rest of the decade, he erected defensive forts and settled frontier posts along the Altamaha River and the offshore islands of St. Simon's, St. Andrew's, Cumberland, and Amelia. To populate these forts and posts, and to defend them against the Spanish, Oglethorpe recruited Highlanders, whose courage and fighting skills he had admired during European campaigns.

To recruit and lead the Highlanders, Oglethorpe selected Lt. Hugh Mackay, the son of a laird from Scoury, Scotland, and Capt. George Dunbar. They attracted about 150 men and another 50 women and children to follow them to the new colony of Georgia. They departed from Inverness in October 1735 and founded Joseph's Town up river from Savannah in early 1736. Lt. Mackay led a splinter group to settle a new town on the Altamaha River. They called it "Darien" in honor of the failed Scottish colony in Panama. The name of the town and its closeness to Spanish Florida invited a repetition of history.

152

Mackay was a professional soldier and his band included hardened Highland fighting men. He also enjoyed the full support of the proprietors. When Oglethorpe visited them in February 1736, he showed his support of them by allegedly wearing "Highland garb," which has been interpreted as the kilt (although it may have been trews and a plaid outer wrap).

Following his visit to Darien, Oglethorpe led Mackay's men on an expedition to the coastal islands, where they built several forts, including Fort St. Andrews. The immediate threat to the colony, however, was not the Spanish but rather internal feuding. Mackay supported Oglethorpe against his critics. His dispute with a Lt. Col. James Cochran was so serious that Mackay was ordered to return to England for a court martial, although he was exonerated and soon returned to Georgia. One issue of contention was black slavery, which many of the Highlanders wished to ban in the colony.

Mackay returned to Georgia in time to take on the Spanish. He participated in Oglethorpe's unsuccessful campaign of 1739-1740 against the Spanish at Fort Augustine. When the Spanish retaliated with their own invasion of St. Simon Island in July 1742, Mackay commanded Fort St. Simon. Upon orders, he evacuated his fort and pulled back toward Fort Frederica at the north end of the island. His Highlanders set up an ambush for the advancing Spanish and shattered them in the so-called Battle of Bloody Marsh on July 7, 1742. It is not known for sure whether Mackay's men were attired in kilts or whether the bagpipes played, but such a scene was entirely possible. The Spanish were driven back and soon retired to their own Fort Augustine. Mackay's Highlanders had achieved the very goal that had been set: they had provided the necessary defense of the frontier from the Spanish, who had twice before (Stuart's Town at Port Royal Sound in 1686 and Darien in 1699) destroyed Scottish settlements in the New World. The Scots won their last encounter with the Spanish, who never again seriously threatened the British possession of Georgia.

After his success in 1742, Mackay returned to Great Britain. He was promoted to the rank of major in 1744, but he retired in 1745 and avoided the Jacobite rebellion that broke out in Scotland in that year. He retired to a plantation on the island of Jamaica, where he died in 1763.

Another notable Highland officer in Georgia was Lachlan MacIntosh, who was born at Raits, Badenoch, in 1725. He was brought to Oglethorpe's colony as a lad by his father, John Mohr MacIntosh, a professional soldier. The boy grew up in Charleston and was trained to become a surveyor. He acquired more than 12,000 acres in Georgia. In 1775 he supported the Patriots and served in the state militia and the Continental Army, in which he rose to the rank of Brigadier General. Today McIntosh County, on the Atlantic coast and on the north side of the Altamaha River, which was the heart of Highlander settlements in Georgia, was named in honor of General MacIntosh and his relatives.

A very prominent extended Scottish family in both South Carolina and Georgia was Stobo-Bulloch-Irvine. In 1700 the Rev. Archibald Stobo, a widely acclaimed minister and a native of Glasgow, accepted refuge for his family at Charleston following their escape from Darien. In 1729 his daughter Jean married James Bulloch, another Glasgow immigrant to Charleston. The Bullochs relocated to Georgia, where they prospered. Their son Archibald Bulloch became a Patriot leader in Georgia and the first "president" and military commander of the state until his early death in 1777. Archibald Bulloch's son James (named for his grandfather) grew up and married Ann Irvine, the daughter of a well respected Scottish-American physician. Their granddaughter Martha Bulloch, an acclaimed beauty of ante-bellum Atlanta, surprisingly wed a Yankee, a wealthy New York businessman of Dutch descent named Roosevelt. In 1858 their son, Theodore, was born in New York City. He developed into the larger than life national hero "TR" and President of the United States from 1901 to 1909.

The pattern of Scottish settlements in Georgia was similar to that in Virginia and the Carolinas, with some variations. Lowlander merchants, professionals, and craftsmen were attracted to the major towns, except in Georgia there were only two, Savannah and Augusta. The Highlanders of Georgia were largely in the Tidewater, as described above. Both Lowlander and Highlander farmers were attracted to the piedmont. And the Scotch-Irish, most of whom were coming into the colony by way of the Great Wagon Road, settled in the mountains and upper piedmont.

Scots played an extremely influential role as Indian agents all along the frontier, especially in the South. Indeed, Scottish Indian agents and merchants frequently intermarried with the Indians and produced generations of Indian chiefs with Scottish roots. Three in particular should be mentioned at this time.

In 1783, Alexander McGillivray was elevated to the status of a chief of the Creek Nation in what is now parts of Georgia and Alabama. McGillivray's father had been a British Indian agent whose wife was half-Creek and half-French. Alexander was born of this union in 1759, and he enjoyed both a traditional Creek upbringing and a colonial education in Charleston and Savannah. Both he and his father were Loyalists during the Revolution. After the war, Chief McGillivray tried to balance the power of the U.S. with the Spanish in Florida to leave his lands as a neutral buffer between the two. He successfully concluded a treaty of peace with the U.S. and with Spain; he also negotiated with the new State of Georgia to recognize the Altamaha River as the boundary with the Creeks. He even accepted a commission as a Brigadier General in the American army. Unfortunately, he died at the age of 34 in 1793 at Pensacola. His efforts to maintain peace and neutrality eventually failed with the loss of Creek lands to Georgia and the new state of Alabama.

Another Creek chief of Scottish heritage was William McIntosh. He was born in 1775 from the marriage between John McIntosh of Borlum, Scotland, who was a British Indian agent, and a Creek princess. His father was a Loyalist during the war, and the boy was raised as a Creek warrior apart from the whites of Georgia. By 1800, William McIntosh, at the young age of 25, achieved the rank of chief of the northern branch of the Creek Nation in what is now upstate Georgia. He saw that the strength and integrity of his people rested with alliance with the Americans, not with the Indian extremists led by Shawnee warrior Tecumseh or the British. In the Creek War of 1813-1814, McIntosh led his Creek warriors against the southern Creeks. He participated in the Battle of Horseshoe Bend on the same side as the Scotch-Irish warriors Andrew Jackson, Sam Houston, and Davy Crockett. The price he paid for his part in this war was death by enemy Indian assassins in 1825, about 12 years after Horseshoe Bend. His heirs continued as chiefs of the northern

Creeks. His son lead the relocation of the tribes to Muskogee, Oklahoma. His great grandson, Waldo Emerson "Dode" McIntosh of Tulsa, served as the principal chief of the Creek Nation in the 1960s and frequently attended Scottish games in tartan kilt and Creek chief headdress.

Perhaps the greatest Scottish-Indian was Chief John Ross (Kooweskowe) of the Cherokee Nation. He was born in 1790 near Lookout Mountain on the border of Georgia and Tennessee. His father, David Ross, had been a British Indian agent and a Loyalist in the Revolution. His mother was Mary McDonald Ross, whose mother was Cherokee and whose father was Scottish. John Ross received both an Indian and a white man's education. He most likely knew well Sam Houston, who spent several years living with the Cherokees. Like Chief McIntosh, Ross sided with the Americans in the Creek War and he, too, saw action with the Americans against the southern Creeks at the Battle of Horseshoe Bend.

Ross was elected the President of the Council of the Cherokee Nation in 1819 and became the principal chief of the east Cherokees in 1828. He opposed Jackson's plan to relocate the Indian tribes from Georgia and Alabama to the west side of the Mississippi River. Yet he knew that war against the U.S. would be disastrous, as it had been for the southern Creeks in 1814. John Ross, therefore, kept his people together and led them on the "Trail of Tears" to the Oklahoma Territory in 1838 to 1839. His stature as an Indian statesman increased further when he became chief of the united Cherokee Nation in 1839. He continued to seek both peace and prosperity for his people. Ross himself owned and managed a large plantation with slaves. At the beginning of the Civil War, his sympathies lay with the South, but his own statesmanship and his Quaker wife persuaded him to remain officially neutral between the North and the South. He and his wife relocated to Philadelphia in 1862, and he died there four years later.

On the eve of the 21st century, the Scottish-Americans of Virginia, North Carolina, South Carolina, and Georgia are vocally proud of their heritage. Many dress in kilts, a Highland attire that their ancestors may have never worn either in Scotland or America. Yet, they are rightfully respectful of the sacrifices and investments that their Scottish ancestors made some 200 to 300 years ago to make their new homes as successful as they became. Today, some of the best attended and most successful Highland games and gatherings occur in the South, such as the ones at Grandfather Mountain in western North Carolina, Charleston, Savannah, and Stone Mountain near Atlanta. Begun in Charleston, St. Andrews societies have spread across the country as a unique Southern contribution to U.S. Scottish culture.

References

Bernard Bailyn, *Voyages to the West. A Passage in the Peopling of America on the Eve of the Revolution.* New York: Vintage Books, 1988.

William R. Brock, *Scotus Americanus.* Edinburgh: Edinburgh University Press, 1982.

Russell M. Chalker, "Highland Scots in the Georgia Lowlands," *Georgia Historical Quarterly, 60* (1976), pp. 35-42.

Desmond Clarke, *Arthur Dobbs, Esquire, 1689-1765.* Chapel Hill, NC: University of North Carolina Press, 1957.

Kenneth Coleman and Charles Stephen Gurr, eds., *Dictionary of Georgia Biography.* 2 vols. Athens, Ga: University of Georgia Press, 1983. (see "Hugh MacKay", Vol. II, pp. 671-672.)

E. Merton Coulter, *Georgia. A Short History.* Chapel Hill, NC: University of North Carolina Press, 1973 (1933).

David Hackett Fischer, *Albion's Seed. Four British Folkways in America.* New York: Oxford University Press, 1989.

Ian Charles Cargill Graham, *Colonists from Scotland: Emigration to North America, 1707-1783.* Ithaca, NY: Cornell University Press, 1956.

R. Edwin Green, *St. Simon's Island*. Westmoreland, NY: Amer Publications, 1985 (1982).

James G. Leyburn, *The Scotch-Irish. A Social History*. Chapel Hill, NC: University of North Carolina Press, 1962.

Hugh Talmage Lefler and Albert Ray Newsome, *North Carolina. The History of a Southern State*. Chapel Hill, NC: University of North Carolina Press, 1963 (1954).

J. P. MacLean, *An Historical Account of the Settlement of Scotch Highlanders in America Prior to the Peace of 1783*. Baltimore, Md: Genealogical Publishing Co., 1978 (1900).

Forrest MacDonald and Ellen Shapiro MacDonald, "The Ethnic Origins of the American People, 1790," *William and Mary Quarterly, 37* (1980), pp. 179-199.

D. MacDougall, ed. *Scots and Scots Descendants in America*. Baltimore, Md: Clearfield Co., 1992 (1917).

Grady McWhiney, *Cracker Culture. Celtic Ways in the Old South*. Tuscaloosa, Al: University of Alabama Press, 1988.

Duane Meyer, *The Highland Scots of North Carolina, 1732-1776*. Chapel Hill, NC: University of North Carolina Press, 1987 (1957).

Richard B. Morris, ed., *Encyclopedia of American History*. New York: Harper & Row, 1976 (1953).

CHAPTER TEN:

THE SCOTS OF NEW ENGLAND
AND NEW YORK

B y the time of the Revolution, New England consisted of four colonies: Massachusetts, New Hampshire, Connecticut, and Rhode Island. The area had had a turbulent history long before 1775 and was still in many ways unsettled. Massachusetts and Connecticut were amalgamations of formerly autonomous communities. Both suffered from social, religious, and territorial disputes. In addition, Massachusetts had never recovered from the experience of having been a virtually independent commonwealth in the 1650s during the English Civil War. It had seized the disconnected northeast section, which later (1820) become the State of Maine. Massachusetts also claimed sections of western and northern New York. Connecticut, too, engaged in border disputes with New York. The land that in 1791 became Vermont was earlier contested by New York, New Hampshire, and Massachusetts.

Despite the territorial and political uncertainties, New England enjoyed great economic growth and attracted many British colonists. Its ports engaged in very profitable trade with the Caribbean and Great Britain. By 1775, Massachusetts had about 475,000 people, second only to the much larger Virginia. Boston, with a population exceeding 15,000, was the third largest colonial city after Philadelphia and New York. Born in Old World religious controversies, the region prospered over the decades until it led the final political break with the Old World. If the first successful English colony took root in Virginia, then the first successful free state emerged in Massachusetts.

In the beginning, during the first half of the 17th century, New England attracted Scottish as well as English religious dissenters. In particular, the Puritans offered sanctuary to the repressed Presbyterians of the Scottish Lowlands and Ulster. But the Scots soon found that the Puritans could be extremely intolerant of any dissenters who differed with their own firmly held beliefs. By the 18th century, Scottish emigration into New England was the lowest for any region in the Thirteen Colonies.

In contrast, New York held much appeal for the Scots. Upstate New York, north of Albany in the Mohawk Valley and the Lake George areas, attracted many Highlanders -- perhaps as many as settled in North Carolina. The city of New York drew numerous Lowland merchants and professionals.

This chapter will provide an overview of the Scots of New England and New York up to 1775.

Regional Statistics

According to the first federal census of 1790, and the subsequent analysis of it, the statistics available on the Scots and Scottish surname descendants of the northeast U.S appear below.

State	%Scots	%Ulster Scots	%Total Scot	Numbers
Massachusetts	4.4	2.6	7.0	26,110
Maine (MA)	4.5	8.0	12.5	12,000
New Hampshire	6.2	4.6	10.8	15,228
Vermont (1791)	5.1	3.2	8.3	7,055
Connecticut	2.2	1.8	4.0	9,320
Rhode Island	5.8	2.0	7.8	5,070
Averages	4.7	3.7	8.4	
Total				74,783
New York	7.0	5.1	12.1	37,994

Sources for the preceding table: Richard B. Morris, ed., *Encyclopedia of American History*. Bicentennial edition (New York: Harper & Brothers, 1976), p. 653; Bureau of the Census, *Historical Statistics of the United States. Colonial Times to 1970*. Bicentennial edition. 2 vols (Washington: Government Printing Office, 1975), Part I, pp. 24-37, and Part II, p. 1168.

While no census figures exist for 1775, these figures for 1790 are reasonable approximations for the Scottish-American population in New England and New York on the eve of the Revolution. These numbers include both Scottish-born colonists and native-born Americans of Scottish extraction with Scottish surnames. The figures for 1790, of course, exclude the casualties of the Revolution and the exodus of Scottish Loyalists. They do include Scottish immigrants after 1783 who may have replaced in numbers the losses of 1775-1783. The figures also do not include Americans whose mothers' families may have been Scottish but whose surnames were English, German, or something else that was not Scottish. The statistics for 1790, if they are not virtually the same as those for 1775 (which do not exist, anyway) may in fact err on the conservative side for what may have been a larger Scottish-American population in 1775.

Combined, New England and New York contained about 110,000 Scots. This number was less than half the number of Scots in the southern states of Virginia, North Carolina, South Carolina, and Georgia (with over 221,000 Scots). Virginia alone was the home of over 113,000 Scots. In New England, the Scots were a small, and probably peculiar minority, with less than 10% of the total populations in Massachusetts, Connecticut, Rhode Island, and what became Vermont.

New York had about 38,000 Scots -- the same as Massachusetts and Maine combined (which they were in 1775). It had a higher percentage of Highlanders and Lowlanders (7.0%) than any other state in the northeast. It had the second largest percentage of Ulster Scots (or Scotch-Irish) with 5.1% (second to Maine, with 8.0%).

Basically, New England was largely English and Puritan (Congregationalists). It was the most homogeneously English of all the colonial regions. Scots, even of the same faith, were not well received. New York, however,

163

was far more cosmopolitan. Originally Dutch, it accommodated many ethnic groups. For example, Massachusetts was 82% English, with the Scots at 7.0% the largest non-English ethnic group. New York was only 52% English, with the Scots at 12.1% and the Dutch at 17.5% of all New Yorkers.

Although the numbers were relatively small, the Scots began to come to New England and New York early in the history of these colonies. A few Scottish families rose to great prominence, so that in general the Scots exercised influence in colonial affairs far beyond their mere numbers.

Scots in Early New England

The various New England colonies started as trading companies with both religious and secular ambitions. The first successful colony in this region (and the second in British North America) was the Plymouth Plantation, founded in 1620, just 13 years after the founding of Jamestown in Virginia. Next came the Massachusetts Bay colony in 1630. Its population grew so rapidly due to immigration from strife-torn England that new colonies were founded to the north (New Hampshire) and to the south (the several towns that merged into the colony of Connecticut and the colony of Rhode Island). But as in the case of Virginia, each private trading company eventually failed and returned to the authority of the Crown. By the 1680s, in the face of vigorous and continual local political opposition, royal power in the forms of royal governors, Lords and later the Board of Trade, and Vice-Admiralty courts had become established throughout New England.

The so-called Pilgrims sought refuge in America from religious repression at home, but they also sought opportunities for worldly wealth. However, they numbered only a few hundred and barely survived as a colony. They struggled for decades and in 1691 their small colony was formally absorbed into the royal colony of Massachusetts.

The largest colony in New England was Massachusetts Bay, founded by the Puritans (a different sect than the Pilgrims) to the north of Plymouth. From 1630 to 1641, when the English Civil War broke out, the Massachusetts colony, centered at Boston, attracted at least 20,000 settlers, primarily from eastern and southern England (East Anglia and Kent). Both religious freedom and economic opportunity provided strong pulls for immigrants. In simple terms, the Puritans were Calvinist in dogma (much like the Scottish Presbyterians), but they technically adhered to the episcopal structure of the Anglican Church. The Puritans sought to "purify" the Anglican Church from within, rather than to escape from it (like the Pilgrims). Largely middle-class in social status, education, and wealth, the Puritans prospered in the trading routes of the emerging English global empire.

During the English Civil War, one solution to disposing of political malcontents and religious dissenters was to exile them to the New World. Oliver Cromwell exiled Scottish prisoners of war to America after his smashing victories in 1651. Following the Battle of Worcester, at least two ship loads of Scottish and English Royalists departed England for Massachusetts. Most if not all were sold as servants; many went to work at the Lynn iron works. While this has become a celebrated incident, largely because some of those prisoners became the progenitors of later powerful families in Boston, the numbers involved were small: 272. Exiling prisoners of war, and common criminals as well, was too expensive to do on a large scale during the 17th century. Very few Scots, certainly fewer than 5,000 and maybe no more than 2,000, were exiled to America against their will during the whole colonial era.

In the early 1640s the Puritans of England, although members of the Anglican Church, allied themselves with Presbyterians (English, Scottish, and Irish) against the "high churchmen" and the Royalists supporting the Crown. For a brief time, Parliament made Presbyterianism the established religion of the British Isles. But the Puritans split with the Presbyterians over details of faith, church governance, and national politics. Many Scots were both Presbyterians and Royalists, supporting the Stuart monarchy against Parliament. The nearly invincible Puritan army under Cromwell crushed the Royalists in England and overran both Scotland and Ireland. In the meanwhile, the Puritans of Massachusetts Bay ran their colony independently of direction from London. But they proved to be no kinder to the Presbyterians and the Scots than the English Puritans.

The Stuart monarchy was restored in 1660, but political and religious turmoil continued until the Glorious Revolution of 1688 drove James II from the throne. During the 1680s the repression of Presbyterians drove a few Scots to America and many more to northern Ireland. After 1688, however, religion became less of a reason for emigration to the colonies, and trade emerged as the single most important reason for Scots to settle in New England, as well as the other colonies.

By 1657 a sense of community among the Scots in Boston led to the creation of the first Scottish social organization in the Thirteen Colonies. It was not a St. Andrews or a Caledonian Society, but rather it was called the Scots Charitable Society. It may well have included members who were concerned about Scottish immigrants but who were English rather than Scottish. Its principal mission was to provide assistance to Scottish newcomers in need. It may have been a social organization as well as a benevolent society.

One early successful Scottish merchant in Boston was Hugh Campbell. He most likely was a leader in the Scots Charitable Society, as he was perhaps the most successful Scot in Massachusetts during the 1670s. In 1679 he initiated a plan to settle Scots in western Massachusetts, near the present city of Springfield. While a few may have come, Campbell's scheme failed to establish a significant Scottish presence on the frontier at that time.

Another prominent Scot in New England was John Campbell, who showed up in Boston between 1695 and 1698. He acted as the postmaster of the city from 1702 to 1718. A printer by trade, Campbell created in 1704 the "Boston Newsletter," the first regular weekly newspaper in America.

In addition to Massachusetts, Scots found homes in Connecticut and a few located in Rhode Island. Stirling Township in Windham County, Connecticut, became a predominantly Scottish community. Another group of Scots or Anglo-Scots settled at Windsor on the Connecticut River. Among these people was the ancestor of General U. S. Grant.

No Scot served as a royal governor or high official of the Crown in the New England colonies. No Scot used a high office to encourage other Scots to come to New England as Spotswood and Dinwiddie had in Virginia or Johnston and Dobbs had in North Carolina. With the lack of friends in very high places, the Scottish immigrants found New England to be the least attractive of the American colonies.

166

The Scots of New England were widely scattered with few communities even mostly Scottish, let alone exclusively Scottish. The Scots from the Highlands and Lowlands who came to New England before the Revolution arrived as individuals, core families, or small groups. With notable exceptions, they did not come to New England as large groups, as did the Scotch-Irish and the Highlanders who came to New York and North Carolina from 1763 to 1775. Two noticeable exceptions were George's Bay, Maine, and Ryegate, Vermont.

A Samuel Waldo, a prominent man in Maine, had an idea similar to that of Hugh Campbell of Boston: to recruit and sponsor Scots to settle on the wild frontier. In 1753 he raised a party of 70 emigrants from Glasgow and Stirling. He offered them rent-free land for 19 years to settle on his property. These people founded a small Scottish community at George's Bay in Maine.

In 1773 a company of Scottish farmers was organized principally by David Allen and James Whitelaw to finance as a business enterprise an agricultural settlement of Lowlanders in upstate New York, where several Highlander communities had already taken root. The company was officially called the Scots-American Company of Farmers, but its popular name was the "Inchinnan Company." As many as 200 families were involved in the enterprise. Unable to find suitable tracts south of Lake George, the company moved further to the east on the banks of the Connecticut River. The territory at that time was claimed by three different colonies: New York, New Hampshire, and Massachusetts. In just two more years, in 1775, it would be in dispute between the colonies and the Crown. Despite political upheavals, the Inchinnan Company founded the town of Ryegate, which in 1791 became part of the new State of Vermont. It was likely the largest Lowland Scot farming settlement in all of New England.

Scotch-Irish of New England

The Scots, largely Lowlanders, experienced relatively few problems blending into the English population of New England. With the matter of religion becoming less significant in both Great Britain and the colonies after 1688, the Scots became more difficult to differentiate from mainstream society. Many were prosperous and highly respected merchants, physicians, teachers, and craftsmen. The Ulster Scots, on the other hand, suffered from the intolerance of both the English and the Scots. They generally considered themselves to be Scots, too, having had a Lowlander heritage, but they were often looked down upon as "Irish." The term "Scotch-Irish" was used as a label for Ulstermen in New England as early as 1695.

In the early 1700s church leaders in Boston became concerned with the plight of Presbyterians in Ulster. By the Act of Union of 1707, the (Presbyterian) Kirk of Scotland was established separately from the Church of England. The Presbyterians of Scotland enjoyed the freedom of their religion, but the Presbyterians of Ulster did not. Northern Ireland, although containing many Lowlanders, was still under the authority of the English and their Church of England, which treated the Presbyterians as disenfranchised non-conformists. The Ulster Scots felt squeezed between the hostile Catholic Irish and the intolerant Anglicans.

With the encouragement of Massachusetts sponsors, five ships with 700-800 Ulster Scots arrived in Boston on August 4, 1718. Unfortunately, the thoroughly English colonists soon rejected "the Irish" and demanded that they move to the colonial frontier. Governor Shute used his authority to force the Ulstermen out of Boston. The Rev. James MacGregor, a Presbyterian leader of the immigrants, protested to the governor that "We are surprised to hear ourselves termed Irish people, when we so frequently ventured all for the British crown and liberties against the Irish Papists and gave all tests of our loyalty which the Government of Ireland required..."

Some of the "Scotch-Irish" relocated to the north at Casco Bay (Portland) in the Massachusetts territory of Maine. Others went west to Wicasset, Worcester, and Haverhill. There had been some Presbyterian presence at the mouth of the Merrimac River since the 1630s. The majority, however, settled in Londonderry, New Hampshire, which became the focus of Scotch-Irish immigration into New England before the Revolution.

The Scotch-Irish of Worcester, Massachusetts, had no better luck with the local population than they had in Boston. Many families moved on to Pelham, Coleraine, Blandford, Warren, and Otsego County in neighboring New York.

The anti-Irish sentiments in Boston flared again in 1723 and 1729. Apparently, the Bostonians objected to the life styles and customs of the

Scotch-Irish. An anti-Ulster riot occurred in 1729 that discouraged further Scotch-Irish immigration to Massachusetts.

The early unhappy experiences of the Scotch-Irish in New England set a pattern for 18th century immigration from Ulster. When they arrived in America, the Ulster Scots rarely settled in the established towns, but relocated to the interior. They were frequently rejected by the established English, as well as other European ethnic groups. They were also roughly treated by many of the Dutch in New York and Germans in eastern Pennsylvania. The Scotch-Irish made their communities on the western frontiers of Massachusetts, New York, Pennsylvania, Virginia, North Carolina, and South Carolina. Discouraged from putting down roots in New England and New York, the Scotch-Irish in large numbers gravitated to western Pennsylvania, Virginia, and North Carolina. Frequently in disputes with their neighbors, the Scotch-Irish were particularly successful in fighting the Indians who threatened the more peace-loving colonists.

Early New York

New York began as a Dutch rather than an English colony. The town and port of New Amsterdam was founded by Dutch families in 1624. The colony grew quickly and spread up the Hudson River to the Mohawk River, to the west banks of the Hudson, and onto Long Island. It conquered the neighboring colony of New Sweden. The Dutch, unlike the Puritans, had few religious reasons for colonies, but were strongly motivated by economic incentives. While their local power was considerable, however, the Dutch of New Amsterdam alone could not redress the shifting of global power to the English.

In 1664, four years after the restoration of the Stuart monarchy, Charles II granted a hugh tract of land west of Connecticut to his brother James, the Duke of York and the heir apparent to the throne. An English task force of four frigates forced the surrender, under generous terms, of the Dutch in New Amsterdam. The English quickly replaced the Dutch politically and renamed their colony "New York," in honor of the Duke. During the Third Anglo-Dutch War, 1672-1674, the Dutch reoccupied New York, but formally yielded it by treaty to the English. Dutch families continued to own large tracts of land and exercise much financial power in the colony, but the Duke's agents attempted to rule the colony as though its were the Duke's own little realm.

In 1685 the Duke of York became James II. His colony, therefore, changed status from a proprietary to a royal colony. Disputes of prerogative continued, in both England and New York, until the Glorious Revolution of 1688 drove James II from the throne. Although he tried to reclaim the crown with his supporters (Jacobites) in Ireland and Scotland, his personal power ended in the New World. There was no Jacobite rebellion in New York.

Apparently, few Scots came to New York before 1707. No evidence exists that significant numbers of Scots arrived in New York during the turmoil between the Dutch and the English and among the English political factions. Yet, one Scot came to New York who exercised great influence and procreated his own clan in the future Empire State.

Robert Livingston entered the Dutch town of Albany on the upper Hudson River in about the year 1674, when the colony of New York was returned to the English. He was 20 years old. He had been born in Ancrum, Roxburghshire, in the Lowlands. His father, a Presbyterian minister, relocated his family to Holland during times of religious repression in Scotland. The young Robert Livingston was raised from the age of 8 to 16 in Rotterdam, where he learned the Dutch language and ways of business.

In 1672, following the death of his father, Robert briefly returned to Scotland, but he emigrated to Boston by 1673. After only one year as a factor serving a Puritan merchant, he was sent to Albany to establish business ties between Boston and that Dutch community. He never returned to Massachusetts and struck out on his own in New York.

Robert Livingston exploited his youth, driving ambition, and business acumen to become a major power in early New York. He began his career as a business manager for Nicholas van Rensselear, a very wealthy and prominent leader of the Dutch Patroons of the Hudson Valley. When his employer and mentor died, he married his widow. Livingston was acceptable to both the Dutch landowners and the English colonial authorities. By 1686, just 12 years after arriving in the colony (and still two years before the Glorious Revolution), Livingston was granted the Lordship and Manor of

Livingston, an estate of 160,000 acres south of Albany. He used his wealth in land to establish many business deals. One of his more unfortunate associations was with a fellow Scot, Captain William Kidd, who was a New York City merchant who turned from commerce to piracy. Despite some reverses, Livingston leveraged his economic and social position for political power. He served as the Secretary for Indian Affairs and as the Speaker of the New York Assembly from 1718 to 1725. By the time of his death in 1728, he had become one of the most powerful colonial politicians in all of the Thirteen Colonies.

Robert Livingston and his wife, Alida Schuyler van Rensselaer Livingston, had three sons, each of whom produced large families. The Livingston families continued to exert great social, economic, and political influence throughout the 18th century. Philip Livingston (1716-1778) was a signer of the Declaration of Independence. Robert R. Livingston (1746-1813) served as Chancellor of New York from 1777-1801 (for which he was respected as one of the greatest legal authorities in the U.S.) and as the U.S. Minister to France, 1808-1803, when he negotiated the Louisiana Purchase from Napoleon. William Livingston (1723-1790) served as the first governor of the State of New Jersey, 1776-1790. And Edward Livingston (1764-1836) was the Mayor of New York City, 1801-1803, a U.S. Congressman and later Senator from Louisiana, 1822-1831, and Andrew Jackson's Secretary of State, 1831-1833.

In addition to Robert Livingston, several Scots played leading roles in the colonial life of New York, much more so than in New England but less so than in Virginia and North Carolina. Only two colonial governors had close Scottish ties. The first was Robert Hunter, who was born in Ayrshire in the southwest Lowlands. He had served as an officer in the English army before the Act of Union, so in many respects he represented a well-born generation of "Anglo-Scots" before the breed became "British." Hunter had acted as the resident governor of Virginia for three years prior to being the governor of both New York and New Jersey from 1710 to 1719.

The other Scottish governor was John Murray, Lord Dunmore, who served just about one year, 1770-1771, in New York before accepting the resident governorship of Virginia. The son of a Jacobite, Lord Dunmore had been a faithful servant of the Crown, which he had supported as a member of the House of Lords. While popular in New York, he proved very unpopular in Virginia with his rigid rejection of colonial demands against London.

In many regards the most influential Scot in colonial New York during the mid-18th century was Cadwallader Colden, who was born in Ulster of Borders Scots and educated at the University of Edinburgh. He was an accomplished physician and a widely respected scholar in botany and mathematics. Colden first settled in Philadelphia in 1710 and relocated to New York eight years later. A man of ambition as well as talent, Colden took advantage of opportunities to become a large landowner (up to 29,000 acres of Skinner's Patent) and colonial politician. He periodically served as Lt. Governor from 1761 to 1774, with brief periods as the acting governor. An agent of the Crown, Colden opposed the Revolution and was forced into retirement in 1775 by his political enemies, including the Livingstons.

The general pattern of Scottish settlements in New York was very similar to that of Virginia and the Carolinas. Lowlander merchants (like Robert Livingston) and professionals (like Dr. Cadwallader Colden) were attracted to the trading cities of Albany on the frontier and New York City on the ocean. New York City rivaled Philadelphia as the greatest port in the colonies; by 1770, with about 21,000 people, it had surpassed Boston. Lowlander farmers and estate-builders came to the Hudson Valley. Highlanders in large numbers settled in upstate New York, west and north of Albany. New York rivaled North Carolina as the colony of first choice for west Highlanders and islanders from 1763 to 1775. Ulster Scots also settled on the New York frontier, especially west of the Hudson Valley.

New York City had the third oldest St. Andrew's Society in the colonies, founded in 1756. By 1776 the society had 21 members, allegedly divided in loyalties between 10 Patriots and 11 Tories. This group, reduced in size, continued its activities while the British occupied the city from 1776 to 1783. Its records for these years were destroyed and the society continued functioning much as before. Its members included several wealthy and powerful New Yorkers, including the Livingstons.

Highlanders of the Argyle Patent. While the story of the Highlanders of North Carolina has been told many times, the trials of the Highlanders of New York has been too often missed. Of particular importance are the Highlander settlers of the Argyle Patent and the veterans of regiments of the French and Indian War who settled in upstate New York.

In 1734, the Governor of New York issued a generous offer to British Protestants to come to the New York wilderness, then a thinly protected buffer between the Europeans and the Indians and between the British and the French. He offered 200 acres free, but with quitrents (a feudal fee much like a land tax), to each family that settled on the Lake George frontier along the Hudson River north of Albany. What the governor failed to make clear was whether the land was to be legally granted to each family in its own name or to the promoter who brought the settlers to New York.

The New York offer attracted the attention of Lachlan Campbell, an ambitious tacksman on the island of Islay. He came to the colony in 1737 to investigate the enterprise. He later claimed that the governor promised him as much as 1,000 acres for each Highlander family that he brought to New York. Families were to receive 150-500 acres each. From 1738 to 1741 he brought a total of 83 Highlander and islander families, numbering 427 people, to the Fort Edward vicinity (in what was then Charlotte County, but now in Washington County). Campbell then claimed up to 48,000 acres for himself, with the apparent intent of becoming a New World laird with the settlers as his crofters.

Captain Lachlan Campbell was in Scotland serving the Crown during the last Jacobite revolt of 1745-1746. His New York "tenants," however, petitioned the colonial government for legal titles to their own land. They argued that they had paid their own passages to America and were entitled to the original offer of 200 free acres per family. "Why would we," they protested, "having freed ourselves from vassalage to Scottish lords, travel all the way to New York to become Captain Campbell's vassals?" They also objected to their paying quitrents (which was a major dispute between landowners and the Crown agents and a contributing cause of the Revolution in many colonies). The principal beneficiary of the quitrents was the governor himself.

As early as 1741, the governor's council, including Philip Livingston (son of the first Robert Livingston) and Cadwallader Colden, rejected Campbell's exclusive claim to ownership of the disputed Fort Edward lands, which were called the Argyle Patent. But Campbell refused to relinquish his control. He appealed his claims to the Board of Trade in London. In the meanwhile, he built an estate house named Campbell Hall near Goshen, in Orange County in southern New York, a long way from Fort Edward. After his death in 1750, the legal dispute between the Argyle Patent settlers and the Campbell heirs continued for 13 years. The Scottish settlers were represented by Duncan Reid, Neal Shaw, Alexander Campbell (no immediate relation of Lachlan Campbell), Neal Gillaspie, and Alexander McNaughton.

Finally, in 1763 the council awarded over 47,000 acres to the trustees, led by Alexander McNaughton, of the Argyle Patent families. The matter, however, was still not settled. During the years of land and rent disputes, several of the original families had drifted on. The situation was so confused that the state held a lottery in April 1764 to distribute the 47,450 acres among 141 claimants.

The ten largest landholders among the original Highlander families were Duncan McArthur (450 acres), Archibald McDougall (450 acres) John McDougall (400 acres), Donald McDougall (300 acres), Duncan McDougall (300 acres), Agnes McDougall (300 acres), Hugh McDougall (300 acres), Elizabeth Caldwell (250 acres), Alexander McDougall, and John McArthur. Apparently, the original settlers included numerous McDougalls and McArthurs, most likely from Islay and western Argyll (Lorn). In the 18th century, these families would have been most likely tenants of (and at a disadvantage to) Campbells, quite possibly Lachlan Campbell himself.

Several parcels of land in the Argyle Patent went up for public sale by those who desired cash more than the land itself. A group of land speculators bought several lots. The largest single land investors were Goldsbrow Banyar, who in 1763 had been the Provincial Secretary and a member of the council, and his business associate Dr. Peter Middleton, a wealthy Scottish physician in New York City. A lesser investor was Philip Livingston, the son of the first Philip Livingston and grandson of Robert Livingston.

The three sons of Lachlan Campbell -- Donald, George, and James -- plus three daughters did not suffer from the settlement of the Argyle Patent controversy. Also in 1763 they received a colonial grant of 100,000 acres north of Albany. The Campbell brothers showed their gratitude by their firm support of the colonial government against the Patriots. Like Cadwallader Colden, they were staunch Loyalists.

Highlander Regiments of the French and Indian War. During the French and Indian War from 1754 to 1763, three Highland regiments served with the British army in North America: the Black Watch (the 42nd), Montgomery's Highlanders (the 77th), and Fraser's Highlanders (the 78th). The Black Watch contained men of many clans. In its early years, the Black Watch had a strong Campbell contingent. Also present were Munroes, Grants, Murrays, and Frasers. Both Montgomery's and Fraser's Highlanders contained predominantly MacDonalds, Frasers, Camerons, MacLeans, and MacPhersons. They included many officers and men who had previously fought with the Jacobites but now served as soldiers for the crown.

The Black Watch was the oldest of the Highland regiments, raised in 1739, and had already demonstrated its valor in European campaigns. It served with great distinction and endured many losses in America. Often thrown into frontal attacks against French regulars in defensive positions, such as Fort Ticonderoga, the regiment suffered heavy casualties. In addition, the men endured physical hardships wearing their regimental kilts in the brutally cold winters of North America.

Montgomery's Highlanders (the 77th) participated in the Indian wars of South Carolina and the occupation of Fort Duquesne in western Pennsylvania in 1758. They were stationed at the fort which was renamed Pitt for the British prime minister in the trading town later called Pittsburgh.

Fraser's Highlanders (the 78th) participated in the campaigns in Canada. Raised by Simon Fraser, the heir of the Lord Lovet who was executed for his support of Bonnie Prince Charlie, the regiment played the leading role in the Battle of the Plains of Abraham, when they scaled the cliffs of Quebec and threw themselves upon the startled French. The subsequent victory led to the French surrender of Quebec and the virtual end of the French and Indian War in September 1759. Coincidentally, Fraser's regiment served the British

General Wolfe who in 1746 had been an officer with the Duke of Cumberland at the crushing defeat of the Jacobite Highlanders at the Battle of Culloden.

With the conclusion of the war in 1763, the British government did not want to pay the cost of returning the three Highland regiments to Scotland. Both the Montgomery's and the Fraser's Highlanders were dissolved while still stationed in North America. Crown agents encouraged the Highlanders to remain in North America as colonists. While the total number of soldiers who did so is not known, it certainly numbered 600-1,000, who settled primarily in upstate New York and western Pennsylvania.

Sir William Johnson, the Irish-born British empire-builder of the Mohawk Valley, personally recruited veterans of the Highland regiments to settle near his estates west of Albany. He sponsored several programs to locate Scots and Scotch-Irish on the frontier. In 1773 he also recruited Highlanders in Scotland to come to America. He is reported to have donated 2,000 pounds sterling worth of cattle, food, and farming equipment for up to 600 Highlanders from Glengarry (largely Catholic McDonnells), Glenmoriston, Glen Urquhart, and Strathglass who lived on or near his estate at Johnstown.

A Johnson ally was the Rev. Harry Munro, a former chaplin in the 77th regiment. He returned to Scotland after the French and Indian War, but came back to Albany as the rector of the St. Peter's (Episcopalian) Church. He arranged for a Daniel Urquhart to petition Johnson for land to locate 17 Rosshire families in 1773. Johnson accommodated them, plus several more families.

In addition to the efforts of Johnson to help the Highlanders, Philip Skene, a native of Fife and the son of a Jacobite, took the initiative to organize a community for regimental veterans. After leaving the army, he obtained a patent for 29,000 acres near Lake George, upon which he founded a community of 30 families called Skenesborough. Once the former soldiers decided to stay in America, many encouraged wives, children, and extended family to join them.

Perhaps not surprisingly, many if not most of the Scots who settled near Johnstown and Skenesborough were Loyalists in the Revolution. The Johnson family remained loyal to the Crown and recruited the same men that they had provided for. Many had no intention of turning their backs on Crown authority; others had little choice under the circumstances than to follow local leaders. The price they paid for their loyalty was their New York homes, as many were forced to relocate to Canada after the victory of the Patriots. Other Scots in upstate New York, particularly the older, better established families and the Scotch-Irish, were largely Patriots.

Scotch-Irish of New York. New York City was a major port of entry for Ulster Scots, although second in volume to Philadelphia. Consistent with the immigration pattern, the Scotch-Irish who entered the port of New York usually moved on to the interior. The principal Scotch-Irish communities were west of the Hudson and north of Albany: Warrenbush in Otsego County, Goshen (Orange County), Wallkill (Ulster County), and Salem and Stillwater in Washington County. They were effective fighters against hostile Indians. The Warrenbush settlement had been encouraged by Sir William Johnson as early as 1741. To the best of our knowledge today, there were 15,000 to 20,000 Scotch-Irish in New York, considerably fewer than the 45,000 to 55,000 in neighboring Pennsylvania. With the coming of the Revolution, the Scotch-Irish generally supported the Patriots, and they provided a critical margin of victory on the frontier against the Iroquois, the British, and the Loyalists.

Conclusions

New England attracted the least number of Scots before the Revolution. The principal attractions were the thriving international port of Boston and opportunities to own farming land. However, Boston became less attractive to enterprising Scots than New York City, Philadelphia, and Charleston. Also, New England land was not as fertile and as inexpensive as farm land in New York, Pennsylvania, Virginia, and North Carolina. Furthermore, the social climate in New England was dominated by southern and eastern English Puritans who were largely indifferent and even hostile to Scottish immigrants, especially from Ulster. Anti-Irish sentiments existed in Boston long before the great potato famine of 1848.

Of course, a relatively small number of early Scottish settlers in New England began families that have now lived in the Northeast for over 300 years. From a few have issued millions of Scottish-American descendants, and the New Englanders of today may be just as proud of their Scottish roots as the Southerners are.

New York, however, did attract many Scots, particularly Highlanders. By 1775 there may have been as many Highlanders in upstate New York as in central North Carolina. The rich farm lands of the Hudson valley and the booming commerce of New York City drew many ambitious Scots, among whom emerged several leaders of colonial New York. The extended Livingston family counted among the pinnacle of New York society.

References

Ian Adams and Meredyth Somerville, *Cargoes of Despair and Hope. Scottish Immigration to North America, 1603-1803.* Edinburgh: John Donald Publishers Ltd, 1993.

William R. Brock, *Scotus Americanus.* Edinburgh: Edinburgh University Press, 1982.

J. M. Bumsted, *The People's Clearance: Highland Emigration to British North America, 1770-1815.* Edinburgh: Edinburgh University Press, 1982.

Eugene R. Fingerhut, "From Scots to Americans: Ryegate's Immigrants in the 1770's," *Vermont History, 35* (1967), pp. 186-207.

David Hackett Fisher, *Albion's Seed. Four British Folkways in America.* New York: Oxford University Press, 1989.

Ian Charles Cargill Graham, *Colonists from Scotland: Emigration to North America, 1707-1783.* Ithaca, NY: Cornell University Press, 1956.

Leo Hershkowitz, "Highland Fling in Washington County: the Argyle Patent," *NAHO* (the journal of the New York State Museum and the State Education Department), Spring 1982, pp. 20-23.

Lawrence H. Leder, *Robert Livingston, 1654-1728, and the Politics of Colonial New York.* Chapel Hill, NC: University of North Carolina Press, 1961.

James G. Leyburn, *The Scotch-Irish. A Social History.* Chapel Hill, NC: University of North Carolina Press, 1962.

J. P. MacLean, *An Historical Account of the Settlement of Scotch Highlanders in America Prior to 1783.* Baltimore: Genealogical Publishing Co, 1978 (1900).

Jack M. Sosin, *The Revolutionary Frontier, 1763-1783.* New York: Holt, Rinehart and Winston, 1967.

Chapter Eleven:

The Scottish Settlements of Pennsylvania, Delaware, and New Jersey

Scottish influence was surprisingly strong in the middle colonies of Pennsylvania, Delaware, and New Jersey. Even though Pennsylvania was dominated by English Quakers and German Mennonites, the Scots represented an influence among the elite of the colony, especially the Patriots on the eve of the Revolution. On the frontier of Pennsylvania, the Scotch-Irish dominated many European settlements struggling for survival against hostile Indians. And in neighboring New Jersey, particularly East Jersey, the Scottish influence was very strong due to the fact that this small colony had once been a Scottish-dominated proprietary enterprise. In fact, East Jersey was the only successful Scottish colony in the New World before the Act of Union of 1707 brought the Scots into the British Empire.

Pennsylvania was the only English colony where the English people comprised less than 50% of the population. According to information from the first U.S. census of 1790, Pennsylvania was the second largest state in population with 434,000 people (Virginia had the largest total population with 692,000 people, of which 442,000 were free whites). Of Pennsylvania's population, 35.3% were English, while 33.3% were Germans. The next largest ethnic group was the Scotch-Irish with 11%. Pennsylvania had by far more Ulster Scots than any other colony, and it was the only colony (excluding Maine, which was a part of Massachusetts) where the Scotch-Irish outnumbered the Lowlander and Highlander Scots. In many ways,

Pennsylvania was the most cosmopolitan, diverse, and tolerant of all the Thirteen Colonies.

According to the census of 1790, and with the presumption that the population did not differ significantly in 1790 from what it was in 1775 (with immigration after 1783 making up for war losses and Tory emigration to Canada), the proportionality of Scots in the middle colonies is shown in Table 1.

TABLE 1, SCOTTISH AND SCOT-DESCENDED POPULATION OF PENNSYLVANIA, DELAWARE, AND NEW JERSEY, 1790
(from: Richard B. Morris, ed., *Encyclopedia of American History*. Bicentennial edition, New York: Harper & Brothers, 1976, p. 653; Bureau of the Census, *Historical Statistics of the United States. Colonial Times to 1970*. Bicentennial edition. 2 vols, Washington: Government Printing Office, 1975, Part I, pp. 24-37, and Part II, p. 1168.)

State	%Scots	%Ulster Scots	%Total Scots	Numbers
Pennsylvania	8.6	11.0	19.6	83,104
Delaware	8.0	6.3	14.3	6,578
New Jersey	7.7	6.3	14.0	23,800
Averages	8.1	7.9	16.0	
Total				113,482

Pennsylvania had the highest percentage of Lowlander and Highlander Scots of any colony outside of the South. It had the second highest percentage of Scotch-Irish (second to Georgia's 11.5%) and was first in total number of Scotch-Irish, over 42,000.

Early Charters of the Jerseys and Pennsylvania

Whereas Massachusetts provided a haven for dissenting Separatists and Puritans, who extended religious tolerance to their own but denied it to others, Pennsylvania provided a haven for British Quakers -- English, Irish, and Scottish -- and many other sects. Denied their freedom of religion, both in England and in Massachusetts, the Quakers founded Pennsylvania as a place of opportunity for both religious and economic reasons. They dominated Pennsylvania society and politics until the 1760s, and they exercised great influence over their neighboring colonies of Delaware and New Jersey.

What became the colony of Pennsylvania was a much disputed territory. In the 1640s, the Dutch and the Swedes had fought for control of the Delaware River valley. The English claimed it following the seizure of New Amsterdam from the Dutch in 1664. Having received a proprietary grant of huge expanses of land between the New England and the Chesapeake Bay colonies, the Duke of York (who in 1685 became James VII of Scotland and James II of England) in turn granted proprietary grants to his closest friends. He assigned lands between the Hudson and Delaware Rivers to Lord Berkeley and Sir George Carteret. Both had been Stuart loyalists during the English Civil War. Berkeley was an English member of the Society of Friends, or Quakers. After about a decade, he sold his proprietary rights in 1674 to two other Quakers, John Fenwick and Edward Byllinge. Following further transactions, the land between the Hudson and Delaware Rivers was divided in 1676 into an eastern and a western part. The dividing line ran roughly from Little Egg Harbor on the Atlantic (near the mouth of the Mulica River north of today's Atlantic City) northwest to the upper Delaware River (therefore, unknowingly forever splitting New Jersey between two future great metropolitan areas of New York and Philadelphia).

Four Quakers, including Byllinge and William Penn, perhaps the most influential English Quaker, dominated the claims to West Jersey, while Carteret controlled East Jersey. When Sir George Carteret died in 1680, the trustees of his estate further sold his interests in East Jersey to a consortium of investors, including Penn. The number of investor proprietors was increased to 24 by 1682. Among them were several prominent Scottish Quakers, who set out to make East Jersey both a Quaker and Scottish colony with the approval of William Penn and the Duke of York.

In 1681 Penn, who held an interest in both West and East Jersey, received his own proprietary land grant from Charles II. According to the popular story, the Crown granted Penn such a large, single-propriety grant, second only in size to that previously accorded the king's own brother, in payment of the Crown's debt of some 16,000 pounds sterling to the famous Quaker's father, Admiral Sir William Penn. Penn claimed all the land west of the

Delaware River between New York and Maryland. Since no one knew exactly where the colonial boundary lines were, territorial disputes with neighboring colonies, including disputes with Virginia over the western mountains, lasted for decades. The new colony was called "Pennsylvania" (meaning "Penn's Woods").

The Scottish Colony of East Jersey

As briefly recounted in Chapter 7, East Jersey was one of four Scottish colonies in the New World prior to 1707. Although it failed as a proprietary enterprise, East Jersey was by far the most successful of all the Scottish settlements in terms of attracting people and encouraging economic growth. The other Scottish colonies collapsed, but East Jersey remained strongly Scottish even after it was combined into the one royal colony of New Jersey.

While Penn was building his own colony, he encouraged Scottish Quakers to invest in East Jersey. By 1684, half of the colony's 24 proprietors were Scots, both Quaker and Episcopalian. The principal was Robert Barclay of Urie (near Aberdeen). A well connected Quaker, Barclay became the first Scottish governor of East Jersey, although he never left the British Isles. The proprietor of highest standing was Barclay's cousin, James, Earl of Perth. It was for him that the earlier settlement of Amboy was renamed Perth Amboy, which in 1683 became the seat of the Scottish plantation. Other prominent Scottish proprietors included David Barclay (Robert's brother), John Drummond (later the Viscount Melfort, the brother of the Earl of Perth), Robert Gordon of Cluny (the uncle of the Barclay brothers), and Arend Sonmons, a Scottish Quaker who had been born in Holland. All were politically acceptable to James, the Duke of York. In fact, after the Glorious Revolution of 1688, several of the East Jersey proprietors became Jacobites.

In 1685 the group of proprietors was enlarged to attract further investors, who became known as "fractioners." The proprietors had grown into a virtual corporation. The new investors included Neil Lord Campbell, a younger brother of the Earl of Argyll (a Presbyterian). The earliest proprietors were primarily from Aberdeen and the north central Lowlands. The addition of Neil Campbell also attracted western Highlanders to East Jersey.

The Scottish town of Perth Amboy on Ambo Point at the mouth of the Raritan River took root by 1683. Within two years at least 700 Scots settled in this area. Perth Amboy was populated with families named Alexander, Barclay, Cameron, Campbell, Drummond, Forbes, Fullerton, Gordon, Haig, Hamilton, Hardie, Henrie, Johnstone, Macgregor, Mackenzie, Riddle, Robertson, and Scott. While the Scots included several gentlemen, they also numbered many more indentured servants recruited as common laborers by the proprietors. Most of the early East Jersey Scottish immigrants were young and single; only about one-fourth of them came with their families.

Several large estates were founded along the Raritan River inland from Perth Amboy. Neil Campbell created "Raritan River," an extended farm of 8,000 acres in today's Somerset County. He clearly intended to create his own small fiefdom in the New World with crofters working his land. Campbell served as the colony's deputy governor, the resident executive, briefly in 1686. John Barclay founded "Plainefield" and James Johnstone established "Spoteswood." One of the largest estates was "Basking Ridge," the manor of James Alexander, a relative of William Alexander, the founder of the first Scottish colony of Nova Scotia in the 1620s. The Alexander family became very wealthy and powerful in both New Jersey and New York. William Alexander, James' son, claimed the title "Lord Stirling" from the earlier William Alexander, although his assertion was rejected by Parliament. This "Lord Stirling" became a Patriot and served as a general in the Continental Army.

From the beginning, East Jersey enjoyed a difficult relationship with New York. Several families, such as the Alexanders and the Livingstons, had land and trading interests in both colonies. Trade was both a source of cooperation and conflict. Governor Edmund Andros of New York attempted to collect duties on goods entering Jersey ports and tried to ban Jersey ships from trade upon the Hudson River. The trading town of Perth Amboy competed not only with New York but with earlier towns on the west side of the Hudson, particularly Elizabethtown. Dutch and English families closer to New York City created numerous difficulties for the proprietors based on the Raritan.

After James, the Duke of York, succeeded his brother to the throne in 1685, he converted his own proprietary interests to the Crown. He also wished to consolidate the many small English colonies into a large, unified colony under one governor accountable only to the king. Acting upon the wishes of his sovereign, Governor Andros of New York created the Dominion of New England by revoking several colonial charters, including those of the two Jerseys and Pennsylvania as well as the New England companies. Although Andros' power collapsed after 1688 without the support of James' court, the proprietors of East Jersey did not recover their powers until 1692. In many respects, they never recovered their ability to govern.

Many of the founding proprietors of East Jersey departed from their colony. Neil Campbell returned to Scotland in 1687. Two principals, the Earl of Perth and Viscount Melfort, remained loyal to James and fled to Europe. Others, including founder Robert Barclay, died. Without their leadership, the remaining proprietors lost their confidence and ability to govern their own colony. A serious riot in 1700 demonstrated the popular alienation from the proprietors. In 1702 the two proprietary colonies of West and East Jersey were combined into the one royal colony of New Jersey. The proprietors, although they lost their power to govern, retained all of their property rights and interests as a private enterprise. Today, some 300 years later, the General Board of Proprietors of the Eastern Division of New Jersey continue their real estate operations from their historical quarters in Perth Amboy.

Following the collapse of Governor Andros' Dominion of New England, the remaining East Jersey proprietors invited Captain Andrew Hamilton, an Edinburgh merchant and investor in East Jersey, to be their governor. Hamilton, acting in the interests of Scottish investors, had served as East Jersey's deputy governor following the resignation of Neil Campbell in December 1686. He served under Governor Andros and returned to Great Britain in 1690. Politically rehabilitated, Hamilton returned to America to serve as the governor of both West and East Jersey until the two colonies were officially united in 1702. He died one year later. In his last two years, he held a third post as deputy governor of Pennsylvania.

Although a minority of the population, the Scots of eastern New Jersey continued to exert much influence in political and economic affairs after 1703. They also spread west and south. A Scottish Quaker from Inverness named William Trent founded a ferry across the Delaware River to facilitate travel from Philadelphia to New York. His inn gave rise to the village and later city of Trenton. Just west of Trenton and about 25 miles southwest of Perth Amboy, a group of Scottish and English Presbyterians in 1746 founded the College of New Jersey, the fourth college established in the colonies. In 1896 it changed its name to Princeton University.

A highly influential Scot before the Revolution was the Presbyterian minister John Witherspoon, who accepted the invitation to become the president of the College of New Jersey in 1768. He had been born and educated in Edinburgh and in 1757, at the age of 34, he accepted a position with a congregation in Paisley, near Glasgow. Witherspoon was socially and politically conservative, a leader of the Popular Party that strongly advocated the democratic rights of each congregation to govern itself. In New Jersey, he became a champion of religious harmony, but continued his defense of democratic rule. He was honored as being elected the moderator of the first General Assembly of the Presbyterian church in America. His beliefs in religious governance crossed over into his secular philosophy. Witherspoon strongly denounced the tyranny of British governance over the colonies. Elected to the first and second Continental Congresses from New Jersey, he advocated withdrawal from the British empire and signed the Declaration of Independence.

One estimate has claimed that 4,000 Scots and Scotch-Irish lived in the colony of New Jersey by the year 1750. They accounted for 20% of New Jersey's total population. By 1790, however, the Scottish population had fallen to about 14% of the total.

The united colony of New Jersey had one Scottish governor before the Revolution. He was Robert Hunter, a former British army officer who had served as the resident governor of Virginia in 1707-1710 before becoming the governor of both New York and New Jersey, 1710-1719.

Having founded his colony in 1681, William Penn vigorously recruited Europeans to settle in his wilderness paradise of religious freedom. He targeted religious dissidents, not just English and Scottish Quakers, but also German Protestants. Penn also recruited ethnic minorities, especially the Welsh. The port of Philadelphia, established on the west side of the Delaware River in 1682, as well as the rich farmland of the interior attracted many Scots as well.

As in other colonies, Lowland professionals, merchants, and tradesmen gravitated to the commercial centers, of which Philadelphia was the center. By 1730, the city on the Delaware River tied with New York as the second largest city in the colonies. Forty years later, with over 28,000 inhabitants, Philadelphia had grown to the largest colonial city.

When Penn departed his colony to return home to England in 1701, he turned the administration of his proprietary rights over to his personal secretary, James Logan. Logan was a Presbyterian of Scottish descent from Ulster who extended Penn's recruitment of English, Welsh, and German Protestants to Irish Protestants.

The large scale Ulster Scot, or "Scotch-Irish," migration into Pennsylvania did not begin until about 1720. Within 50 years, a torrent of Scotch-Irish flooded Pennsylvania. They typically entered the colony in Philadelphia, where they were no better treated than in Boston. In most cases, they quickly moved on to the Susquehanna Valley, where they often ran into conflicts with the well-ordered farming communities of the German Mennonites and Amish. From Lancaster to York, the Scotch-Irish penetrated the frontier up the Juniata Valley and west across the Alleghenies. Another branch of migration went south into the Shenandoah Valley of Virginia and into the mountains of North and South Carolina.

At first, Logan encouraged his fellow Ulster Scots to come to Pennsylvania. Oppressed as dissenters in Anglican dominated Ireland, yet feared and despised by many Irish Catholics, the Presbyterian Scotch-Irish were strongly attracted to the religious toleration and economic opportunities of Penn's woods. They craved owning their own farms. They even desired other people's farms, as the Scotch-Irish of Pennsylvania were notoriously careless in respecting formal land rights. Many Scotch-Irish families would carve from the wilderness their own modest farms only to discover later that they were infringing upon other's land rights when they had not bothered with legal papers and formalities. By 1730, Logan wrote in near despair that "a settlement of five families from the North of Ireland gives me more trouble than fifty of any other people."

The Scotch-Irish of early Pennsylvania carried with them centuries of beliefs and folkways from the Scottish Lowlands. The 16th century had been a particularly violent period in the Borders, frequently raided by English and Scottish bandits. The Borderers were forced to live a hardened life, often living in poverty. Homes were often burned and crops destroyed. Yet in their political and social turmoil, many Lowlanders turned to the absolutes of Presbyterian faith -- faith in a righteous God who expects both right thoughts and right deeds from his elected following.

When the Lowlanders shifted from the Borders to Ulster, they continued to live in a hostile environment, where Irish Catholics bitterly resented their presence. The English Civil War turned into a brutal civil war in Ireland. After the Restoration of 1660, the English often treated the Presbyterian Ulstermen with as much contempt as they did the Catholic Irish. With religious and political difficulties combined with periodic economic depressions, many Ulster Scots gave up on their first colonial attempt and turned to another colony across the ocean.

The Ulster Scots who came to America were largely farmers and craftsmen. They came to escape oppression in Ireland and to seek better lives in the New World. Most were simple people, and many were poor, even relative to colonial standards of living. Part of their great unpopularity in New England and Pennsylvania was their reputation for careless hygiene. In fact, many Scotch-Irish were basically poor with many characteristics associated with 18th century rural British commoners.

The Scotch-Irish believed in God and in themselves. They frequently fought with neighbors, to the great distress of Logan, who repeated tried to preserve peace between Scotch-Irish and Germans and Scotch-Irish and English settlers. They were relentless in their restlessness, moving from farm to farm and community to community, always seeking some more perfect spot to put down their roots, as if they had any. Despite their many flaws, however, the Scotch-Irish were well suited for fighting hostile Indians when the Quakers would not. All in all, the Scotch-Irish were as tough as the great American wilderness itself.

An example of frontier violence were the incidents of the so-called Paxton Boys, consisting of many Scotch-Irish frontiersmen. In December 1763, at the end of the Indian revolt on the western frontier, they massacred 20 peaceful Conestoga Indians in Lancaster County, far from the scenes of Pontiac's Rebellion. When confronted with legal actions against their crimes, they turned on the authorities by staging a threatening march on Philadelphia in February 1764. They demanded not only better colonial protection from the Indians but political reforms to allow better representation of the interior counties in the colonial assembly. Echoing their religious beliefs in the self-governance of congregations, they asserted that "We apprehend that as freemen and English subjects, we have an indisputable title to the same privileges and immunities with his majesty's other subjects...and therefore ought not to be excluded from an equal share with them in the very important privilege of legislation." No less a figure than Benjamin Franklin negotiated with them to return home without harming the colony's capital. In part the incident marked the collapse of the Quaker domination of Pennsylvania government.

The Scotch-Irish community was strongly Presbyterian, with a dour Calvinist view of predestination and salvation by grace. Philadelphia hosted the first American presbytery, founded in 1706 by Francis Makemie, a Scottish-educated minister from Ulster.

By 1790, about one-third of all Pennsylvanians were English and another one-third were Germans. About 11% were Scotch-Irish, making it the third largest ethnic group. The proportion of Scotch-Irish in Pennsylvania was second only to Georgia (with 11.5%), but in absolute numbers, about 47,000, there were more Scotch-Irish in Pennsylvania than in any other state. This was likely the case in 1775, too.

When the Revolution erupted in 1775, the frontier Scotch-Irish strongly supported the Patriot cause. Lowlanders were divided in their loyalties --

some Scottish merchants and virtually all Scottish agents of the Crown in Pennsylvania, Delaware, and New Jersey remained Loyal, but many others, including the famous case of Dr. John Witherspoon supported the Patriots. The Scotch-Irish, on the other hand, were solidly for the Patriots.

A very prominent Pennsylvania Patriot was James Wilson, who had been born at Carskerdo, Scotland, and educated at St Andrews, Glasgow, and Edinburgh. He emigrated to New York in 1765 and within a year relocated to Philadelphia. Having tried teaching, he studied law and was admitted to the Pennsylvania bar in 1767. He became a civic leader in Carlisle, where the Scottish community founded Dickinson College. He shared many political and religious ideas with Dr. John Witherspoon of New Jersey -- Wilson, too, became a signer of the Declaration of Independence. He also became a signer of the Constitution in 1787 and sat as one of the first associate justices of the U.S. Supreme Court.

The Scots of Delaware

In several respects, the colony of Delaware was an extension of Pennsylvania. Settled first by Swedes and then by Dutch, the west side of the Delaware River was claimed by William Penn far south of Philadelphia. Following a charter of 1701, the colony of Delaware was granted the right to have an assembly separate from that of Pennsylvania, but the governor of Delaware was the same person as the governor of Pennsylvania up to the Revolution.

By the census of 1790, Delaware had the smallest population of any state. Its white population was only 46,000. Scots comprised the second largest ethnic group (a distant second to English) with 8% of the population. Most of these Scots would have been Lowlanders, as very few Highlanders came to Delaware. The Lowlanders were primarily professionals, merchants, and tradesmen in the towns and farmers in the countryside. The Scotch-Irish were in third place with 6.3%.

The most influential Scot in colonial Delaware politics was Thomas McKean, who had been born in Pennsylvania of Scotch-Irish immigrants. He became a Patriot leader and a signer of the Declaration of Independence.

Conclusions

The Scots enjoyed considerable influence in the Mid-Atlantic colonies of New Jersey, Pennsylvania, and Delaware. New Jersey had been the scene of perhaps the most successful Scottish colony in the New World: East Jersey. Although the Scottish proprietors lost their hold within about 20 years, the Scottish settlers of the Raritan River Valley continued to enjoy economic and political control beyond their numbers. In Pennsylvania, numerous Lowland Scots achieved success in the professions (particularly religion, law, and medicine), business, and the trades. Pennsylvania also attracted Scottish farmers, especially land-hungry Ulster Scots. Perhaps in no other colony did the Scotch-Irish make themselves more felt in day-to-day affairs than in frontier Pennsylvania.

References

William R. Brock, *Scotus Americanus*. Edinburgh: Edinburgh University Press, 1982.

John T. Cunningham, *The East of Jersey. A History of the General Board of Proprietors of the Eastern Division of New Jersey*. Newark, NJ: New Jersey Historical Society, 1992.

Wayland F. Dunaway, *The Scotch-Irish of Colonial Pennsylvania*. Baltimore, MD: Genealogical Publishing Co., 1992 (reprint of the University of North Carolina edition, 1944).

David Hackett Fisher, *Albion's Seed. Four British Folkways in America*. New York: Oxford University Press, 1989.

Ian Charles Cargill Graham, *Colonists from Scotland: Emigration to North America, 1707-1783*. Ithaca, NY: Cornell University Press, 1956.

Carlton Jackson, *A Social History of Scotch-Irish*. Lanham, MD: Madison Books, 1993.

Ned C. Landsman, *Scotland and Its First American Colony, 1683-1765*. Princeton, NJ: Princeton University Press, 1985.

James G. Leyburn, *The Scotch-Irish. A Social History*. Chapel Hill, NC: University of North Carolina Press, 1962.

Richard B. Morris, ed., *Encyclopedia of American History*. Bicentennial Edition. New York: Harper & Row, 1976.

CHAPTER TWELVE:

THE SCOTS OF THE AMERICAN REVOLUTION

Many conflicting opinions have been published about the role of Scots in the American Revolution. Some authors have claimed that "most" Scots were Loyalists, or Tories. Others have asserted that they were usually Patriots. The confusion in accounts reflects accurately the confusion of the American Revolution. Some Scots were Loyalists, and others were Patriots. The hard part to explain is why some were on the King's side while others were on the side of independence.

The temptation to draw stereotypes is almost too strong to resist. It would be easy to say simply that Highlanders, in the spirit of the Jacobite revolts, were mostly Patriots because they loved the cause of freedom and they hated Hanovarian tyranny. But such a generalization cannot be supported. The Highlander communities of upstate New York and Cross Creek, North Carolina, were largely Tory, at least in the beginning of the conflict. The most famous Highlander in all of the colonies, John Murray, Lord Dunmore, remained an uncompromising Loyalist in his capacity as the resident governor of Virginia. On the other hand, Arthur St. Clair, a Highlander from Thurso and a British veteran of the French and Indian War, became a general in the Continental Army.

Another generalization might be that all Lowlanders were Loyalists, because the Lowlands had been extensively Anglicized and had remained loyal to the Crown in the last Jacobite revolt of 1745. In the case of Tidewater Virginia, the Lowlander merchants were mostly Tory, but the Lowlander Scot communities of New Jersey were solidly Patriot.

The one generalization that has withstood close scrutiny is that the Ulster Scots, or Scotch-Irish, of the American frontier were overwhelmingly Patriot, although exceptions did exist. They hated heavy-handed Royal authority and taxes. They also hated the Indians, especially the Iroquois, who allied themselves with the British.

This chapter will examine the role of the Scots in the American Revolution from 1775 to 1783 and briefly mention the post-war period that completed the 18th century.

The Loyalist Scots

Having just admitted that generalizations have been misleading, a broad profile of the Loyalist Scots is offered here, at least as a contribution to a better understanding of why some Scots remained loyal to the Crown while others did not.

The typical Scottish Tory fit this profile:

1. A servant of the Crown. As discussed in previous chapters, several prominent Scots served as colonial civil and military servants of the Crown. If the reason for the individual's coming to the colonies originated as an assignment of duty, then that individual almost always remained faithful to his patron. This rule explains the Loyalist role of Lord Dunmore, the resident governor of Virginia. British agents to the Indian tribes on the frontier remained mostly Loyalists. So did British officers from Scotland who were in America, some on active duty and others on half-pay.

2. A recipient of a previous Crown pardon for past offenses. Few Highlanders after "the '45" were ready to fight the Crown again. After Culloden, several prominent Highland clan chiefs were in jeopardy of permanently losing their titles and lands, not just for themselves but also for their heirs. The Government facilitated the pardoning of many of them in

return for future political favors. Once pardoned, the former Jacobites and their families could hardly risk further treasonous offenses at home or in the colonies. For example, Lord Dunmore's father had been pardoned and the family estates passed to him upon his father's death only because Lord Dunmore was 100% reliable to the Government. He remained so in Virginia. Another example was Allan MacDonald, the husband of the Jacobite heroine Flora MacDonald, who had enjoyed the grace of His Majesty and fought with the Tories in North Carolina, although it cost them their home in the New World.

3. A recent immigrant to America who received land grants or pensions from the Crown or from colonials loyal to the Crown. Many of the Highlanders of upstate New York had been former veterans of Highlander regiments engaged in the French and Indian War. They had been encouraged to stay in America and many had received generous land offers. The officers in particular felt allegiance to the Crown and were socially and politically close to influential Loyalists, such as Sir John Johnson (the son of Sir William Johnson, who had displayed many kindnesses to Highlanders) and Ulster-Scot Lt. Governor Cadwallander Colden (a famous, but isolated, exception to the generalization about the Patriotism of the Scotch-Irish). In addition, Johnson actively recruited hundreds of Highlanders, as families and whole communities, to resettle in the Mohawk Valley. Many of these Highlanders, although far from most, had Loyalist sympathies early in the Revolution.

4. An agent of Scottish economic interests closely tied with the British Empire. Lowland merchants with a vested interest in trans-Atlantic trade stayed loyal to the Crown. Their future lay with the mercantile system, which was interrupted by the Revolution. The factors (managers) of the Glasgow tobacco lords largely remained Loyalists. They owned fine homes and even their own plantations in America, but their wealth was invested in the Empire. The Virginia tidewater Scots who were employed in Scottish trading firms were Tories, and they lost everything when he Patriot legislature confiscated all Loyalist properties and nullified debts to British creditors.

5. Very socially and politically conservative. Scottish Tories were ideologically tied to the principals of the British constitution, including the prerogatives of the Crown and the powers of parliament. They opposed the Revolution because it threatened political chaos and social disintegration. They were men of deep conviction who abhorred disloyalty and disorder. Lord Dunmore, who was incapable of making any concessions to the Patriots, was an example of this type as well as a servant of the Crown and the beneficiary of a past pardon.

Scottish Tories of New York. As mentioned earlier, one of the two hotbeds of Scottish Loyalism was upstate New York, including the upper Hudson River Valley from Albany to Lake George and the eastern Mohawk River Valley. Following the conclusion of the French and Indian War in 1763, the Crown dissolved the 77th (Montgomery's) and the 78th (Fraser's) Highlander regiments while its men were still in North America. Colonial agents in New York, including the very powerful Sir William Johnson, encouraged the men to settle on the frontier. In addition, veterans of the 42nd (Black Watch), the third Highland regiment that had served in that war, were enticed to remain in North America. It is estimated that at least 1,000 former Highlander soldiers settled in New York, Pennsylvania, and North Carolina.

The Highlander veterans had deep feelings of loyalty to the Crown based on past military service and land grants. Yet without strong leadership, they might not have stayed loyal for long under intense pressures from the Patriots (including the great Dutch-American families of the Hudson Valley and Albany). One such leader was Alexander MacDonald, a kinsman of Allan MacDonald from Skye. Born in the Highlands, he had served as a junior officer in Montgomery's Highlanders in the French and Indian War. Although his regiment was disbanded in 1763, as an officer he retained his commission while on inactive service, still receiving half-pay. In 1772 he even received a promotion to captain. Meanwhile, he acquired land, on Staten Island rather than in the Mohawk Valley, engaged in some trade out of New York harbor, and married into a lesser branch of the prestigious Livingston family.

MacDonald felt strong bonds with the British army and the trade routes of the Empire. Although his wife's relatives recruited him for service with the Patriots, he remained steadfastly loyal in the hopes of achieving yet higher rank in the British service. His Highland kin had had very strong ties of loyalty to the Stuart monarchy, and Alexander MacDonald by 1774 had transferred these sympathies to the Crown of the Hanovarian dynasty. He traveled north to influence his former men to stay loyal, too. In addition to the former soldiers of the French and Indian War, MacDonald contacted the communities of about 300 MacDonnells of Glengary, who had immigrated to the Mohawk Valley as recently as 1773 under the sponsorship of Sir William Johnson, whose family supported the Crown.

MacDonald moved on to Boston, where he urged the British military commander, General Thomas Gage, to authorize him to raise a regiment of Scottish Loyalists. His idea, however, was not original to him. Also seeking General Gage's support for a Highland regiment among American Loyalists was Lt. Colonel Allan Maclean, the son of Maclean of Torloisk on Mull and a pardoned Jacobite. The efforts of MacDonald and Maclean resulted in the creation in June 1775 of a Loyalist Highlander regiment, called the Royal Highland Emigrants, later designated the 84th Regiment of the regular British army. It was to consist of two battalions drawing upon Scots, particularly recently arrived Highlanders and islanders, in both New York and North Carolina. As the senior officer, Maclean received command of the regiment and its 1st Battalion. The command of the 2nd Battalion went to Major John Small, a veteran of the Black Watch. Much to MacDonald's disappointment, he received a lesser assignment.

Maclean displayed vigorous leadership by going immediately to the Mohawk Valley to raise his battalion, which consisted of just 200 recruits, a distinct minority of former Highlanders in the region. He took his men north to participate in the battles to defend Quebec against the American invasion. His battalion served well, but suffered numerous casualties. Most of the men who served in it, however, were not Highlanders -- by the end of the war, maybe no more than 25% of the whole regiment consisted of Highlanders.

While Maclean saw action along the Canadian border, MacDonald served at the remote garrison of Halifax on Nova Scotia. He continued his contributions to the King's cause by recruiting and training men of the Royal Highland Emigrants (spelled as "Emigrants" rather than "Immigrants," reflecting their ties with Scotland). His men provided garrison services in New York after the British retook the city in September 1776 and participated in the Southern campaigns of 1780-1781. The North Carolina contingent never joined up with the regiment, having been destroyed by the Patriots in February 1776. The ranks of the regiment were filled with Tories from various parts of the colonies and Canada.

The entire 84th regiment was dissolved in 1783 and most of its veterans relocated to Canada.

Meanwhile, Sir John Johnson, the eldest son of Sir William Johnson, raised his own regiment, called the King's Royal Regiment of New York ("The Royal Greens"). It included some Scottish settlers of the Mohawk, especially some MacDonnells of Glengarry, but it was not particularly a Highlander regiment. Johnson allied himself with the brothers John and Walter Butler and the Iroquois warrior Joseph Brant, but they could not contend with superior Patriot numbers. In the spring of 1776 they retreated to Canada, with some of them returning to New York in support of the British invasion which ended in the decisive American victory at Saratoga in October 1777.

After their victory at Saratoga in October 1777, the Patriots dominated upper New York, although acts of war continued on the frontier. The Scots with Patriot sympathies had remained quiet during the recruiting campaigns of MacDonald, Maclean, and Johnson. After Saratoga, they became more outspoken in their support of independence, while the Tory Scots took their turn being quiet.

In the summers and autumns of 1778, 1779, and again in 1780, the New York Tories and allied Indians conducted very nasty raids into New York and Pennsylvania, but they could not affect the course of the war. They were soundly defeated by Patriot forces in August 1779 and October 1780. The British continued to hold New York City, but the rest of the state fell to the political control of the Patriots.

New York City remained in British hands from September 1776 (following their victory at the Battle of Long Island) until April 1783. Loyalties had been divided in the city prior to 1776, but the Tories dominated the city under British protection. The St. Andrews society of New York had ceased operations in 1776 and did not reorganize itself until 1783. It was said that the renewed membership consisted of both past Patriots and past Tories. But as many as 7,000 Loyalists, including Scots, evacuated the city along with British troops. All Tories by 1783 had only two basic choices: pledge alliance to the U.S. or relocate to other British colonies. Throughout the old 13 colonies, from 60,000 to 100,000 Loyalists resettled in Canada, the British West Indies, or returned to Great Britain.

Scottish Tories of North Carolina. As briefly recounted in Chapter 9, central North Carolina attracted numerous Highlanders before the Revolution. Cross Creek, now Fayetteville, was the hub of as many as 20,000 Scottish settlers in the Cape Fear River valley. In the years immediately before 1775, North Carolina had attracted immigrants from the west Highlands and islands, especially Skye. Numerous MacDonalds had left their ancestral homes out of disgust for lairds, rents, and Redcoats. Although many had Jacobite sympathies, some remained solidly loyal to the Crown, especially those, like Allan and his wife, Flora, MacDonald of Kingsburgh, who owed gratitude for prior pardons from the King.

In the summer of 1775, Governor Josiah Martin attempted to raise Loyalist companies in North Carolina to supplement the British army. He hoped for as many as 3,000 Scottish recruits. To help Governor Martin, General Gage in Boston dispatched two officers to North Carolina. They were Lt. Colonel (promoted to Brigadier General) Donald MacDonald and Captain (promoted to Colonel) Alexander Macleod. They set about organizing a battalion of the Royal Highland Emigrant Regiment. By mid-February 1776, they had enlisted a Loyalist force that may have numbered as many as 1,300 men -- a figure higher than the number of Highlander Loyalists enlisted in New York, but less than half as many as Governor Martin had sought.

Governor Martin advocated a plan by which the Highland Loyalists would march on Patriot-held Wilmington, take the port, and receive reinforcements of regular British troops to campaign against Charleston, the largest port in the South. The Cross Creek Loyalists began their march down the Cape Fear River Valley on February 18, 1776. The column was apparently headed by pipers, although it is not clear that the troops wore kilts. The campaign lasted just nine days. About 20 miles northwest of Wilmington, the Highlanders were ambushed by Patriot militia, including Scots, at Moore's Creek Bridge. The engagement broke the back of the Scottish Tories. About 50 were killed, including Captain Macleod. As many as 850 were captured, including Major Allan MacDonald.

Patriots soon replaced Loyalist leaders along the Cape Fear River Valley. Like the New York Tories, the North Carolina Loyalists stayed at home rather than risk death at the hands of hostile Patriot neighbors. The Cross Creek Highlanders had been bitterly divided in their political views in 1775, but after the Battle of Moore's Creek Bridge, the Patriot Highlanders took control of local political affairs. Even when regular British forces swept into North Carolina in 1780, the Cross Creek Scots remained passive to the King's call.

In May 1780, Charleston, the largest port in the South, fell to the British. Among the British forces were five companies of the Royal Highland Emigrants from Halifax -- men recruited and trained by Alexander MacDonald. Three months later the American Patriots suffered a humiliating defeat at the Battle of Camden. With much of coastal Georgia and South Carolina under their control, the British launched an invasion of North Carolina from the exposed southern flank.

The invasion, however, ended almost as abruptly as it had begun. The Tories proved to be more of a military liability than an asset. On October 7, 1780, a force of about 900 Patriot militia led by Col. Isaac Shelby and Col. William Campbell, a Scotch-Irish frontiersman, attacked a larger force consisting mostly of Southern Tories under the command of Major Patrick Ferguson, a Scottish officer of the British army, at King's Mountain. After intensive fighting, the Tory strength collapsed and virtually Ferguson's entire command was killed, wounded, or captured (119 killed, including Ferguson, 123 wounded, and 664 captured). The regular British army, under the command of Lord Cornwallis, was unwilling to risk exposure to further Patriot attacks and retreated back into South Carolina for the winter. The following year, Cornwallis launched another invasion that penetrated North Carolina but ended in the decisive British defeat at Yorktown, Virginia, in October 1781.

Scottish Tories of Virginia. The outspoken leader of the Virginia Loyalists was the resident Governor Lord Dunmore. Having been driven out of the colonial capital at Williamsburg during the autumn of 1775, he reestablished his base of operations at Norfolk under the protection of British ships. On November 7, 1775, he declared martial law throughout the colony. Among his supporters were the Scottish tobacco merchants of the Chesapeake Bay. Yet Dunmore had too few friends and allies in colonial Virginia. He completely alienated the large planters and most European whites by offering freedom to slaves who joined the King's cause. He further raised a black military unit to fight the Patriots.

On December 11, Dunmore's small force of Loyalists was decisively defeated by Patriots from Virginia and North Carolina. After evacuating the town, Dunmore returned with soldiers on January 1, 1776, to burn Norfolk. By February, he was again forced from his colony, never to return. Most of the Scottish merchants also evacuated their homes and businesses. The Tories of Virginia lost everything as the price of their loyalty to the Crown. The Patriot legislature confiscated all property belonging to Tories and cancelled all debts owed to British, including Scottish, creditors. After the elimination of Lord Dunmore early in the war, the Tories exercised little influence in Virginia and could offer no support for Lord Cornwallis when he invaded the state in 1781.

Lord Dunmore was the most influential of all Scottish Tories during the Revolution. The Scots played supporting, but not leading, roles within the English-dominated British army. And the Scottish leaders among the Tories never enjoyed as much influence with the British as the Scottish leaders of the Patriots did with the American colonials.

Scottish Regiments in the Revolution.

In addition to numerous Scots in British regiments, there were four Highland regiments raised in Scotland and sent to America to fight in the Revolutionary War. The first was the 42nd, or the Black Watch. It had seen extensive service in North America during the French and Indian War. It participated in several of the greatest British victories against the Continental

Army: the Battle of Long Island and the subsequent New York and New Jersey campaign (August 1776 to January 1777), the Battle of Brandywine (September 1777), the Battle of Germantown (October 1777) and the consequent fall of Philadelphia, and the successful siege of Charleston (April-May 1780). But it also suffered the humiliation of defeat and surrender at Yorktown, Virginia, in October 1781.

Fraser's Highlanders also saw action in both the American Revolution and the French and Indian War. As mentioned above, as the 78th Regiment it had been dissolved in 1763, leaving many of its men in America. But the regiment was reconstituted as the 71st Regiment in 1775. In both cases, the man most responsible for the regiment was Simon Fraser of Lovet, the son of Lord Lovet, who had been executed for his role in the Jacobite Rebellion of 1745. In return for his military service, Simon Fraser had been promoted to the rank of Major-General and allowed to recover his father's forfeited estates. The new Lord Lovet raised over 2,300 Highlanders to fight in America. His regiment included six clan chiefs plus numerous chieftains and sons of chiefs.

The 71st failed to duplicate the distinguished record of the 78th. A major blunder occurred when the transport ship carrying the 2nd Battalion landed in Boston after that city had already fallen to the Patriots. The entire ship of troops was taken as prisoners of war. The other battalion served well in the New York campaign of 1776 and the Southern campaigns of 1780-1781. Like the Black Watch, Fraser's Highlanders were also present at the Yorktown surrender. The men were returned to Scotland, where the regiment was formally disbanded after the Treaty of Paris.

The Argyll Highlanders, designated the "Old 74th Highland Regiment," was raised late in 1777 by Colonel John Campbell of Barbreck, a veteran officer of Fraser's Highlanders. Numbering not quite 1,000, the men hailed from Glasgow as well as the western Highlands. In contrast to the Black Watch and Fraser's Highlanders, it saw little action in America from 1778-1783. In one of its few engagements, it participated with the Fraser's in the siege of Charleston in 1780.

MacDonald's Highlanders ("Old 76th Highland Regiment") was raised by the first Lord MacDonald of Sleat (Skye). Command was passed to Major

John MacDonell of Lochgarry, a veteran officer of Fraser's Highlanders. He, however, was captured by the Americans before he formally took command, so the 76th passed to a Major Donaldson, a veteran of the Black Watch. The regiment was sent to Canada in 1779 and later joined Lord Cornwallis' campaign. It was one of the three Highland regiments to surrender at Yorktown.

In addition to the Highlander regiments, the 3rd Guards and the Royal Scots Fusiliers also served in America, while the Cameronians served in Canada.

Scottish Views of the American Revolution

Initially, the Scots "back home" were largely unsympathetic with the Patriot cause. Loyalty to the Crown was the order of the day following the Culloden disaster of 1746. Many Scots were eager to prove their reliability and participate in the economic gains of the British Empire.

Under the surface, however, the Scots most likely felt very mixed feelings about the American Revolution. Many had family and friends in America, some Patriots and some Loyalists. Some Scots were in sympathy with the democratic ideals of the Patriots, and some may have believed (as Robert Burns dared to write, but years later) that the American Declaration of Independence expressed in the same nationalist spirit as the Declaration of Arbroath of 1320 during their own War of Independence. The religious and political views of Francis Hutchinson, a professor of moral philosophy at the University of Glasgow from 1730-1746, had had a deep influence on Scottish-born Patriot leaders James Wilson and John Witherspoon. Their political views, as incorporated in both the Declaration of Independence and the Constitution, had a strongly Scottish, even Presbyterian, flavor that would have appealed to many Scots as well as Americans. Yet other Scots had brothers and sons serving in the British army and hoped that they would once again return as winners from a foreign war.

There were no anti-war protests in Scotland. Those who opposed the war or favored the American cause simply stayed quiet and went about their daily business. But as the general British population grew weary of the war, undoubtedly so did the Scots. Surely everyone was relieved when the Treaty of Paris officially ended the war in 1783 with recognition of the sovereignty of the United States of America.

War sentiments were deeply divided in Glasgow, which dominated the American tobacco trade at that time. Some of the tobacco lords had desired political concessions to avoid violence, while others wanted a heavier British military hand to protect their property interests. The war had a devastating economic impact on the Clyde. Scottish tobacco imports from the colonies (primarily Virginia, Maryland, and North Carolina) fell from a high of 45.9 million pounds in 1775 to just 5 million pounds by 1780. Several major tobacco trading companies went bankrupt. In the meanwhile, several state legislatures, including Virginia's, confiscated British and Tory property and nullified debts to them. The elaborate Scottish "store system" that supported the highly profitable tobacco trade totally collapsed. The Scots lost virtually all of 1.3 million pounds sterling of colonial debts. Even though some of the "Tobacco Lords" tried to restore the Virginia tobacco trade in the 1780s, political problems and hard feelings blocked business. Because of the war, many Virginians hated all Scots -- especially Lord Dunmore, his Tory friends, and Scottish creditors -- and refused to resume trade with Glasgow. Likewise, people in Glasgow felt deep resentments against the Americans, especially Virginians.

Scottish Immigration to the U.S. from 1775 to 1800

Scottish immigration to America remained heavy during the spring and summer of 1775, despite the violence in Massachusetts. Immigrants were arriving in North Carolina, for example, as late as the autumn of 1775. In September British officials closed all immigration to the Thirteen Colonies. Undoubtedly, some ships avoided the ban, but for the most part Scottish immigration to the U.S. ceased for eight years.

Scottish immigration into the U.S. resumed by the mid-1780s and continued into the 1790s, although not as heavily as the flow from 1763 to 1775. It fell off again during the wars with France and did not resume until after the War of 1812. But the political climate of Scottish immigration had totally changed. Prior to 1775, the Scots were moving from one part of the British Empire to another -- from the homelands of Great Britain to the British colonies of North America. After 1783, however, immigration to the United States was moving to a foreign country. It carried the implication of becoming an American, a new national identity outside of the British world. In addition, for decades the U.S. was hostile to Great Britain and not a friendly refuge for British, including Scottish, immigrants.

Prior to the Revolution, the Thirteen American colonies had been the principal target of Scottish immigration outside of Europe (and second perhaps only to Ulster for total Scottish immigration). But after independence was recognized in 1783, the chief target of Scottish immigration became Canada.

The first Federal census was taken in 1790. Over a century later a group of scholars studied the names reported in it and deduced the ethnic composition of American society. They determined that 8.1% of Americans in 1790 were Scots (either Scottish born or descendants of Scottish immigrants) and 5.9% were Ulster Scots (Scotch-Irish). Together, the two Scottish groups comprised about 14%, or about 479,000 out of 3,172,000 white Americans. That number is the closest figure available to the number of Scots in the Thirteen Colonies before the Revolution. It is not known how many Scots died during the Revolution or how many Scottish Loyalists left. It is also not known how many new Scottish immigrants replaced them by 1790 or how many children were born to Scottish parents in the U.S. In the absence of data, a reasonable estimate is that there were more Scottish-born colonists in 1775 than there were Scottish-born Americans in 1790. Considering that there may have been as many as 20,000 Scottish Loyalists who left the colonies and that relatively fewer Scots entered the U.S., the proportion of Scots in colonial society may have been as high as 20% in 1775.

The Scottish Patriots

In contrast to the Loyalists, the Scottish Patriots generally fit the following profile:

1. Those who had arrived early in the colonial experience and had had time, perhaps generations, to develop a national identity independent from "Scottish" or "British." Timing of arrival alone is not a reliable predictor of loyalties in the Revolution, but identification of being American as opposed to British was a determining factor in political sympathies. For example, Robert Livingston arrived in Albany, New York, from Scotland (via Boston) in 1674. His grandsons, Philip Livingston and William Livingston and great-grandson Robert R. Livingston sat at the top of colonial society and resented bitterly the privileges of the British aristocracy and the Crown. Also many new arrivals, even within 15 years of the Revolution, were Patriots rather than Loyalists.

2. Those who had immigrated into the colonies with their own resources and who believed that they were "self-made," owing no debts of gratitude to the Crown or other British interests. A large number of Lowlander agriculturalists came to America to establish their own farms. Likewise craftsmen, tradesmen, and professionals typically made their own ways to America and established their own enterprises. They opposed the taxes and arbitrary powers of Crown officials. By 1775 many of these Scots supported the Revolution, and by 1776 they advocated independence. As a generalization, people who had their own means were Patriots and those who remained dependent upon the Crown for salaries and pensions were Loyalists. Also, people in business for themselves tended to be Patriots, while the representatives of British firms or those heavily involved in the trade routes of the Empire favored the Loyalist cause.

3. Those who ideologically opposed the arrogant and heavy-handed governance of the British in the colonies. Some Presbyterians, such as the highly regarded Rev. John Witherspoon, went so far as to draw a parallel

between the self-rule of the congregation and the self-governance of free men. The large number of colonial Presbyterians, Scots and Scotch-Irish, who supported the Patriots led some British authorities to dismiss the American Revolution as little more than Presbyterian agitation. Several Scots saw the cause of the Patriots to lead to the independence once championed by Scottish national heros William Wallace and Robert Bruce.

4. Those Scots who were proximate to and highly affected by strong Patriot leaders tended to go with the Patriots; likewise, those exposed to vigorous Tory leaders (as in upstate New York and Cross Creek, North Carolina) gravitated to the Loyalists.

Lowlander farmers, craftsmen, and tradesmen were typically Patriots, from New England to Georgia. Lowlander professionals, likewise, heavily supported the Patriots. Lowlander merchants were divided in loyalties, especially in New York City and Charleston. Both Lowlander and Highlander merchants in the employment of Scottish tobacco companies were primarily Loyalists. Highlander farmers were largely divided, even within their own settlements, particularly in New York and North Carolina. Highlanders who had come to the colonies as self-reliant individuals rather than as members of a group tended to be Patriots rather than Loyalists.

Too many Scots supported the Patriot cause to discuss them in detail. This narrative will focus on a few, but very famous Patriot political leaders and military commanders. As mentioned above, the Scottish leaders of the Patriot cause were far more influential and famous than the Scottish leaders among the Tories. The great Scottish Patriots in political affairs included Patrick Henry, the Livingston family, John Witherspoon, and James Wilson. The prominent wartime commanders included John Paul Jones of the Navy and a cluster of Scottish generals who served General George Washington: Arthur St. Clair, Henry Knox, Hugh Mercer, William Alexander, Alexander McDougall, and Alexander Hamilton.

Famous Scottish Patriots: The Political Leaders

Patrick Henry. Perhaps the most inflammatory oratory leading up to the Revolution was Patrick Henry's declaration, "Give me liberty or give me death!" Henry was born in Hanover County, Virginia, in 1736. His father, John Henry, had left Scotland to begin a new life in America. He may have had a strong sense of identity in his Scottish heritage, but he surely was thoroughly Virginian. He studied law and was admitted to the Virginia bar in 1760. He served many years in the House of Burgesses, where he became an outspoken opponent of Crown prerogatives. He had a very strong dislike for Lord Dunmore. Henry vigorously supported the war against the British and he advocated the independence of Virginia. He was elected the first governor of the state in 1776, and re-elected in 1777, 1778, and 1784. In many regards, Henry's political and social views were considered "radical," even compared with Witherspoon and Wilson. He was a radical in regard to the sovereignty of Virginia and opposed the Constitution of 1787 as providing too much central government authority without protecting the rights of individuals or the power of the state.

The Livingston Family. The Livingstons were large land owners, merchants, and lawyers with great power in New York and New Jersey. Robert Livingston, the progenitor of his own colonial Clan Livingston, had amassed a fortune. Both he and his sons intermarried with the wealthy Dutch landowners and merchants. The family had been in New York for a century before the Revolution and thought of itself as thoroughly American, a national identity of its own far removed in time and space from Great Britain. Among the numerous Livingstons, three played critical roles in the Patriot cause for independence.

Philip Livingston (1716-1778) was the fifth son of Philip Livingston, the eldest son and business manager of the first Robert Livingston. Although a merchant with an interest in British trade, Philip opposed London-directed policies in New York. He served as a delegate to both the First and Second Continental Congresses, where he supported independence. In 1776 Philip Livingston was a signer of the Declaration of Independence.

William Livingston (1723-1790) was Philip's younger brother. Educated at Yale (as was his brother) and admitted to the New York bar, William became a wealthy landowner and businessman in New Jersey. He, too, served as a delegate to the First and Second Continental Congresses. He was elected the first governor of the sovereign New Jersey, although the British held large parts of his state during his tenure. He used his considerable influences to keep the state in the Patriot ranks, in the face of strong Tory opposition from the former Crown governor of New Jersey, William Franklin (the illegitimate son of Benjamin Franklin).

Perhaps the most famous of the clan was Robert R. Livingston (1746-1813), the nephew of Philip and William and the great-grandson of Robert Livingston. Also a lawyer, he served as a New York delegate in the Congress from 1775-1785. In 1781-1783 he served as the Secretary of Foreign Affairs and guided the negotiations that culminated in the Treaty of Paris. He also held the highly prestigious position of the Chancellor of New York from 1777-1801. As the Chancellor, Livingston was the principal authority in civil (as opposed to criminal) law. Initially, he supported the Constitution and the Federalists, but he deeply resented President Washington's appointment of John Jay, and not him, as the first Chief Justice of the U.S. Supreme Court. Livingston also hated Alexander Hamilton. As a Jeffersonian, he served as minister to France, where he finalized the Louisiana Purchase in 1803.

John Witherspoon. When he arrived in 1768, the Rev. Witherspoon likely had no idea that he would become a colonial political figure. He was a highly regarded Presbyterian minister, a graduate of the University of Edinburgh in his home city. He had acquired a national reputation as a theologist while serving the congregation in Paisley. His stature was so great that he was vigorously recruited as the President of the College of New Jersey (later named Princeton University). He continued his work with the church in America and rose to Moderator of the First General Assembly of the Presbyterian Church in America. Witherspoon was thoroughly Calvinist in both religious dogma and social views. He believed that each individual was responsible for his soul and each congregation for the well-being of the church. He carried the same views over to politics, arguing that a nation must govern itself to protect its own interests (the secular soul). As an elected delegate from New Jersey to the Second Continental Congress, he strongly supported independence: "Our civil and religious liberties, and consequently in great measure the temporal and eternal happiness of us and our posterity depend on the issue." With great satisfaction, Witherspoon was a signer of the Declaration of Independence. While retaining his positions of responsibility at the university and in the church, he participated in state politics throughout the Revolution and supported the ratification of the Constitution.

James Wilson. In addition to Witherspoon, James Wilson was also a principal Scottish ideologist of the Revolution. Born in Carskerdo and educated at St. Andrews, Glasgow, and Edinburgh, he came to America in 1765 at the age of 23. He taught Latin at the College of Philadelphia while studying colonial law. Admitted to the Pennsylvania bar, he set up his practice at Carlisle, where there was a strong Scottish and Presbyterian presence. Wilson wrote several influential tracts in which he laid out philosophical and legal reasons why the parliament of Westminster had no legislative powers over the colonies. He not only favored independence, but he also advocated a strong national government beyond the divided authorities of the states (a matter in which he clashed with Henry of Virginia). Wilson, like Witherspoon, must have signed the Declaration of Independence with great delight. He participated in Pennsylvania state politics, in which he defended the rights of property as a civil liberty (a point he would have shared with another legal and social conservative, Robert R. Livingston). Wilson was one of the few men to have signed both the Declaration of Independence in 1776 and the Constitution of the United States in 1787. In return for his past services and political reliability as a conservative Federalist, Wilson was appointed by President Washington to serve as an Associate Justice on the U.S. Supreme Court, where he served from 1789 until he died in 1798.

Famous Scottish Patriots: The Naval and Military Leaders

In addition to the political leaders, several Scottish-born or Scottish-descended men provided invaluable leadership in the navy and the army of the

United States during the Revolution. Among the naval leaders, the one who stands virtually in a class by himself was the principal American hero John Paul Jones. Among the numerous Scottish officers of the Continental Army and the state militias, six stand out as particularly key military figures, not just because of their military talents but also because of their closeness to General Washington. Three of them continued their relationship with Washington and participated with him in the first Presidential administrations of 1789-1793 and 1793-1797.

John Paul Jones. "John Paul" was born in Kirkbean, near the Solway Firth, in the southwestern Lowlands. He immigrated at the age of about 26, believed to be 1773, to Virginia, where a brother had settled. John Paul "Jones" had already seen extensive sea duty with the British navy and with merchant ships, including slave ships. He was commissioned a lieutenant in the newly created American navy on December 7, 1776 -- one of the first if not the first American naval officers. He quickly rose to the rank of captain. At first he seized British merchant ships, then he confronted British war ships. He even raided the coast of Scotland, not far from where he had grown up. He left the American service after the Revolution to become an admiral in the Russian navy. He died in Paris in 1792, but in 1905 his remains were relocated to the chapel crypt at the U.S. Naval Academy in Annapolis, MD.

Hugh Mercer. Mercer is an example of a Scottish Jacobite who fled Scotland in 1746 and relocated in the colonies, first in Pennsylvania and later in Virginia. He was a native of Aberdeenshire and a physician by education. He served as a field officer in a colonial regiment during the French and Indian War, during which he befriended Colonel George Washington. Before the Revolution, Mercer practiced medicine, operated a pharmacy, and engaged in several enterprises in Fredericksburg, VA. He remained a close friend of Washington's, whom he supported as commander of the Continental Army. Mercer was given the rank of Brigadier General and participated in the very difficult New York and New Jersey campaigns of 1776-1777. He was killed at the Battle of Princeton on January 3, 1777, and quickly became a hero of the Patriot cause. Years later he became famous once again as the Scottish forefather of another famous American general, George S. Patton, Jr.

Alexander McDougall. McDougall represents a Highlander who fought for the Patriots. Born on the island of Islay, he was brought to New York at the age of six by his immigrating parents. He went to sea as a boy and engaged in privateering and merchant trade. He became a wealthy New York City businessman, and although he had extensive interests in the British mercantile system, he strongly opposed British policies in the colonies. McDougall became a leader of the Sons of Liberty in New York and an influential propagandist (much like Wilson in Pennsylvania). A colonel of New York militia, he was appointed a Brigadier General (1776) and promoted to Major General in the Continental Army. He was personally and politically loyal to Washington. He was also close to Washington's young Scottish aid, Lt. Colonel Alexander Hamilton. Toward the end of the war, McDougall served as an elected delegate to Congress. A conservative Federalist, he became the first President of the Bank of New York and supported the policies of the first Secretary of the U.S. Treasury, fellow conservative Federalist from New York, Alexander Hamilton.

William Alexander, "Lord Stirling". Alexander was born and raised in the colonies. His father, who as a young man had been a Jacobite in 1715, had become a great land owner and businessman in New York and New Jersey. Both the father and the son were leaders of the East Jersey proprietors, who continued their land transactions after they lost proprietary control of East Jersey. Although William Stirling was thoroughly American, he pursued the British title "Lord Stirling" because an ancestor, John Alexander, had been the uncle of the famous William Alexander, first Earl of Stirling, a favorite of James I. His claim to the title was formally recognized in Scotland but rejected by the House of Lords in 1762. In the meanwhile, Alexander had become a man of wealth and influence in his own right. He married the sister of William Livingston, the future Governor of New Jersey. Like the Livingstons, Alexander became a Patriot. He was appointed a Brigadier General in 1776 and promoted to Major General in 1777. He participated in several major campaigns and remained a staunch friend and ally of General Washington.

Arthur St. Clair. The name "St. Clair" was a variation on the Scottish clan name of "Sinclair" from the far northern Highlands. Arthur St. Clair was born in Thurso in 1736. Although few details about his family have survived, he apparently was a relative of the Earl of Roslin who came into an inheritance from his mother in 1757. St. Clair reputedly attended Edinburgh University and studied medicine in London. He purchased a commission in the British army and served in America during the French and Indian War. Having married the niece of the governor of Massachusetts in 1760, St. Clair decided to remain in the colonies after 1763. He established himself as a businessman, farmer (owning over 1,000 acres), and civic leader in the Ligonier Valley of western Pennsylvania. Although a Highlander and a former British army officer, he sided with the Patriots rather than the Tories. With prior military experience, he rose quickly as an officer in the Continental Army, achieving the rank of Major General by 1777. He brought with him excellent political connections in Pennsylvania and he was totally dedicated to General Washington. He remained in the army after the Revolution and in 1787 he became the first Governor of the Northwest Territory. Despite a humiliating defeat by the Indians, he remained territorial governor under President Washington's protection. He resigned from the army in 1792, but did not resign his territorial title until 1802.

Henry Knox. Knox was the son of a Ulster Scottish bookseller who had immigrated to Boston. The family was strongly anti-British and Knox joined the Continental Army early in the war. He commanded the cannons that forced the British evacuation of Boston. Through the remainder of the war, he served as Washington's chief commander of artillery. He held the position of Secretary of War under the Congress from 1785 to 1789, when he became the first Secretary of War of the U.S. government. He served in the first Washington administration, resigning his cabinet position in 1794. Of all the Scotch-Irish who fought with the Patriots, Knox rose to the highest position in the army and the government.

Alexander Hamilton. According to John Adams, Hamilton was "the bastard brat of a Scottish peddler." His father, James Hamilton, was the fourth son of an Ayrshire laird who became a merchant in the West Indies, where he lived with a French Huguenot woman who was legally married to another man. Alexander Hamilton was born on the island of Nevis in 1755 and raised by his struggling mother at St. Croix. In 1773 he came to New York City to receive an education at King's College (later Columbia University). He joined the Patriot cause in 1775 at the age of 20. His intelligence and vigor brought him to the attention of General Washington, who made Hamilton his personal aide in 1777. Over the years, Hamilton became like a son to the childless Washington. Hamilton reached the rank of Lt. Colonel and commanded troops in combat at Yorktown in 1781. After the Revolution, Hamilton became a highly influential lawyer and political leader in New York City (and an enemy of the Livingstons). He married into a wealthy Dutch family, maintained his close association with General Washington, and allied himself with the influential Jay family. He played an aggressive role in the drafting and ratification of the Constitution. He served Washington again as the first Secretary of the Treasury, 1789-1795. A man of great energy and purpose, he became most famous because of his one personal friend and his many political enemies, both Jeffersonians and Federalists. He was killed in a dual by Aaron Burr, his bitterest political foe, in 1804.

Conclusions

The population of the 13 colonies was bitterly divided in loyalties at the beginning of the American Revolution in 1775. It has been said that of the entire colonial population one-third supported the Patriots, one-third the Tories, and the rest were indifferent or non-committal. Much can likewise be said about the colonial Scots. Certainly there were Scottish Loyalists, especially in upstate New York, tidewater Virginia, and the upper Cape Fear River Valley of North Carolina. There were also Scottish Loyalists in New York City and Charleston. But it is a gross exaggeration to say that "all" or even "most" colonial Scots were Tories. There were just as many, if not more, Scots who sided with the Patriots, and the prominent Scots enjoyed far more power and influence among the Patriots than they did among the British. Patriot Scots played vitally important roles in New York, New Jersey, and Pennsylvania; Scots were also indispensable to the Patriots of Georgia, South Carolina, and New England. Along the frontier, the Ulster Scots were overwhelmingly Patriots. Despite religious or national biases, they felt that their interests as farmers, tradesmen, and businessmen on the frontier were best protected by independence rather than subservience to larger British imperial interests.

The American Revolution was a defining event for Scots in America. As Loyalists, they identified themselves as "British" -- as subjects of the King and as residents of the British Empire if not Great Britain itself. As Patriots, however, the Scots identified themselves as "Americans," of Scottish extraction but not as Scots of Scotland. The Scottish Patriots may have believed that they were truer to historical Scottish values, especially personal and religious freedoms and national self-determination, than the Scots of Scotland who fought for the King. The great contribution of Witherspoon and Wilson was the concept that the American Scots could be thoroughly American without jeopardizing earlier cultural values. To many, being an "American" in 1783 was at that time the realization of being "Scottish" in times past.

References

Ian Adams and Meredyth Somerville, *Cargoes of Despair and Hope. Scottish Emigration to North America, 1603-1803.* Edinburgh: John Donald Publishers, Ltd, 1993.

J. M. Bumstead, *The People's Clearance: Highland Emigration to British North America, 1770-1815.* Edinburgh: Edinburgh University Press, 1982.

Linda Colley, *Britons. Forging the Nation, 1707-1837.* New Haven: Yale University Press, 1992.

T. M. Devine, *The Tobacco Lords. A Study of the Tobacco Merchants of Glasgow and Their Trading Activities, c.1740-90.* Edinburgh: Edinburgh University Press, 1990 (1975).

Ian Charles Cargill Graham, *Colonists from Scotland: Emigration to North America, 1707-1783.* Ithaca, NY: Cornell University Press, 1956.

Bruce Lenman, *Integration, Enlightenment, and Industrialization. Scotland, 1746-1832.* The New History of Scotland, Volume 6. London: Edward Arnold, 1981.

James G. Leyburn, *The Scotch-Irish. A Social History.* Chapel Hill, NC: University of North Carolina Press, 1962.

J. P. MacLean, *An Historical Account of the Settlement of Scotch Highlanders in America Prior to the Peace of 1783.* Baltimore, Md: Genealogical Publishing Co, 1978 (1900).

D. MacDougall, ed. *Scots and Scots Descendants in America.* Baltimore, Md: Clearfield Co, 1992 (1917).

Duane Meyer, *The Highland Scots of North Carolina, 1732-1776.* Chapel Hill, NC: University of North Carolina Press, 1987 (1957).

Christopher Moore, *The Loyalists. Revolution, Exile, Settlement.* Toronto: McClelland & Stewart, Inc., 1994.

Richard B. Morris, ed., *Encyclopedia of American History.* Bicentennial Edition. New York: Harper & Row, 1976.

W. Stanford Reid, ed., *The Scottish Tradition in Canada.* A History of Canada's Peoples. Toronto: McClelland and Stewart, 1976.

Charles Royster, *A Revolutionary People at War. The Continental Army and American Character, 1775-1783.* New York: W. W. Norton, 1979.

Jack M. Sosin, *The Revolutionary Frontier, 1763-1783.* New York: Holt, Rinehart and Winston, 1967.

Chapter Thirteen:

Summary and Conclusions

The Scots played a leading role in the settlement of the American colonies during the 17th and 18th centuries. They were among the "ground floor" investors in the American national enterprise. The principal themes of the Scottish experience in the making of the United States are captured by the following generalizations.

1. *The principal motivation for emigration was self-improvement and economic gain.* The search for religious liberties was certainly a major reason for the earliest European immigration to America. In general, however, the religious reasons for settling the New World have been exaggerated. It certainly was a principal issue for the very early Pilgrims of Plymouth colony. It was also an issue for the Puritans of Massachusetts Bay, New Hampshire, and Connecticut; for the non-conformists of Rhode Island; for the Quakers and German Mennonites of Pennsylvania; and for the Catholics of Maryland. Among the Scots, religion also played a part in the settlements of Stewart's Town (as a Covenanter haven in the Carolinas) and in East Jersey, where Presbyterianism was very strong. But most Scottish settlements concerned owning land and making money, and those were the great issues for a majority of American colonists before the Revolution.

221

Religious toleration was definitely America's "first freedom," because without it so many different faiths, ethnic groups, and races could have never lived in a condition even approximating peaceful coexistence. Religious toleration, however, was a rarity within the religiously motivated colonies. For example, Boston was seen as primarily a refuge for Puritans experiencing difficulties with Anglicans, not as a center of religious opportunity for those who were not Puritans. Militant faiths, exclusive and hostile of other sects, constituted a major barrier to colonial union. Once people accepted religious toleration, following the example of Pennsylvania, then the colonists could move on to pursuing their material interests. Among those who were particularly interested in material pursuits were the Scots.

In the early colonial years, prior to 1688, when religion played a leading role in settling the American colonies, the European population of the American colonies was barely 200,000, or less than 10% of the colonial white population by 1775. A vast majority of American colonists, including the Scots, arrived during the 18th century, when religion provided only a minor reason for coming to America. Among the Scots, religion played a very small role in the failed Scottish colony of Darien and the successful Scottish settlements of upstate New York, tidewater Virginia, central North Carolina, Charleston, and the coast of Georgia. These Scottish communities were founded by settlers wishing to own and work their own farms, to practice their trades and professions for their own profit, to engage in money-making trade, and generally to make their fortunes for themselves and their prosperity.

Next to religious reasons, political causes of emigration from Scotland have been overrated. Some histories have emphasized the political turmoil of the British Isles during the 17th century as a reason to escape repression at home and to find refuge in the New World. While it certainly is true that Cromwell exiled a few hundred Scots to the American colonies, the number of political refugees to America from Scotland was relatively few. Some histories have also left the impression that the failed Jacobite revolts from 1689 to 1746 provided a push for emigration. Yet one reasonable estimate is that no more than 1,000 Jacobites were forced to go to the colonies. Many more may have elected to emigrate to avoid political repression -- even jail -- but the total number pales in comparison with the number of families which emigrated with absolutely no demonstrated political motivations.

Looking at 200 years of colonial history, the principal reason why the Scots left Scotland for the Thirteen Colonies was the pursuit of self-advantage. Most Scots were not forced to leave Scotland -- they chose to leave. They left because of economic hard times in Scotland due to rising rents, lack of opportunity to own land, and occupational shifts caused by the early stages of the Industrial Revolution. The emigration from Scotland prior to 1775 has been characterized by one scholar as the "people's clearances." They came to America because the colonial "pull" matched the Scottish "push." For every reason to leave Scotland there was an opportunity in America: to acquire high quality land at low prices; to engage in one's own chosen trade or profession; to own a house and to build an estate; to pursue, quite literally, one's own happiness. In economic terms, one Scottish immigrant to the New World called America "the best poor man's country in the world."

2. *The Scottish settlers were ambitious and self-reliant.* The image of the poor, oppressed, and downtrodden Europeans sailing by the Statue of Liberty into Ellis Island is based on the millions of south and eastern European immigrants who flooded into the U.S. from 1890 to 1915. Many of these immigrants were indeed poor with few skills and fewer prospects. But, generally, the colonial settlers were a different lot. They suffered hardships, too, but they were also middle class by the standards of their own day. The Scots in particular were not the desperate poor, but rather they were ambitious craft, trade, farming, soldiering, and professional men and their families. Very few of the Scottish settlers came from the wealthy class; likewise, very few came from the working class -- the former lacked the incentive and the latter lacked the means to emigrate. The Scots who arrived in America before the Revolution were largely "men on the make," with some resources to invest, a lot of energy and drive to succeed, and education and skills that were wasted in the Scotland of limited opportunities for advancement. No wonder, then, that the Scottish settlers did remarkably well in colonial society, with several rising to prominent leadership positions in colonial commerce, politics, churches, education, and law.

Colonial statistics are very rare and limited in explaining the social composition of early American society. The few sets of numbers that do exist, however, are mostly consistent in the profiles of typical Scottish immigrants before the Revolution. About one-quarter of all Scots in the colonies were farmers, and most of them did or would eventually own their own land. One-fourth to one-third of the Scots were craftsmen and artisans (including weavers, tailors, and various smiths and wrights). Therefore, it is safe to say that roughly half of all Scottish immigrants into the Thirteen Colonies were either farmers or lower middle-class skilled workers. The proportion of unskilled laborers ranged from as high as one-third to as low as one-fifth. The middle class merchants and professionals have been estimated from as high as one-fifth to as low as less than one-tenth of the Scottish immigrants. Although a small group, the merchants and professionals exercised power and influence in the colonies far beyond the proportions of their numbers.

3. *The Scottish settlers came in families to stay.* Most Scots, like most colonial settlers prior to the American Revolution, immigrated as families and small communities. There were, of course, many immigrants who were single men and women, particularly those in their late teens and 20s. More commonly, the Scots immigrated as young families of husband, wife, and a few children. There were also extended families and small communities. And they came with the intention of staying in America. Again, naturally some individuals returned to Scotland, but the returns were rare.

Once established in America, the Scots attracted more family members, friends, and neighbors. One of the great attractions of colonial America was the existence of previous Scottish immigrants who had successfully planted roots in the new soil and were now drawing more Scots to them. The Scottish soldiers who remained in upstate New York after 1763 attracted several hundred, if not a thousand, more Highlanders. The early Highland settlements in Cross Creek (later Fayetteville), North Carolina, attracted several thousand more settlers before 1775. The Scottish proprietary colony centered at Perth Amboy, East Jersey, became the magnet for many Scots to settle around the New York estuary. And the numerous Scotch-Irish of the Pennsylvania frontier drew tens of thousands of Scots from northern Ireland to the Allegheny rim.

James Boswell commented frequently on Scottish emigration in his account of his tour of the Highlands and islands with Samuel Johnson in 1773. On the island of Skye, "Mrs. M'Kinnon told me, that last year when a ship sailed from Portree for America, the people on shore were almost distracted when they saw their relations go off, they lay down on the ground, tumbled, and tore the grass with their teeth. -- This year there was not a tear shed. The people on shore seemed to think that they would soon follow." And many did, until British authorities in the autumn of 1775 closed emigration to the rebellious colonies.

4. *The Scots comprised one of the three dominant ethnic groups of colonial America.* The number of Scottish immigrants into the American colonies before the Revolution has been much debated. No one knows for sure what the number was. According to an authoritative analysis of the first U. S. census in 1790, Scottish and Scotch-Irish immigrants and their descendants numbered about 480,000 people, or 15% of the national population. The number of Scots born in Scotland was likely higher in 1775 than in 1790, but the total number of Scottish-Americans, including American-born descendants of Scots, was likely higher in 1790 than in 1775. During the Revolution, Scottish immigration virtually stopped and resumed only gradually after 1783. Also during the Revolution, a significant number of (but no one knows how many) Loyalist Scots were forced to flee the thirteen states. It is possible that the number of Scots and Scotch-Irish who immigrated to the colonies may have numbered as many as 250,000. Evidence strongly suggests that the Scots were the second or the third largest European ethnic group that comprised colonial society, following the English and possibly also the Germans. In most colonies the Scots were second, although often a distant second, to the English. In four colonies the Scots (including Ulster Scots) represented 20% or more of the white population: Pennsylvania (20%), North Carolina (21%), South Carolina (25%), and Georgia (27%). In absolute numbers, the most Scottish-Americans lived in Virginia (over 100,000), Pennsylvania (over 80,000), and North Carolina (nearly 60,000).

5. *The Scots favored certain areas and colonies over others.* The principal areas of Scottish settlements before 1775 were as follows:

Upstate New York, from Albany to Lake George and along the Mohawk Valley west of Albany (primarily Highlanders and Scotch-Irish)
New York City and vicinity (Lowlanders and Highlanders)
Perth Amboy and the Raritan River Valley, New Jersey (Lowlanders)
Philadelphia (Lowlanders)
The Pennsylvania frontier, from the Susquehanna Valley to the Ohio River (Scotch-Irish)
The Chesapeake Bay area and Tidewater Virginia (Lowlanders).
Frontier Virginia, including the Shenandoah Valley and the mountains (Scotch-Irish)
Cape Fear River Valley and Cross Creek, North Carolina (Highlanders)
Frontier North Carolina, especially the upper piedmont and mountains (Scotch-Irish and Lowlanders)
Charleston, South Carolina (Lowlanders)
Frontier South Carolina (Scotch-Irish)
Coastal Georgia, from Savannah to Darien (Highlanders)

6. *While the early Scots, especially the Highlanders, experienced some hard times, most Scottish settlers assimilated very well into colonial society.* While many Scots arrived in this country in family and even small community units before 1775, the Scots quickly diffused into colonial society. With a few exceptions, they did not keep to themselves within ethnic communities. They also lived in small towns and rural areas. There were no "Little Scotlands" in the first half of the 18th century like there were "Little Italies" or Irish neighborhoods as existed in the first half of the 20th century.

The Lowlanders experienced the least difficulty assimilating into American society, the Highlanders had the most difficulty, with a mixed story for the Scotch-Irish.

Most of the Lowlanders already spoke English and were largely Anglicized in their manners. They may have spoken with a Scottish accent, but regional dialects were spoken all over the British Isles; the Puritans from East

Anglia had their own style of speaking as did the West Country yeoman who settled Virginia. The Lowlanders, as a general rule, were the most educated, the most well-to-do, the most influential, and the most successful of the Scottish settlers of colonial America. They crossed easily into mainstream colonial society, which was dominated by the English. Lowlander Scots shared similar values and cultural traits with the colonial Dutch and Germans. Perth Amboy and the Raritan River valley of New Jersey was a rare concentration of Lowland Scots, and they were hardly the majority ethnic group. Another atypical settlement of Lowlanders was Ryegate, VT, which had been founded by the Scots-American Company of Farmers, an enterprise to relocate Lowland agricultural hands and managers onto their own farms in America.

The Highlanders, on the other hand, had more trouble assimilating into colonial society. Many spoke only Gaelic and had to learn English in the colonies. Some continued to wear distinctively Highland garb, although the kilt was worn more for special occasions than as everyday attire. The Highlanders and western Islanders tended to move and settle in small communities. Small towns in the Argyll Patent of New York were dominated by Highlanders. They also were a significant minority in central North Carolina and may have been a majority, at least for a while, in Cross Creek. Darien, GA, began as a Highlander settlement, although it attracted many other colonists after the defeat of the last Spanish incursion in 1742.

Highlanders may have attracted much ill will from the Patriots before and during the Revolution. Many volunteered for Tory regiments. They also may have looked and sounded too much like the Highland regiments from Scotland that served with the British army. Patriot Highlanders would have been quick to hide their origins and change over to Anglo-American customs (just as German-Americans did in World War I).

By the second and third generations, the descendants of Highlanders would have become thoroughly American. They lost the ability to speak and understand Gaelic. They also became very reluctant to wear the kilt or play the bagpipes. Only several generations later would Highlander traits become the re-adopted rage of thoroughly American Scottish-Americans.

227

The Scotch-Irish had a mixed experience assimilating into American society. The Ulster Scots were very unpopular in New England, as explained in previous chapters. They were pressured to leave Boston and settle along the wild frontier. Several communities in remote Maine, New Hampshire, and western Massachusetts were Scotch-Irish. Yet they spoke English and in many respects behaved in typical British fashion. They were also Protestants -- overwhelmingly Presbyterians. There were Scotch-Irish communities in the Mohawk Valley of New York. In both New England and New York, the Scotch-Irish blended into frontier society. During the Revolution, their loyalty to the Patriot cause further accelerated their assimilation into mainstream American society (in contrast to their neighboring Highlanders near Johnstown, NY.)

When the Ulster Scots first came to Massachusetts Bay, they were called "Irish," a name that they deeply resented. They thought of themselves as being Ulstermen of Scottish or English extraction whose ancestors had relocated to northern Ireland during the 17th century. The Ulster Scots, largely of Lowland descent, were quick to differentiate themselves from the subjugated Irish, who were typically landless, poor, ill educated, anti-British, unable to speak the King's English, and Catholic. The American descendants of the Scotch-Irish became thoroughly American by the 19th century, and many were very successful. When the great Irish immigration into Boston and other American cities began in 1848, the Americans of Ulster extraction wanted nothing to do with the new arrivals. They were just as intolerant of the Irish as the earlier Puritans had been of the early Ulster immigrants. They were most emphatic to call their colonial ancestors "SCOTCH-Irish" and not just "Irish." Many of these Americans still practiced Presbyterianism, which retained its strong ethnic associations with Ulster and Scotland; but others joined mainstream New England Congregationalism. In the middle states and in the South, many Scotch-Irish descendants joined the very American churches of the Methodist and Baptist faiths.

The Scotch-Irish of Pennsylvania ran into many difficulties with the Germans. Their styles of life apparently clashed. So the Scotch-Irish moved beyond Lancaster County into the frontier regions of central and western Pennsylvania. There were Scotch-Irish settlements throughout the Appala-

228

chian Mountains, especially in the Juniata Valley. In most cases, the early Scotch-Irish merged with other ethnic groups and lost their uniqueness. But some Scotch-Irish began two very serious challenges to local authority. One incident involved the so-called Paxton Boys, who nearly toppled the colonial government of Pennsylvania in 1763. The second disruption came 31 years later, in 1794, when western Pennsylvania farmers, including many Scotch-Irish, organized the "Whisky Rebellion" against federal taxation of distilled spirits. In the face of the national army, however, the insurrection melted away with little violence.

The Scotch-Irish of frontier Virginia, North Carolina, and South Carolina played leading roles in the development of those states. They not only assimilated into society, in many cases they led it. Their prominent military contributions to the U.S. during the Revolution leveraged them into leadership roles in the political and economic affairs of the New Republic era. From the vigorous Scotch-Irish communities both east and west of the Blue Ridge Mountains emerged Andrew Jackson, John C. Calhoun, James K. Polk, Davy Crockett, Sam Houston, and Andrew Johnson.

7. The principal sources of identity for Scots were surname and family.
Immigration is always frightening. Leaving one's ancestral homeland and crossing the ocean into an untamed land was both exciting and scary. Some immigrants tried to hold onto to their Old World ways and experienced great difficulties adjusting to American culture. Some could not adjust to America, and established Americans could not accommodate them, either. The degree to which the immigrant's adjustment was easy or difficult depended a great deal upon the psychological sense of identity and flexibility within the immigrant.

One historical account of Irish immigration to the U.S. has explained that the Irish people have historically had a deep sense of personal identity with the land. To many Irishmen, their very existence was the land they worked -- an Irishman parted from the land was like the soul being parted from the body. In Ireland it was the custom to hold a party for emigrants the night before their departure. This party was called an "American wake," symbolizing the death of the old life and the transition to the "afterlife" of America.

Many Irish experienced great psychological distress leaving their homes and land and their distress often continued in the New World. Not feeling identified with the American land, many Irish felt alienated from American society. In general, the assimilation of the Irish was slower and more painful than that of the Scots.

Certainly there were Scots who felt great distress leaving Scotland for America. But the historical record reflects that most Scots wanted to leave Scotland and chose to come to the U.S. The victims of the great Highland Clearances, which began in earnest in the 1790s and lasted until the violent evictions on Skye in the 1880s, were forced to emigrate, but most of them went to Canada, Australia, and New Zealand. The earlier Scottish settlers of America, as mentioned before, were "self-cleared." As in Ireland, many traditionalists in the Highlands felt a deep sense of personal identity with the land. But an even stronger sense of identity existed in the assumed blood ties of surname and family. The Scots definitely agreed with the saying that "Blood is thicker than water." Blood ties meant pride and security. The Scottish obligations of family support were assumed to exist among all with the same surname, whether an actual blood relation existed or not. This sense of identity, far more flexible than that with the land, was the very core of the clan system.

Samuel Johnson observed during his tour of Scotland in 1773 that "The inhabitants of mountains form distinct races, and are careful to preserve their genealogies....They who consider themselves as ennobled by their family, will think highly of their progenitors, and they who through successive generations live always together in the same place, will preserve local stories and hereditary prejudices. Thus every Highlander can talk of his ancestors, and recount the outrages which they suffered from the wicked inhabitants of the next valley."

This comment holds for Lowlanders and Ulster Scots as well as Highlanders. During the very turbulent 16th century, Lowlanders were repeatedly burned out of their homes and driven off of their land by clan feuds and border reivers. A century of chaos was ended only after 1603 when the King of the Scots and the English king became the same person. At the same time that order was restored on both sides of the Tweed, many Lowlanders were encouraged by the king and his agents to relocate to Ulster. In the face of political and social disorder and much random violence, these Lowlanders developed a strong sense of identity through other related individuals -- security was found in blood lines and family. The sense of belonging and the badge of honor became the family surname. Lowland families could be just as tight knit and inclusive as any of the Highland clans.

When Lowlanders and Ulster Scots came to America, they brought with them their sense of identity in surnames and families. It made little difference where they lived, they were always of the same stock. So a Johnston was always a Johnston whether living in the Borders, Ulster, or America. This sense of identity with blood facilitated emigration and eventual assimilation into American society.

The heart of the Scottish-American community, which is and always has been a virtual rather than spatial community, remains the feeling that common names mean common blood; that there are bonds of friendship and support in same surnames. While some Americans may make too much of the historical, social, and genetic significance of a surname, the fascination with clan identity is a reflection of our ancestors' emphasis on blood lines. An individual only has to have a drop of Scottish blood, only one ancestor, no matter how distant, male or female, to claim to be Scottish.

In the traditional Highlands, affiliation with a clan depended only upon acceptance by the chief, who was often willing to accept unrelated renters and retainers as clansmen as well as distant cousins. In the U.S. today, membership in a clan society depends upon nothing more than an individual having had, or believing there was, any ancestor, from any branch of the family, who had the clan's surname. And paying the dues, too, of course. Clan societies do not request genealogies or blood tests to prove any member's assertion that he or she wants to belong to a clan society. Even more important than actual blood ties has been the state of mind of being Scottish and wanting to be with and help other Scots as though they were real family.

8. The Scots made several distinctive contributions to early American culture. Clearly the greatest contribution of Scotland to the U.S. is its people, the settlers who came and built the emerging American society. These people made their lives as Americans, but they also made distinctively Scottish contributions to American culture.

231

The Highlanders brought to this country their unique style of clothing and music. Americans associate kilts and bagpipes with the Scottish Highlands, but these cultural attributes did not become common to American society. More importantly, both Highlanders and Lowlanders gave American culture their colorful tartans, or what we typically call "plaids" (a "tartan" consists of the colors and sett associated with a particular clan, while a "plaid" is a generic style). Even when the Highlanders exchanged their kilts for pants, which were much better suited for the extremes of the North American climate, they continued to wear tartan or plaid shirts, pants, wrap-arounds (which were technically "plaids," pronounced with a long *a*), and jackets. Lowlanders and Ulster Scots also wore plaids, whether or not they had any specific family or clan association. Scottish plaids were much admired by other colonial ethnic groups, including the English, and were worn generally in the U.S. by the late 18th century. By 1815 Scottish plaids had become standard clothing styles in both North America and Europe.

More significant than the bagpipes was the fiddle-based folk music of the Scots and their particular style of folk dancing. The Scots loved music and dancing. Their tradition of the spontaneous gathering, called the *ceilidh*, became the American country hoedown. The rhythms and melodies of the 18th century Scottish settlers of Virginia, North Carolina, and South Carolina provided the foundation of what has become known as "country music." The Scottish country dancing, including reels and strathspayes, likewise contributed to American country dancing, including "square dancing."

In religion, the Scots influenced American society with the institution of the Presbyterian church. The Lowlanders and Ulster Scots held a strong faith in Calvinist teachings and congregational (rather than hierarchical) governance. They founded Presbyterian churches in every locale where there were enough of them to support them. The Presbyterian church originated with a very strong Scottish identity (after all, it was the Church of Scotland), but with time it attracted others, too, so that it acquired a general American appeal. Today, the Presbyterian Church ranks among the most popular Protestant denominations in the U.S.

The 18th century Lowlanders brought the sport of golf from Scotland to America. The game was played in New York City and Charleston by the time of the Revolution. American newspaper ads document the existence of golf equipment and organizations in the 1790s. But the game virtually disappeared during the War of 1812, a period of intensive Anglophobia and anti-Scottish sentiments in the U.S. The sport matured in Scotland and spread to England. It was re-introduced to this country after the Civil War. Golf, as brought to the Americans by Scottish professionals, became a national pastime by the turn of the last century.

Finally, the greatest contribution that the Scots made to early American society was the fulfillment of their own Scottishness in the rich opportunities of the New World. The robustness of Scottish intelligence, hard work, determination, and ambition became fully realized in this country more so than most Scots could have ever achieved within the limitations of Scotland. In fulfilling their potential, the Scots became thoroughly American, because their dreams and values were so compatible with those of the U.S. In many respects to be a Scottish-American is just to be thoroughly American with a slight brogue.

References

J. M. Bumstead, *The People's Clearance: Highland Emigration to British North America, 1770-1815.* Edinburgh: Edinburgh University Press, 1982.

Roger Daniels, *Coming to America. A History of Immigration and Ethnicity in American Life.* New York: Harper, 1991.

Kerby A. Miller, *Emigrants and Exiles. Ireland and the Irish Exodus to North America.* New York: Oxford University Press, 1985.

Eric Richards, *A History of the Highland Clearances. Agrarian Transformation and the Evictions, 1745-1886.* London: Croom Helm, 1982, and *A History of the Highland Clearances. Emigration, Protest, Reasons.* Vol II. London: Croom Helm, 1985.

Allan Wendt, ed., Samuel Johnson's *A Journey to the Western Islands of Scotland* (1775) and James Boswell's *The Journal of a Tour to the Hebrides with Samuel Johnson, LL.D.* (1785). Boston: Houghton Mifflin, 1965. (The quote by Johnson is on p. 35; quote by Boswell, p. 296.)

www.ingramcontent.com/pod-product-compliance
Lightning Source LLC
Chambersburg PA
CBHW071856270326
41929CB00013B/2254